THE
French Revolution
AND THE
Meaning of Citizenship

Edited by
Renée Waldinger, Philip Dawson,
and **Isser Woloch**

Contributions in Political Science, Number 330
GLOBAL PERSPECTIVES IN HISTORY AND POLITICS
GEORGE SCHWAB, SERIES EDITOR

Greenwood Press
Westport, Connecticut • London

Library of Congress Cataloging-in-Publication Data

The French Revolution and the meaning of citizenship / edited by Renée
  Waldinger, Philip Dawson, and Isser Woloch.
      p.   cm.—(Contributions in political science, ISSN 0147–1066
; no. 330. Global perspectives in politics and history)
    Revised versions of papers presented at a conference held May 1992
at the City University of New York Graduate School.
    Includes bibliographical references and index.
    ISBN 0–313–28829–1 (alk. paper)
     1. Citizenship—France—History—18th century—Congresses.
    2. France—Politics and government—1789–1799—Congresses.
    I. Waldinger, Renée. II. Dawson, Philip. III. Woloch,
Isser.   IV. Series: Contributions in political science ;
no. 330.   V. Series: Contributions in political science. Global
perspectives in politics and history.
    JN2921.F74   1993
    323.6'0944—dc20   93–12517

British Library Cataloguing in Publication Data is available.

Library of Congress Catalog Card Number: 93–12517
ISBN: 0–313–28829–1
ISSN: 0147–1066

First published in 1993

Greenwood Press, 88 Post Road West, Westport, CT 06881
An imprint of Greenwood Publishing Group, Inc.

Printed in the United States of America

The paper used in this book complies with the
Permanent Paper Standard issued by the National
Information Standards Organization (Z39.48–1984).

10 9 8 7 6 5 4 3 2 1

The editors and publisher gratefully acknowledge the Bibliothèque Nationale (Collection De
Vinck) for permission to reprint the engravings included in Chapter 5.

CONTENTS

ILLUSTRATIONS

All the engravings are from the Collection De Vinck in the Print Department of the Bibliothèque Nationale, Paris.

PREFACE

Renée Waldinger

This book focuses on the practical meaning and implications of the concept of citizenship. When the millions of subjects of the king of France were transformed into citizens at the time of the French Revolution, the word itself acquired new meaning and significant implications. The practical consequences of these changes on the lives of ordinary French people deserve additional study in the kind of collective effort this volume represents.

The need for this book became apparent to me in the summer of 1989 when I directed an institute on "The French Revolution: Texts and Contexts," sponsored by the National Endowment for the Humanities. As a historical event, a literary or philosophical referent, or a creative impulsion, the French Revolution has relevance to every discipline; thus it offered an illuminating focus for an institute at the Graduate School of the City University of New York, bringing together thirty college and university humanities professors from all over the United States for one month of intensive interdisciplinary study. The overarching aim of our institute was to enrich the teaching of our participants by leading them to understand better the climate of ideas and the social conditions that shaped the French Revolution and the ideology and political forces that propelled it. Our approach was based on the belief that literature offers a privileged entry into a culture, and that therefore the thorough analysis of major literary works within a contextual framework is an effective conduit to an understanding of the period.

In building this framework, we immersed ourselves in historical texts. Questions on citizenship during the Revolution surfaced again and again in our discussions, but we found that the literature on the issue was widely scattered. Our research indicated a number of publications that dealt with varying aspects of the question and that approached it from very different directions. None dealt precisely with the issue itself, and none addressed what we considered the most important practical achievement of the Revolution—the transformation of subjects into citizens.

During the eighteenth century, the concept of "citizen" slowly lost its traditional connection to *ville* and "bourgeois" and acquired a broader meaning in relation to the political community and the fatherland. The Revolution enlarged the concept further by substituting the notion of the citizen as a free actor in the political life of the state. It is this modern meaning of the citizen as the focal point of political activity that has resonated with such force, in so many venues and circumstances since the French Revolution. The consequence of conceiving the citizen as the agent of political life is a fundamental question of modern society and remains at the very core of our political discourse. What does citizenship encompass? What are the rights and duties of citizens?

We wanted to know how the Revolution confronted these issues, what it actually accomplished, and how its responses affected the different segments of French society. We were interested in finding out what citizenship meant to ordinary French people and how citizenship worked in practice. Yet these questions were not the object of scholarly enquiry and interpretation in the wide-ranging activities in honor of the bicentennial of the French Revolution between 1987 and 1989. The focus of the numerous symposia and conferences, and the historical writings resulting from them, was on dramatic incidents, ideology, revolutionary ritual and symbolism, and social class. They emphasized ideas and sought to show how ideas are related to one another and to the major events of the Revolution. In that historical arena the ordinary man and woman get lost.

I concluded that our understanding of one of the essential contributions of the Revolution to the future would be greatly enhanced if we could have a group of scholars address this subject. The most efficient means for achieving this goal was to plan an international conference that would bring together the major scholars working on revolutionary activities and where the question of citizenship would be pertinent. Thanks to the support we received from the Florence Gould Foundation and the Graduate School of the City University of New York, we were able to carry out this project; a conference on "The French Revolution and the Meaning of Citizenship" brought together an international group of scholars in May 1992.

The conference, held in the auditorium of the CUNY Graduate School, was planned as a collaborative workshop and a presentation to the larger scholarly community. Papers were distributed in advance to all participants, as well as to a number of distinguished scholars in the field, who had agreed to chair or act as commentators for one of the four sessions scheduled over a period of two days. There were many lively and informed exchanges during the conference, but this book is not a verbatim report of those proceedings. We particularly regret that we could not include in the volume the remarks of the session chairs, Robert Darnton, Patrice Higonnet, Emmet Kennedy, Charles Tilly, or of commentators Keith Baker, Colin Lucas, Simon Schama, and Donald Sutherland, who placed the papers in a broader context and showed how they were related to each other. Lack of space prevents the inclusion of their comments here, but the success of the conference itself owed much to their contribution. The conference attracted a large audience of faculty and graduate students from the New York metropolitan area, including many specialists in the field. The publication of the participants' revised papers now brings their work to a much wider audience.

I should like to acknowledge publicly the debt I owe to all those who contributed to the realization of this project. Support from the National Endowment for the Humanities allowed me to concentrate my research on the French Revolution, and I want to thank that organization and the participants at the 1989 NEH Summer Institute, whose probing questions spurred me on. I also wish to express my gratitude to the scholars who responded so positively to my invitation to address the topic of citizenship and the French Revolution at a conference in 1992 and who prepared such excellent presentations. Without the generous support of the Florence Gould Foundation and that of my own institution, the Graduate School of the City University of New York, that international conference could not have taken place. Let me say, too, how much I valued the gracious cooperation I received from all those who contributed to this volume. It was a signal pleasure to work with them. Above all, I owe a special debt to my two coeditors, Philip Dawson and Isser Woloch. Their advice and steadfast encouragement were invaluable and much appreciated.

ABBREVIATIONS

A.D.   Archives Départementales

A.N.   Archives Nationales

B.H.V.P.   Bibliothèque Historique de la Ville de Paris

B.N.   Bibliothèque Nationale

THE REPUBLICAN CALENDAR

We have used the revolutionary style of dating for the years following 1792. Year I began September 22, 1792, and ended September 21, 1793; Year II began September 22, 1793, and ended September 21, 1974; and so forth. In some chapters we have followed the revolutionary date with a "translation" into the date according to the Gregorian calendar. In other chapters we felt that the revolutionary date ("Year II of the Republic") was clearer than the date using our current calendar ("1793–1794").

INTRODUCTION

Philip Dawson

Violent events dramatized the French revolutionaries' emphatic rejection of long-established authority. Not as obvious, but as important, was the constructive side of the Revolution—the extensive and continuing effort to create a new political and social order. In this effort, citizenship became a central idea from the beginning, and was an evolving practical reality throughout the 1790s.

The men who drafted the Declaration of the Rights of Man and of the Citizen in August 1789 evoked the natural rights of man partly in order to establish the standard by which the old regime would be condemned. They had to clear the ground. But the Declaration was also intended to provide the guiding principles by which the new regime would be shaped. The preamble, written by Mirabeau, explained what this would mean:

[This] declaration, constantly present to all members of the social body, will ceaselessly remind them of their rights and their duties; . . . legislative and executive acts, being susceptible of instant comparison with the purpose of every political institution, will consequently be the more respected; . . . the citizens' complaints and demands, being based henceforth on simple and incontestable principles, will always tend toward the maintenance of the constitution and the happiness of all.

Reciprocity of obligations, adaptation of law and policy to the fundamental purposes of a social existence, rational criteria on which to evaluate the claims of conflicting interests, a self-restoring equilibrium, public felicity: these would be the permanent characteristics of the citizens' common life.

The expectations and the hopes of the revolutionary lawmakers were not forgotten during the ensuing century. The exponents of civic education under the Third Republic were consciously the heirs of everything public-spirited in the great Revolution, and sought to imbue the young with a republican morality. Alphonse Aulard's history of the Revolution, published in 1901, carried the same theme into the realm of professional historical writing. He pictured the Revolution in a frame defined by the struggle to establish and defend the rights of citizens and the struggle over their meaning and extent.

All French historians in the first part of the twentieth century were familiar with Aulard's history. One may wonder, then, why citizenship, as an idea and a practical reality during the French Revolution, has recently been so little studied—why only a few bold sketches and several fainter outlines were to be seen on the canvas on which the authors of this book propose to fill in some parts of a complex picture.

A satisfactory answer to this question would have to be based on a comprehensive view of the evolution of historical writing on the French Revolution. One reason is doubtless the very nature of its headline events: their drama and complexity absorb attention. This was even true of Aulard, who found that he had to devote many pages simply to recounting events. Another reason is that writers on the Revolution usually offer explanations of its general character and significance, and in doing so they have often placed parentheses around the revolutionaries' conscious motive of creating a nation of citizens. Some historians present the revolutionaries and the counterrevolutionaries as actors expressing one or another of the ideologies that so strongly marked the late eighteenth century. This sort of explanation is given by Alexis de Tocqueville, to select an eminent instance.[1] Writers wanting to expound their own political philosophies have turned to the French Revolution for illustrative material; they tend to see the Revolution above all as ideological conflicts. Other historians have sought general explanations of the Revolution in the class structure of the Ancien Régime and the rapidly developing class conflicts of the revolutionary period. Since the 1950s, this type of explanation has been the subject of debates that have generated much heat and some light. Facts uncovered through research and logical analysis have combined to render untenable any simple depiction of a rising middle class overthrowing an obsolete ruling class. More recently there have been tentative efforts at reformulation, for, after all, France in the eighteenth century was not a classless society. From the perspective of this book, however, the important point is that both these pictures—the Revolution as the acting out of ideology and the Revolution as the realignment of class struggle—have drawn attention away from a purpose that the revolutionary leaders tried most seriously to achieve: the definition of civic rights and obligations and the creation of an environment in which they could and would be fulfilled.

With an additional two hundred years' hindsight, we know that only in certain circumstances is that kind of social order possible. Economic interdependence; a normally adequate food supply; a shared culture not riven by ethnic or sectarian hatreds; public, or at least community, control of lethal weapons: these are conditions whose absence renders citizenship a purely hypothetical idea in parts of the world in 1993. And in the history of Western Europe, even before the construction of modern states, a key prerequisite for citizenship was the growth of a legal tradition that assessed conflicting claims by reference to impersonal and factual modes of proof and argument.

In the French Revolution, the process of transforming citizenship was shaped by conditions that could not be quickly changed. Four such conditions may be singled out here. Most obviously, France was not merely a city with surrounding cultivated land but a vast state in which messages required three days to travel between Paris and Marseilles or Bordeaux and several additional days to reach villages in the hinterland. The centralized bureaucratic monarchy had been built up as a political response to this, among other reasons. In any new political system, too, citizens' participation was bound to be limited. A population of 25 million people could take a continuous part in national decisions only through representation.

Second, France had extensive land frontiers that had to be defended. The old royal government had imposed heavy burdens of taxation and military service, which had become sources of obvious injustice. In the European system of independent, competitive states, however, these burdens could not be renounced for very long. How they were to be borne would be an inescapable question.

Next, the handling of information, the means of communication and record keeping, had grown elaborate and fairly reliable. The information that a local community possessed was not limited by how fast its young men could carry news nor by how much the oldest inhabitants could remember. Widespread literacy, rapid and inexpensive printing, and large elements of bureaucratic organization combined to enable official networks to receive reports, keep records, and send messages. The king's council, with the intendants and their subdelegates, constituted one such network. The parlements with the lesser royal courts and seigneurial courts formed another, the bishops and local priests yet another. Thousands of small towns and many thousands of villages could thus be connected. These networks themselves were not immutable. On the contrary, they were all going to be abolished or drastically modified during the Revolution. But the whole social system had come to incorporate intensive communication and record keeping. A new political order would be affected by this established social reality, even while making use of it.

Finally, France was an old society with a rich and complex symbolic life. Much communication occurred in rituals or in extremely formal and rule-bound settings. Many men and women went regularly to mass where they saw and heard a representation that was intended to tell and remind them of fundamental meaning. Lawsuits were frequent and reached far down in the social hierarchy. They provided means of expression and formal controls and supported the expectation (sometimes met) that decisions would be disinterested and based recognizably on evidence and impersonal rules. At the top of the national political system, the ceremonies at the royal court no longer constituted the crushing routine of a hundred years earlier, but they still expressed relations of authority and subordination, the existence of political will and the claims of acknowledged custom. Religious, juridical, and political culture was usually represented in traditional and largely unobtrusive ways. It was available to be transmuted and used in the elaboration of new symbols and new rituals that could supply depth and permanence to a new way of life.

The chapters in this book seek to elucidate aspects of the French revolutionaries' efforts to define citizenship anew and to put it into practice. The authors approach the subject from different standpoints, and they bring forward varied evidence. The following comments are meant to indicate the relation of each contribution to the general theme of the volume and a few specific ways in which certain chapters are related to each other. In the first chapter, Pierre Rétat reminds us that modern citizenship was invented through transformation rather than original creation. The late eighteenth century had inherited an extensive body of thought on the topic; ideas drawn from Aristotle, Cicero, Montesquieu, Rousseau, and others were widely familiar. At the very beginning of the Revolution, in 1789, however, the word "citizen" itself underwent significant changes, which Rétat analyzes on the basis of usage in a large number of newspapers. The word "citizen," he finds, derived its force initially from contrast with its opposite: the privileged, the aristocrat, the member of a faction, the troublemaker. With the formation of the National Assembly and the capture of the Bastille—in short, the conquest of sovereignty by the patriots—a citizen became one who took part in ruling the nation. Finally, where the bourgeois had been distinguished by his respectability, the citizen manifested civic virtue and the desire to be socially useful. The characteristics of the citizen of classical antiquity, Rétat concludes, were thus to be revived in a regenerated France.

At the same time, Enlightenment thought limited the application of the concept of citizen largely to men. Madelyn Gutwirth argues that the misogyny of some of the leading Enlightenment writers, and the faithful adherence to it of most revolutionary spokesmen, were major factors resulting in the exclusion of women from full citizenship during the Revolution.

Defining the rights of citizens in law involved much more than drafting a Declaration of Rights. Michael Fitzsimmons points out important steps: the merging of all three Estates to form a single National Assembly at the end of June 1789; the abolition of privileges on the night of August 4, 1789; the reconstruction of local and provincial administrative and judicial systems; and the abolition of the legal differences between nobles and commoners. In all these actions Fitzsimmons sees the underlying aim to eliminate objects of loyalty other than the nation and criteria of rights other than citizenship. The result was a fundamental change in the practical reality of civic life, even for those who were not given the right to vote.

Yet this sunny picture, seen from Harriet B. Applewhite's perspective, contained some ominous clouds. The relationship between the citizens and their representatives was going to be crucial, and the National Assembly was divided throughout the years 1789–1791 by political attitude and ideology. (It was there, in August 1789, that the terms "left" and "right" were first used as descriptions of political positions.) Questions at issue were not only how one might qualify as a voter, but also whether the electors could impose binding instructions on the representatives and how restrictive would be the limitations on the right to petition the legislature. Left-wing and right-wing legislators reacted differently to these issues. Yet, Applewhite finds, left and right implicitly agreed in important respects. During the very period when many ordinary men and women were being drawn into political activity and given a feeling of power, the national legislature was excluding them from the lawmaking process while asserting its own sovereign authority to make laws binding them.

While the legal outline of the citizen took shape, so did his image in the popular press. In caricatures, Antoine de Baecque shows, the citizen was first of all not the anti-citizen, not the privileged aristocrat or clergyman of the old regime. The citizen appeared in a visible environment that was historically specific, having been created by a rupture of continuity. The new politics were a decisive break with the past; the contrast was expressed as a change from corruption and social pathology to health. The viewer's awareness of the old regime and of the counterrevolution allowed the difference between the citizen and his opposite to be depicted in bodily appearance.

In the theater, the citizen could be represented as a character developing with the vicissitudes of a dramatic plot. In his discussion of the enormous output of plays in Paris during the revolutionary period, Marvin Carlson sketches some changes in the ways in which plot and characterization were used. In the first years of the Revolution, the aristocrat could be seen renouncing his privileges in order to make possible reconciliation of all citizens. Later, in Year II of the Republic, it was more usual to see the citizen represented on stage with a single-minded devotion to the Republic. Still later, the theater became a weapon used by political factions in their struggles with one another.

Modern citizenship had not only to be invented and depicted; it also had to be learned. Its meaning appeared to the citizens themselves in their own actions. The Revolution as a whole raises the question of the extent to which the changes in the political system were results of deliberate choices by individual partici- pants. This question comes sharply into focus in the study of elections, to which two chapters are devoted.

The Revolution created many opportunities to vote. The new political map of France brought with it thousands of governmental positions. The National As- sembly drew new boundaries, initially creating 83 departments, each of which was subdivided so that there were 545 districts and approximately 4,700 cantons. About 44,000 municipalities subsisted, for which the medieval term ''com- munes'' was revived. A department administration had ten elected officials, a district administration had six, and a commune from three to twenty-one, de- pending on its population. A department had a criminal court judge and pros- ecutor; a district had a civil court of five judges and four alternates; and a canton had at least one justice of the peace. All these administrative and judicial officials were elected, and so too, later on, were the bishop of each department, the priest of each parish and the postmaster of each canton, as well as the national legislators.

Elections were conducted according to procedures very different from those used in twentieth-century France. In his chapter, Patrice Gueniffey emphasizes some specific features of the elections in the Revolution. Individuals did not cast their votes in a voting booth but in a local assembly when summoned by roll call. Results were determined by majority vote on each of the first two ballots, then by plurality on the third ballot. Candidacies were neither declared nor avowed, but only perhaps implied by a man's public behavior or rumored by his friends. Gueniffey argues that this combination of circumstances delivered the elections into the hands of organized, active minorities. Officials were elected; there was a lessening of the political uncertainty which had been created by the new democratic politics. But, Gueniffey contends, the electoral system did not provide for the exercise of real choices by the voters.

It took a couple of years to enact all the legislation creating the new governmental posts. Accordingly, elections were frequent in that period. Melvin Edelstein shows that the extent of participation was highly variable—except in Paris, where it generally involved fewer than 20 percent of the voters. Outside Paris the elections in 1790 brought out substantial numbers of voters: on the average about 35 percent of those eligible to vote in the municipal elections in twenty-six cities, and more than half for the departmental and district elections in twenty-five departments. In 1791, however, the national legislative elections witnessed a sharp decline in rural participation. Historians disagree about how to explain the chronological and geographic differences in voter participation rates. Edelstein favors an explanation that emphasizes the self-consciousness and solidarity of the local community as the chief factors leading to a large turnout.

In order to exercise effective choice, a citizen needed knowledge: the whole Enlightenment movement pointed to this necessity. The required knowledge would include general information and analytical capacity—the skills presumably acquired through schooling. It would also include news about very recent events, personalities, and issues. But the revolutionary leaders did not begin by formulating these exigencies in such functional terms. Rather, as Jeremy Popkin points out, they spoke of the citizen's right to express his (or her) thoughts and opinions. The exercise of this right would allow the citizen to attempt to influence others. The revolutionary leaders thought that the press would provide a substitute for the Agora and the Areopagos, supplying that difficult link between the citizens and their representatives. But the newspaper business was called into being by a market in which profits could be made. Popkin outlines the two major dilemmas that were therefore inescapable: Success in newspaper publishing could create a new kind of privilege and infringe upon the equality of political rights that was supposed to prevail, and unpatriotic readers might be willing to buy unpatriotic newspapers. Popkin elucidates the story of the revolutionaries' struggles with these problems, and shows them continuing to declare their loyalty to the freedom of the press in principle, even while they were driven to limit it in practice.

The Revolution had begun with a vast outpouring of new periodical and ephemeral publications. In contrast, there was no comparable creation of primary schools. For the long run, a nation of citizens required a population that had learned to read, write, and calculate, and that had absorbed the mental discipline that those skills entail, but attempts to devise a new system of elementary education encountered major obstacles. Primary schooling would shape the young citizen; in legislative bodies, unavoidably, it evoked conflicting utopian visions. Unlike the printing press, the school did not produce a physical object to be transported and distributed; rather, its continuing activity was itself the medium of information, and the organizational aspects as well as the costs of this proved wholly intractable for several years after 1789.

In his examination of primary education during the Revolution, Isser Woloch focuses on the law proposed by Joseph Lakanal and adopted at the end of 1794 by the National Convention. The intention was to institute primary schooling for all children, with teachers salaried by the national government. Woloch shows the difficulties that the Lakanal plan encountered: the pressure to establish more schools than the number that the Convention had voted; the shortage of teachers, especially women; and—the fatal problem—the fixed salary paid in paper money (the assignat), which was just undergoing its most rapid decline toward final collapse during 1795. The Convention had to retreat. It abolished salary payments to teachers and instead granted them a small indemnity for the cost of lodging. In almost 90 percent of the municipalities, it eliminated the requirement to maintain a school. Woloch concludes, however, that the experience of the Lakanal law also left as a legacy the ideal of universal education.

The right to vote and the opportunity for one's children to be educated were prospects that aroused the aspirations of many thousands of people. For many men and some women, the freedom to own and carry firearms was also an important mark of political maturity and full membership in a community. This had been revealed in the countryside all over France during the summer of 1789 in the rush to acquire weapons. The revolutionary lawmakers did not declare any such thing as a right to keep and bear arms, but they regarded bearing arms as a valuable privilege of citizenship. This is confirmed by their early legislation limiting membership in the local militia units, the National Guard.

Possessing firearms was one thing, military service quite another, for it entailed using the weapons as and wherever one was commanded to do so. It meant obedience and absence from home. When, with Alan Forrest, we turn to the topic of military service, the emphasis has shifted from the citizens' rights to their duties. The revolutionary lawmakers held on as long as they could to the image of an army of citizen volunteers. Forrest tells us that once—in 1791— this idea worked tolerably well, and produced a fifty-thousand–man net increase in the size of the army at the time of a scare that had not yet turned into actual war. Two years later, however, conscription raised three times as many new soldiers and touched off an exceptionally cruel civil war in western France. In reality, as Forrest's account makes clear, some felt neither eagerness to serve nor fixed determination to evade or even resist conscription. There was a contingent willingness to serve if, for instance, it was clear that defending France meant defending one's own locality. Even within a local community, the impact of military service could be very unequal, depending on one's normal occupation in civilian life. An obligation that appeared equal in the enactments of the legislature did not seem so to all the citizens who had to bear it.

Among many discoveries, revolutionary leaders found that civic spirit is not automatically created by establishing constitutional government and that it cannot be commanded into being. The unwillingness of some ''active'' citizens to fulfill their obligations was troublesome, and it also appeared that civic spirit might arise and flourish where many leaders did not welcome it. The willingness, even eagerness, of some women to act as full citizens was awkward from the viewpoint of the many men who believed what Rousseau had written about women. In her contribution, Darline Gay Levy discusses two telling instances of civic spirit among women. One is an address to the Cordeliers Club in Paris in February 1791 from a group of nineteen women who described themselves as ''les citoyennes de la rue du Regard.'' They noted that they had been relegated to the roles of wives and mothers but said that they were ready, if necessary, to step forward into the public sphere and defend freedom or perish with it. Levy shows the context of political tension at that moment and examines a hostile commentary on their address that appeared in the *Révolutions de Paris*, a paper definitely of the left. In effect, there was a brief but real exchange on what citizenship should mean for women. Levy's other example of civic spirit among women consists of episodes in the political activity of Constance Evrard, whose feeling of her obligations as a citizen can be studied in the interrogation conducted after her arrest in July 1791. The women of the rue du Regard and Constance Evrard made their own choices and sought an active revolutionary role for themselves as citizens.

The experience of these women dramatizes the fact that the creation of modern citizenship in the French Revolution had necessarily to proceed through the definition of a new relation between the self and the social order. In part the working out of this definition depended on the expectation that the social order would be framed by rights. In the preamble of the Declaration of Rights, Mirabeau had written that henceforth citizens' complaints and demands would have a clear and rational basis. In reality, though, a distressed group might not be able immediately to see its most persuasive basis for a claim to public attention, sympathy, or assistance. It needed new self-representation. Allan Potofsky shows us the groups in the building trades in Paris trying out first one idea, then another. In their series of communications to the National Assembly and to the public, there is no single philosophy to which the building trades steadily adhere. Even the list of groups included within the trades varied. The old privileges had been overthrown and they were finding their way in a new world. New reasons for special consideration and new ways of extracting benefits from public authority had not yet been established. It was necessary to try various approaches: limit exploitation by creditors, stimulate private building, finance public building. Among these approaches, one was that the civic aspirations of the nation would be embodied in the public monuments that the builders would construct. This was, however, not their standard or dominant self-representation.

The concept of citizenship in France in the 1790s centered on the individual and his or her rights and obligations. Society was thought of as a compact among individuals. A different version of the composition of society, put forward more than a century earlier by Jean Domat, for instance, and before that by Jean Bodin, had held that society consisted of groups, and that the basic group was the married couple with their children. In 1797, after a major victory in the annual spring elections to the national legislature, right-wing politicians mounted an attack on individualism and sought to revive the concept of society as an aggregation of nuclear families. This maneuver took the form of a critique of the divorce law of 1792, which allowed incompatibility as a ground for divorce. Suzanne Desan's contribution studies the debates of 1797 on the divorce law. They reveal, predictably enough, a Roman Catholic premise that marriage is a sacred bond as well as a legal contract, followed by the resurrection of the argument that the marriage bond is the basis of every other social bond, and if it is not a lifelong commitment then society is in danger of crumbling. Desan finds that the defenders of the 1792 divorce law replied not with a defense of individualism, but rather with the argument that the possibility of divorce protected domestic morality and made possible the termination of a marriage in which one spouse was mistreating the other. These moderate republicans did concede, however, that the viability of the household formed around the marriage bond was a fundamental value. Their position, with its slight emphasis on individual rights, seems almost an echo of the definition of citizenship as bourgeois respectability, which was one of the meanings in current usage when the year 1789 began.

The retreats and compromises of the late 1790s were only one part of a complex legacy of that decade of intense debate and practical experience. Every reader of the chapters that follow will find it possible to draw a variety of lessons from them.

NOTE

1. Alexis de Tocqueville, *L'ancien régime et la Révolution française*, pt. 3 (Paris), chap. 3.

PART I

Toward New Conceptions of Citizenship

1

THE EVOLUTION OF THE CITIZEN FROM THE ANCIEN RÉGIME TO THE REVOLUTION

Pierre Rétat

Citizenship assumes its fullest meaning whenever it is coupled with popular sovereignty and the affirmation of political rights. The Revolution provided a link to the concept and image of the citizen of antiquity, to his rights and duties. This image, which had been presumed lost, was often evoked in monarchical Europe, in the midst of what Montesquieu referred to as "the dregs and corruption of our modern times." It was a central concept that helped regulate a renewed form of political life, a restored legitimacy, which Jean-Jacques Rousseau had posited as both absolutely fundamental and irredeemably absent in *Social Contract*.

The lexicon of the Ancien Régime, however, not only included the citizen but granted him an increasingly important place as the Revolution drew near. The word should not be understood in the radical sense that it would finally assume during the Revolution, but in the sense of the reformist ideology of the Enlightenment and a progressive monarchy where everyone, from the most obscure individual all the way to the king, would contribute to the public good without challenging current political practices, at least insofar as the word is commonly understood.

Elsewhere[1] I have attempted to trace the semantic evolution of this word from the end of the seventeenth century to the beginning of the nineteenth, the broadening of the number of concepts to which it referred (society, the state), and the growing insistence on the need for social utility by which the term was defined after 1750. Taken in its most general sense as the individual's position with respect to his peers and the state, it was initially defined as the expression of a need for sociality. If we set aside the political and radical usage of the term, which grew more forceful with the final crises of the Ancien Régime, beginning with Maupeou's coup d'état, the notion of citizenship had, through well-estab-

lished habits of language and thought, become subordinated to the idea of a
social whole. When the notions of sovereignty and equality were added in 1788–
1789, there occurred a dynamic association between the citizen and the nation,
the exultant rise of the citizen as the executor of national unity and freedom.

Through the use of material drawn largely from the newspapers of 1789, I
would like to examine the way in which the word entered the language of the
first stage of the Revolution and the elements of permanence and change that
characterized this moment of rupture and transition. My approach will not take
the form of a theoretical analysis based on political concepts. The large number
of occurrences supplied by a vast corpus of material from the press not only
provide an overview of ordinary usage, but also contain a number of unexpected
discoveries. They present the word in various situations when it was used,
together with the lexical relationships that restore the context of contemporary
historical and political events. Through them we can track the word "citizen"
from the outset of its truly revolutionary career when, still following in the traces
of previous usage, it was in the process of establishing itself at the core of the
representation of social and political behavior and ideals.

Toward the beginning of June 1789, in the *7e Lettre à ses commettants*,
Mirabeau attacked the bishop of Langres with these words: "Doesn't it seem
absurd to you, Monsignor, to place the interests of two-hundred thousand privileged individuals in opposition to those of twenty-five million citizens?" (p. 6).
This statement perfectly expresses the polemical value of "citizen" for the Third
Estate during this moment of struggle for political equality that had begun prior
to the meeting of the Estates-General and had culminated in Sieyès's *Qu'est-ce
que le Tiers Etat?* In January Mangourit's *Héraut de la Nation* had opposed
"the opinion of the nobility" to the "opinion of the citizenry" (no. 1, p. 13),
and in May, addressing itself to "good citizens," it formulated the desire that
the representatives chosen by them would "forever eliminate oppression and
uncivil pretensions" (no. 41, p. 642). Affiliated with concepts such as people,
nation, country, communes, and liberty, the word "citizen" entered into the
extremely active lexical composite that stood in opposition to the "aristocracy"
and ministerial "despotism." The antonymic couple "citizen/aristocrat" would
last for a long time, but with increased significance following the July victory.
It designated the special locus of combat for or against the Revolution, for or
against the "popular party" at the National Assembly. In a language that is both
simple and repetitious, the small, sensationalistic newspapers continuously appeal to the "citizens" to remain alert, to be on the lookout for the insidious and
omnipresent intrigues of the aristocracy, encouraging them in a fantastic struggle
between Good and Evil. The anxiety of conspiracy was occasionally answered
by the dream of a more auspicious conclusion: "When will Aristocracy expire
at the feet of public spirit? Oh good, free, and generous Citizens! Do not grow
discouraged. Your efforts to achieve that which is good, beautiful, and true,
must certainly triumph over evil and disorder" (*Révolutions nationales*, no. 30,
Dec. 5, p. 22).

The word's polemical value, although vague, penetrated the language of the revolutionary newspapers of 1789 and was concretized as a form of address—even if the latter concealed a more specific meaning, which I will analyze later on. Three concepts, however, both together and separately, are often found associated with the notion of the citizen. They differentiate its meaning while they point to the confrontational nodes that dissociate it from other meanings: union, sovereignty and freedom, virtue and social usefulness. I will make a distinction between them, especially between the first two, simply for the purposes of this chapter.

Brissot responded to Bernardin de Saint-Pierre, who wished to maintain the social "orders," that "class distinctions" would destroy social bonds: "These are truths which have been felt and recognized, and have led to the destruction of the social orders in France. Only one order is needed, that of the Citizen" (*Patriote français*, no. 65, Oct. 9). The abolition of distinctions served as the basis for what was then the most commonly accepted and one of the most emotionally charged meanings of "citizen." The excited account of the revolutionary week of July in *Révolutions de Paris* owes much of its emotional force to the representation of civic unity as the real motor and guiding principle of the Revolution:

Citizens of every rank, every age, who were capable of bearing arms, showed up in their districts; it is the voice of the nation, the bonds of blood that command; they are defending their friends, their brothers, and themselves. . . . Everyone was together, in a single group, without distinction; all were friends; all were citizens. . . . The rich graciously welcomed the poor; rank did not exist, all were equals. (no. 1, July 12–17, pp. 4, 32)

In this state of grace, political unity ("all were citizens") goes hand in hand with a unity of class and feeling. Shortly after, Tournon, the editor of *Révolutions de Paris*, suggested a way to ensure and perpetuate this unity. With the help of a "national register" of their motions and deliberations, the districts "would effortlessly rally to the revered and imposing voice of public opinion, the general welfare would be heeded, . . . the citizens, united by common interest, would soon be united in thought, and all would soon constitute a single and undivided body" (no. 5, Aug. 7–15, p. 12). Prudhomme, the "citizen-patriot," offered to print the register, but it was never published. It should come as no surprise to see "public opinion" joined with the "body" of citizens in a revolutionary composite of great and all-encompassing ideas. That is why it was so difficult to accept the notion of political parties in 1789, and why such frequent mention was made both of their existence and of the danger they entailed. Together with the various factions, they were reserved for a political hell of intrigue and personal interest. Denouncing "the party spirit," Brissot stated that "good Citizens still exist who do not belong to any party" (*Patriote français*, no. 109, Nov. 25). Despite the evidence, many still attempted to contrast the reality of political division with the pure image of a National Assembly unified in its devotion to the public good, the permanent symbol of national unity. Regnaud de Saint-Jean d'Angély, deputy and author of the *Journal de Versailles*, felt it served as a "poor response to the wishes of the prince and the nation" to remind us of "separate orders, a split in opinion over which every citizen's hand should draw the heaviest veil."[2]

This wonderful cohesion—celebrated, postulated, desired—was unable to resist the internal tensions acting upon it. The evidence shows that the notion of the citizen was often given a discriminatory social and cultural meaning as well as a conflicting political meaning. The term was dissociated from "the people" and referred only to the most enlightened segment of the populace. The *Héraut de la Nation*, in its account of the uprising at Rennes that took place toward the end of January, contrasted the "upper Third" with the "lower Third," the "Citizens" with the "lackeys," the nobility here playing both sides against one another. Once again public opinion was closely associated with the concept of the citizen: "What is public opinion? Everything. The cry of the multitude? Nothing" (no. 16, pp. 243–45). Even more revealing were the writings that appeared during the July revolution, especially during the summary executions and the period of the "great fear." Justifying the "legitimate insurrection" that took place in Paris, Poncelin wrote in the *Courrier français* of July 16 that "some virtuous and enlightened citizens, masters of the public opinion that they have earned through their patriotism, hold order above anarchy; the slightest misdemeanor is a crime in the eyes of the multitude that has been enlightened by these generous Citizens." Tournon expressed similar feelings in the *Révolutions de Paris*, where the "citizens" shuddered with "horror" after the murders of Foullon and Bertier: "The people are not sufficiently enlightened to lead themselves and should follow the guidance of the citizens. Our cause is the same, we are unable to betray it; and it is this union—why not say it—that has contributed to our success" (no. 2, July 18–25, p. 6). Brissot announced this "great political truth" just as clearly:

All authority comes from the People. But the People can only maintain this authority through its obedience. For if it allows itself to disobey the Citizens to whom it has given power, then everything is lost, there will no longer be Laws, or peace, or public safety. The citizen who disobeys public authority disobeys himself. (*Patriote français*, no. 35, Sept. 5)

There is a shift of meaning in these lines, which corrects but does not cancel the lexical separation that allocated to the citizen alone, as a limiting category, the exercise of power. In fact, those who were most strongly opposed to the distinction between active and passive citizens—and Brissot belonged to this group,[3] as did nearly all journalists—betrayed, at least through their language, their resistance to a universal extension of the word "citizen," and virtually excluded an entire segment of society.

The principal division, the one that is lexically the most telling, it that which opposes the "good," "honest," "peaceful," "zealous," and "true" citizens to the "bad," the "false," the "enemies of public welfare" (or "disturbers of public peace"), the "factious." This double set of qualifications proliferated after the riot of August 30. It proved that the citizen, from the very beginning of the Revolution, was an object of partisan rivalry in the conflict of opinions. The word became a concept to be argued back and forth and was viewed as evidence of political virtue, a form of privilege that could be denied an adversary. If we attempt to introduce some order into the large number of statements that were made, two separate categories appear: one, which was dominant and inspired by a kind of defensive reflex, was politically moderate, the other activist and, occasionally, extremist.

The "good" citizens sought in this designation a refuge against the dangers of "license" and anarchy. They displayed a wise and enlightened concern for the public welfare and the normal operation of the institutions established by the Revolution. They willingly cast into the shadows any idea of sovereignty and placed the emphasis on order and peace. The author of the *Journal du Palais-Royal* writes with indignation about the "seditious events" that occurred on August 30:

And they dare assume the honorable title of Citizen, these factious men, who have probably been sold to what remains of the most tyrannical Aristocracy. . . . They should more appropriately refer to themselves as our most determined enemies! Does being a Citizen mean introducing despair, terror, and defiance into the hearts of one's brothers[?] . . . Enlightened Frenchmen! those of you who truly desire public welfare, keep your distance from these men. (no. 4, Sept. 4, p. 27)

He appealed to "honest citizens" to "rally for the sake of all."

Mlle de Keralio reacted similarly in the *Journal d'Etat et du Citoyen*:

The revolutions that occurred last Sunday, August 30, terrified all good Citizens. Public calm cannot be established in the midst of riots and insurrections . . . Paris is full of good Citizens who seek only calm and public safety, but a crowd of aristocrats and despots have managed to slip into all the societies. (no. 5, Sept. 10, supp., p. 97)

Here, as elsewhere, it is the aristocrat and not the "bad citizen" who persecutes the "good," a reflex that was, perhaps, destined to preserve the word and its value. With some difficulty a category of evil entered the national body. Everything and everybody deemed contrary to the public good, and especially "paid" provocateurs like Marat were lumped into this category. As often happens, however, the "bad citizen" soon made his appearance. "May bad citizens not take advantage of this to cause disorder and spread rumors that might light the fire of sedition! May honest people show them no welcome," wrote Gorsas in his *Courrier* of July 13 (I, no. 8, p. 118). There were many statements of this kind, and they could be found not only in the small, moderate newspapers but in the patriotic ones as well, though differently expressed, and in Gorsas and Brissot, who exhorted "every honest citizen" to help calm the disturbances at the Palais Royal and confront the "tumultuous mobs" with "reason" and freedom of opinion in the regular assemblies (*Patriote français*, no. 32, Sept. 2). Even the *Révolutions de Paris* claimed, "We can only join with all the other good citizens against the instigators of disorder" (no. 9, Sept. 5–12, p. 11).

"Good" and especially "true" citizens, however, could also be the most active revolutionaries, the most outspoken in their demands for freedom and sovereignty, who always sided in the Assembly with the "patriotic" or "popular" party, still referred to as a "minority." The *Chronique de Paris* clearly established the polemical and political value of the expression: "Our only hope is in the courageous minority, supported by all the strength of public opinion and by the unanimous voice of true citizens" (no. 35, Sept. 27). Brissot reproached Mounier for his beliefs, which he felt were dangerous to the people's cause: "It is the duty of every good citizen to fight against you and unmask your errors" (*Patriote français*, no. 36, Sept. 7, p. 6). Shortly afterward he called upon "good citizens" to denounce the stratagems of the "party" formed at Versailles around this same Mounier (no. 45, Sept. 17, p. 3). And it was in a similar context that Marat, in the *Ami du peuple*, often contrasted the "true citizens" (or "honest," or "good"), who were still referred to as "good patriots," with an "aristocratic faction" of uncertain proportions but definitely sinister intentions. To pull France back from the abyss, "the only hope is in the energy of true citizens, who are courageous enough to instill in the people a distinct awareness of its rights and encourage it to take revenge" (no. 18, Sept. 28, p. 154).

The "bad citizen" began to take shape. He hid among the citizens themselves and took his place in the very heart of the National Assembly. Desmoulins assured his readers in *Révolutions de France et de Brabant* that the decree concerning the *marc d'argent* "constituted an aristocratic government in France, and was the greatest victory that bad citizens have had in the National Assembly" (no. 3, Dec. 12, p. 108). He announced that he would display "every Saturday throughout France" the "canvas of bad citizens" (no. 4, Dec. 19, p. 157). The journalist-censor became the judge of civic duty or, rather, of the political behavior of the deputies. Robespierre was an "excellent citizen" (no. 4, Dec. 19, p. 162). Public denunciation, once again restored to a position of honor, will lead "as many accusers as there are good citizens" to stand up against crime (no. 5, Dec. 26, p. 233).

When the *Actes des apôtres* ironically presented its pompous parodies of the "good" or "virtuous" citizen, or the *Journal de la ville* its own parody of the "bad" citizen, they recorded the necessary and foreseeable fragmentation of a notion that claimed to be unitary, and because of that very unity could be used in so threatening a manner.

The most explicit definitions, the clearest lexical associations of the word "citizen," place it in extremely close contact with the concepts of civil and political freedom, with equal rights and sovereignty. This semantic base can be perceived in a number of contexts, but its constituent elements are often incompletely or barely articulated. The *Révolutions de Paris*, especially after October, in keeping with the didactic and theoretical role its editors assigned it, provides the most accurate and rigorous definition of the term: "whoever is a citizen is everything because he enjoys all the rights of man" (Tournon, no. 21, Nov. 29–Dec. 5, p. 9); "we refer to a citizen as someone who carefully observes the sense of equality among all men" (no. 22, Dec. 6–13, p. 13); "the word *citizen* expresses the quality of an individual considered as a participant in legislative or sovereign power" (no. 6, Aug. 16–22, p. 10).

It is this citizen whom the journalist salutes, somewhat dramatically: "People of France . . . ! for I can no longer call men destined for slavery *citizens*. People of France! you were free for only a few days" (no. 21, Nov. 28–Dec. 5, p. 2). The citizen, here degraded but within view of a redemptive ascension, provides the support for public speeches in the patriotic papers. His fictional presence is the promise or certainty of a deep unity of feeling and a warm reception. The name itself was a source of energy; in the popular imagination it actualized the courage that was inseparable from freedom. The distinctions in forms of address should also be analyzed, for they frequently reveal a political attitude. To "Citizens!," which resonated constantly in the pages of the *Révolutions de Paris* and occasionally in the *Patriote français*, the *Chronique de Paris*, and the *Révolutions de France et de Brabant*, can be contrasted Gorsas's "Oh fellow citizens!" and "Frenchmen!" which appeared in the *Gazette de Paris* or the *Lettres de M. le Comte de B****.[4]

It was to this superlatively active citizen that the call to arms was addressed, for arms alone enabled him to win his freedom and maintain it. The "citizen soldier" (and the collective "citizens guard" and "citizens militia") held an important place in the earliest revolutionary papers. Through their driving spirit and numbers, calculated with a certain frenzy and growing sense of menace, they ensured the Revolution's victory over its enemies. "Citizens! to Arms. Yes, to arms. You must remain armed at all times. Are we so far from slavery, or are you already tired of your freedom?" cried Guffroy in October, writing in his *Tocsin*, so frequently cited in the patriotic press. According to the *Révolutions de Paris*, Paris alone would be able to save France. "The Romans were never better citizens or really freer than when clouds of Gauls swept through Italy and advanced right to the gates of Rome" (no. 10, Sept. 12–18, p. 5).[5] Freedom and sovereignty were, nevertheless, capable of certain modifications, which often revealed the ambiguous and archaic aspects of citizenship.

The union between nation and king was a commonplace theme often heard in the months preceding the July revolution and remained firmly anchored in popular feeling until shortly after the events of October.[6] It perpetuated, often in an extremely clear manner, the association between the subject and the citizen that characterized the ideal of a legitimate monarchy during the Ancien Régime and was one of the fundamental aspects of the classical configuration of the citizen. Toward the beginning of June, Mangourit expressed this as follows:

"Those of us who are citizens, say respectfully to the best of Princes: do what is best for the Empire; but, Sire, your Majesty must do it alone. Show yourself to your subjects, come down into their midst" (*Héraut de la Nation*, no. 50, p. 786). This position is relatively atypical in the sense that it encloses the citizen within fairly narrow limits. We should take a closer look at Gorsas's declaration in his *Courrier* of July 20, where he states that the king, who had arrived in Paris on July 17, had cemented "an inviolable pact between the Prince and his subjects, a union whose basis is the freedom of the French Nation" (I, no. 13, p. 200). It was as a result of this "pact," and through the support it provided for the people's cause and for liberty, that Louis XVI was so often referred to as the "citizen king" throughout 1789, when it appears to have become a common epithet at the August and September flag ceremonies. In his address to the people of Paris in October, intended to calm and reassure them, Brissot asked "Isn't your King among you! Isn't he a citizen?" (*Patriote français*, no. 73, Oct. 19). Unlike the others, however, the man who stated "The word *subject* is odious, revolting, disgusting" (no. 41, Sept. 12) was not prepared to combine the two expressions. Feydel, however, could write calmly in the *Observateur* of October 29, "People of France, unite . . . People of France, there is still time to choose. Let us be free men, subjects of a Citizen King, or we shall become slaves of the Emperor" (no. 35, p. 274). And Brune, reminding the king to what extent the French "idolized" their kings, addressed Louis XVI as follows: "August and powerful leader of a free people, there is not one of your subjects who wouldn't be proud to spill his blood for the honor of his Prince and the glory of his Country." This obedience to the king in no way precluded being a citizen, and an ancient form of legitimacy was renewed and fulfilled through the French constitution. The author of the *Rôdeur français* could, therefore, dare to use the plural when he recalled the love of the people for "its Citizen Kings" (no. 5, Dec. 6, p. 74).

But what about the notion of citizenship as the source of political legitimacy? Gorsas's *Courrier* is, in this sense, extremely informative. In conformity with the request of the permanent committee at the Hôtel de Ville, the author's name is included with his title following number 19 on July 26, but the attribution that follows is quite significant: "By M. Gorsas, Citizen of Paris." Denounced in the district of Saint-Roch in December, he rebuffed his accusers, claiming "thirty-five years of the most honorable existence, as well as being the father of a family, a Citizen enjoying all his rights, the most peaceful of men, a respected man" (VI, no. 28, Dec. 11, p. 438). We find here all the old bourgeois privileges; honor, family, and civic responsibility are intimately connected with the concept of citizenship, an association that the dying Ancien Régime had not completely forgotten. Perhaps it was of Gorsas that Tournon (who disliked him) was thinking when he wrote in the *Révolutions de Paris*:

"Most people," wrote J.-J. Rousseau, mistake a town for a "City, and a bourgeois for a citizen." . . . The word "citizen" expresses an individual's social position when he is viewed as a participant in legislative or sovereign power. It is, therefore, absurd to say that one is a "Citizen of Paris," for example, or of any other city. We are "citizens of France," because it is as French people that we participate in legislative power. . . . It is not as citizens that we make decisions in the districts, for we are not referring to matters that are of interest to France, but as members of the Commune. (no. 6, Aug. 16–22, pp. 10–11)

In 1789 there was some value in following Rousseau's example of critical rigor and recalling the principles that had led to abandoning the binding mandate on the deputies by their constituents. As Tournon said, it was necessary to teach people "the art of being free." The bourgeois had disappeared for the sake of the citizen, with all the changes in social and political position that such a change assumes. But the bourgeois could occasionally be seen hiding behind the citizen, a fact often made clear in revolutionary literature. Gorsas accused Marat and other yellow journalists of wanting to "incite the people against the Bourgeoisie" (*Courrier*, IV, no. 94, Oct. 10, p. 135). His intentions become clear when he remarks that the Café de Foi in the Palais-Royal "is the ordinary meeting place for those Citizens who are best known for their patriotism, and they shouldn't be confused with other disturbers of the public peace, whose civil existence is unknown"—that is to say, foreigners without rights (*Courrier*, Sept. 3, no. 58, III, p. 34). We should also bear in mind that the "bourgeois" guard was the first and traditional name of the militia, or "citizens" guard, later referred to as the "national" guard, and was formed, as the author of the newspaper *Assemblée Nationale* states, from the "elite bourgeois" (issue of July 20). He goes on to say that it was due to the "diligence of the bourgeois" that the towns owed their safety during the insurrection of "brigands" in July and the disturbances of the following months. Many of these "good citizens," who appeared so frequently in the literature, seem to be twins of the bourgeois who were busy defending their "hearths." Their interests are in any event the same.

A small and very violent royalist paper that appeared toward the end of 1789, entitled the *Vrai bourgeois de Paris*, provocatively claimed this bourgeois status for itself and also tried to ban the "title" of citizen, which was "devoid of meaning in a monarchy:"

When I say "true bourgeois of Paris," I am referring to all those who have a position, a house, a business, and a family. This collection of provincials and foreigners swarming around Paris, living any which way they can, should not be honored with the title of bourgeois. Let them assume the vague and ridiculous title of "citizen," which can have no meaning in France. (no. 1, p. 7)

This opposition expressed a political radicalism that was antithetical, but exactly homologous, to the patriotic radicalism of the supporters of the "general will."

"Free men place good sense, the love of freedom, and the virtues of a good citizen above all else," wrote Brissot in the *Patriote français* of December 31 (no. 145, p. 4). "Virtue" and freedom are, therefore, inseparable. The Revolution produced a virtuous energy, it supplied the individual with motives and ends capable of raising his social position. Goodness is an inherent quality of a community of citizens: "The Citizen, the Patriot, are they capable of not being virtuous? Isn't vice the implacable enemy of society and the citizen? . . . They would sacrifice what they hold most dear for the safety of their country" (*Le Solitaire*, no. 1, Dec., p. 7). According to Tournon, the people should not choose men over forty years old to be representatives, for they had been corrupted by the Ancien Régime, but "citizens, who were born into the social order and bore equality in their souls and freedom in their hearts" (*Révolutions de Paris*, no. 16, Dec. 24–31, p. 4).

There were several aspects to the eminently moral quality that characterized the citizen. The aspect of social usefulness was of particular importance during the Enlightenment. It maintained its importance in 1789 but changed noticeably through an association with revolutionary ideals. When Mlle de Keralio defined herself as "quite simply a good citizen," implying that her aim was "public usefulness" (*Journal d'Etat et du Citoyen*, no. 14, Oct. 22), there were models and goals for that usefulness other than those pursued by the good citizens of the last decades of the Ancien Régime. The Revolution made possible a return to the virtues of antiquity. Lafayette declined the salary that was offered him: "That is how one serves as a Citizen. Thus served the virtuous Cincinnatus, whose portrait our worthy general does not wear in vain on his chest" (*Révolutions de Paris*, no. 9, Sept. 5–11, p. 28). Loustalot proposed to the "legislators" that they embrace the lofty ambition of uniting virtue and happiness: "Ah! Isn't being a citizen the most important thing? If the duties that are attached to this title become, as they do with all free people, the most intense pleasure we can experience, do not fear that individual duty will be neglected." This utopia of civic pleasure tended to absorb the majority of "private pleasures" in the customary preoccupation with "public happiness," and placed a moral cost over all experience by placing it at the service of society.[7] The formation of "morals," the "institution" of a free people was the aim of the most demanding ideal of the citizen: for some the moment seemed to have arrived to give substance to the fascinating images that classical culture and the reading of Montesquieu and Rousseau had kept alive in their memories.

There were several immediate opportunities for citizens to exercise their virtue in 1789. Beginning in September, the movement of patriotic gifts supplied the National Assembly with marginal but steady work and the press with an edifying headline. The offer of their jewelry by the wives of artists, the "new Roman women," is one of the most frequently discussed events of the period and marks the entrance of the *citoyenne*, in the positive sense of the word, onto the stage of history. With singular intensity, women developed a heroism of devotion; it was their individual lot as citizens, as in other respects. Tournon's *Révolutions de Paris* published a charming letter from a "Society of 22 young Citoyennes of Civray, in Poitou, a generous region of citizens. We come from generous families, we are gentle, we are citizens, we are a society of individuals and prepared to sacrifice ourselves.'' But they shared their fears with the journalist: ''In a time of patriotic contribution, how can we turn rich property owners into citizens, for he who is too attached to his gold does not deserve the name citizen, nor the right to belong to the nation.'' If, through some unfortunate coincidence, they were later to marry an avaricious husband, how could they turn him into a ''generous man and a citizen'' (no. 23, Dec. 13–19, pp. 45–47)? The *citoyenne* didn't always give off this fragrance of naive patriotism, however. On October 6, Le Hodey stated that the women of Paris ''have shown under the present circumstances that there are an infinite number of Jeanne Hachette and virtuous citoyennes in France, who are ready to risk death for their country'' (*Journal des Etats Généraux*, IV, p. 414).

Could priests become citizens, and how could this be accomplished? In 1789 the clergy appeared to respond encouragingly to this Voltairian question. Although a fruitful marriage could not be expected, an active collaboration with the national cause could. Concerning a speech given by a canon during the flag ceremony, Brissot wrote, ''Finally our Priests have become good Citizens, the Apostles of Freedom,'' and suggested that they become ''political teachers'' (*Patriote français*, no. 73, Oct. 19). When the clergy's wealth was turned over to the nation on November 2, Talleyrand, who had initially suggested it, was warmly praised: ''What an excellent Citizen, what an ardent Patriot, this Bishop of Autun! How many wise, profound, and disinterested insights has this respectable Prelate offered the country into making the clergy useful to the Nation, which has been harmed for so long by their scandalous opulence'' (*Courrier français*, no. 126, Nov. 8).

After 1789 *citoyen* became one of the words of the sacred language of the Revolution. As an adjective it easily grafted itself onto other words, and anyone who used it became a hero of freedom or social utility. Necker was referred to as a ''Citizen-Minister,'' Lafayette a ''Citizen-Hero,'' Talleyrand a ''Citizen-Bishop'' (even as ''a great ecclesiastical Citizen'') Monsieur (the comte de Provence, brother of the king) a ''Citizen-Prince,'' and Louis XVI a ''Citizen-King.'' The general category of civism,'' a word that was relatively new, appeared often enough to designate the qualities and virtues of a citizen. There was even a doublet, unconsecrated by usage and not recorded in any dictionary— *citoyenisme*—which was a kind of crude, popular version of the word (*Journal général*, no. 54, Nov. 11).

The newspapers of 1789 provide insight only into the beginnings of the revolutionary apogee of the citizen. They display the ambiguities and contradictions that surround the concept and the traces of earlier meanings conveyed through lexical usage, and they help situate chronologically this important phase of the word's metamorphosis.

And it was a metamorphosis to the extent that the burning issues of the moment (which themselves changed or shifted rather quickly) gave the citizen a meaning and effective value that were not altogether new (the word was first used in the struggle against ''despotism''), but were mobilized to a greater extent than ever before in the struggle against the "aristocracy" and finally against "bad" or "perverse" citizens. The sign of a postulated social unity, of liberty and equality, the citizen was by necessity a part of the Revolution but was quickly confronted with the problem of political schism; he opposed it in a variety of ways with his magical strength of denial and resisted it with his totalizing values. When he allied himself with sovereignty once and for all, he entered a political hell and lost the serenity he had cloaked himself in during the Enlightenment through a form of political abstention that had now become untenable.

The traces of former usage were in evidence everywhere. Nearly synonymous with bourgeois, citizen had gradually freed itself of its earlier prerogatives through its new association with society and the state. The movement was completed with the Revolution, but certain vestiges of the old formula remained, and within the new context that arose, the good citizen seemed to some—and in a language that was politically defined—to be a substitute for the bourgeois. The urban elite, dissociated from the violent, credulous, and ignorant "people," not to mention the "brigands" from the countryside, often received the implicit privilege of civic status. In this way there endured the complex relationship between the two categories, political man and economic man, that Max Weber developed in his comparative study of the city of antiquity and the medieval city.[8]

Sovereignty was generally admitted although unequally invoked as a condition of the citizen's liberty. There was hardly a single journalist, however, who did not protest the decree concerning the *marc d'argent* and the rejection by the National Assembly of the amendments intended to soften its impact. Some of them, though, had no difficulty in uniting the status of being a citizen with that of being a subject of the king. It seems that for a significant part of public opinion, the figure of the citizen-king, himself obedient to the law and the nation, helped perpetuate the model of a "legitimate" monarchy, in spite of the fundamental transformation that had occurred. The compromise between the earlier royalty and popular sovereignty satisfied the desires of the "good citizens." It was a major factor in the first Revolution, which many consider to be a reestablishment of the monarchy. "The law and the king," the inscription on the medal that the porters of Port-aux-Blés, "brimming with *citoyenisme* and honor," asked to wear, was the formula for this delicate synthesis.

Beginning in the 1750s, citizen had become, together with such expressions as nation, patriotism, interest, and happiness, one of the standard words in the ideology of the Enlightenment. The concepts of public usefulness, social service, and progress, which it consolidated and promoted, were apparent in the language in use at the beginning of the Revolution. But the conquest of sovereignty profoundly altered the position these concepts held in the overall linguistic configuration. The values they represented tended to fuse with the image of morality and virtue taken from classical antiquity. That which, in a great, modern monarchy, could only be evoked, though often passionately and through nostalgia, had taken root in a regenerated France.

Translated by Robert Bononno

NOTES

1. Pierre Rétat, "Citoyen-Sujet, Civisme," in *Handbuch politisch-sozialer Grundbegriffe in Frankreich 1680–1820*, ed. R. Reichardt and E. Schmitt (Munich: Oldenbourg, 1988), vol. 9, 75–105.

2. No. 38, Sept. 25, supp. See Pierre Rétat, "Partis et factions en 1789: émergence des désignants politiques," *Mots*, 1988, no. 96: 69–89, especially 72–74.

3. See *Patriote français*, no. 91, Nov. 7. "Active citizen" is a pleonasm; "passive citizen" is a contradiction in terms: "We should no longer give the name Citizen to anyone who lacks civil and political rights. We must not deceive the People with words."

4. Marat generally wrote, "Oh, my fellow citizens!" The "Citoyens!" of the more assertive small papers such as the *Observateur* or the *Journal universel* had a very different value than when it was used in the *Révolutions de Paris*.

5. Many texts expressed similar views: see Pierre Rétat, "Aux Armes, Citoyens! 1789 ou l'apprentissage de la guerre," *Commentaire*, 1988, no. 42: 526–33. Some journalists considered themselves soldiers in their own way, and Marat's pen was worth an "army" (*Ami du peuple*, no. 18).

6. Articles in the press provide ample evidence for this. See Claude Labrosse and Pierre Rétat, *Naissance du journal révolutionnaire, 1789* (Lyon: Presses Universitaires de Lyon, 1989), 253–56.

7. *Révolutions de Paris*, no. 17, Oct. 31–Nov. 7, pp. 4–6. The text continues with the image of "civic enrollment" treated as a living "canvas" (p. 7). Concerning celebrations as a moment of civic thanks, see Rétat, "Aux Armes Citoyens," 603.

8. See *La Ville*, trans. Philippe Fritsch (Paris: Aubier Montaigne, 1982), 173–93; and Philippe Fritsch, "Le Citoyen, le bourgeois et le citadin," in *Regards sociologiques* (Université de Strasbourg), 1991, 2: 1–30.

2

CITOYENS, CITOYENNES: CULTURAL REGRESSION AND THE SUBVERSION OF FEMALE CITIZENSHIP IN THE FRENCH REVOLUTION

Madelyn Gutwirth

In 1799 Germaine de Staël would write:

Someday, I believe, a time will come when philosophic legislators will grant serious attention to the education women ought to receive, to the civil laws to protect them, to the duties that ought to be imposed upon them, to the happiness that may be guaranteed them; but in the present state of things, they belong . . . neither to the order of nature nor to that of society. In some respects their destiny resembles that of the freed slaves under the emperors: if they want to acquire influence, they are reproached with committing a crime unauthorized by law; and if they remain slaves, their lot is to stay oppressed.[1]

Inherent in Madame de Staël's musing over women's fate is the paradox that women's status presented to her generation, born after mid-century. As she summons up the kind of measured consideration legislators ought to bring to thinking about her sex, she is reduced to perplexity as to how to categorize its situation. By the year of the Consulate's onset, she finds the freed slave to be her closest analogue. Such a slave stands upon a threshold, free to go where no slave has gone before, in a liminal position but ready for nothing. Primarily, she finds herself in this posture because she belongs neither to nature, an imaginary construct to which she cannot turn for comfort, nor to society, which rejects her impulse to participate actively in its re-creation in ways responsive to her needs. She remains a member of an instrumental class, unentitled under law to be seen as an individual.

What troubles Staël here is the great problem of her life. She speaks of it openly by way of exception: Ordinarily, she chooses the more politic tactic of saying whatever she needs to say on this issue only covertly. What puzzles her is the plethora of imperatives aimed at her sex by male culture: to be virtuous, but not to the point of grimness; to please by their talents, but not to cultivate them to excess. Staël's perspective is that of a woman of the privileged class, for whom politics was the elixir of life: for her, privation of a participatory role in society betokened an annihilation of her energies close to the extinction of life itself. By the century's end, her claim would be that the Revolution had reduced women to the most absurd mediocrity (*Litt.*, pp. 359–60). The gulf between her understanding of herself, women's understanding of themselves, and Revolutionary male culture's insistent pronouncements about what they were and should be was a wide and jagged one.

I argue here that a long series of regressive ideological steps, from well before 1789, had prepared the way for the First Republic's shunning of women's claims to active citizenship. These moves had so effectively engineered a climate in which women's demands would be received as "out of order" that subsequent history would all but bury the evidence of the force and variety of their activities under the illusion that nothing (or nothing of consequence) had transpired in the struggle for gender parity of the Revolution.

In referring to "regressive ideological moves," I mean to summon up to scrutiny the tactic employed by male culture in the battle for women's full status as cultural beings of reverting to alleged previous models of female subordination, whether in nature or in culture, so as to authorize its present campaign to maintain its own sex privilege.[2] These reversions, in their implicit assumption that what was once must inevitably persist in being, possess a psychically retrogressive power: they hold that only in a pastorale of the past can we uncover a true (that is, strongly sexually dimorphized) promise of gender harmony in the future.

Christine Fauré divines such an unconscious trend to dimorphism in Voltaire's reaction to the *puella campanica*, or wild girl, captured in 1731. In anger, she had struck a companion who then died in her arms. "As soon as she saw her companion's blood flow, she was sorry, she wept, she staunched the wound, she placed herbs on it. . . . Call reason and remorse what you like, they exist, and they are the foundations of natural law."[3] Voltaire read into her spontaneous recognition of the significance of her act an alternative to Christian pessimism: a benevolent human nature that might release humankind from the curse of Eve. Sexual temptation, projected onto our original mother, had by tradition, rendered woman quintessentially evil. But now, as Fauré puts it, "the female sex was becoming naturally good."[4] Voltaire's assessment of the *puella* takes an alle-gorical form: the girl, representing *human* goodness, assumes for her sex the burden of conscience for humankind. For women themselves, however, the association of women with pity, charity, and conscience represents them as subject to a series of vulnerabilities: to a permanent childlikeness and dependency; to inarticulateness before overwhelming emotion; and, of course (and this is capital), to helplessness before their own sexuality. We discern the problem inherent for women in internalizing this division of labor: how to accept what is proffered to them as their sphere without losing all grasp on cultural aspiration or power. Appeasement of these needs will be found in the fact that clustered within the qualities proposed to them as theirs lay a set of values that would ultimately be rejected by the *demos*, but to which it continued to pay pious tribute. Women, while yet dispossessed, could thus become, as a sex, inspirators to the new national dispensation. Buoyed up as they might be by this inflated role for their gender, they might yet despair as individuals of their personal capacity to contribute to the common good.

The progressive tendency in the whole of the eighteenth century to break the growing identification of women with culture, of which we still find vestiges in its folklore of "women's reign,"[5] is imprinted in the works of all of the *philosophes*. Theirs was a campaign, albeit only a semiconscious one, undertaken under the banner of Reason, to reassign women *qua* gender to their sexual and maternal functions, and to force them into themselves with respect to their own cultural pretensions.

Carol Pateman has posited the thesis, apposite to the French Revolution, that "at the turning point between the old world of status and the modern world of contract," a new story of "masculine political birth" was told. Locke and Rousseau had created a new form of political right via the concept of a contract to be entered into exclusively by men, who would thereby exercise a "patriarchal or sex-right" over women. In this story, "the women are already defeated and declared procreatively and politically irrelevant." In the new civil society, "all men, not just fathers, can generate political life and political right. Political creativity belongs not to paternity but to masculinity." Pateman argues that our very notion of civil freedom for the individual is embodied as a wholly masculine attribute: "the sons overturn paternal rule not merely to gain their liberty but to secure women for themselves."

At the same time that it locked women out of rights in the polis, contract theory, she tells us, "was yet the emancipatory doctrine *par excellence*, promising that universal freedom was the principle of the modern era." The salient civil difference between men and women is that the former may obtain rights via contract, while the latter "are born into subjection." Here we sense the regressive tendency alluded to in our title: men's potential for citizenship, while it is presented as rooted in ancient precedent, lies open to future development in contract law. Women's subordination, posited as "natural," is destined for infinite repetition, authorized by history as well as theory.

Any threat of women's independence, sexual or social, appears as a permanent fount of disorder. "Women," writes Pateman, "their bodies and bodily passions, present the 'nature' that must be controlled and transcended if social order is to be created and sustained."[6] Thus Montesquieu gives to a brief passage of his *Spirit of the Laws* the title, "Of Public Continency." Here he offers this amazing pronouncement: "So many are the imperfections that attend the loss of virtue in women, and so greatly are their minds depraved when this principal guard is removed, that in a popular state public incontinency may be considered as the last of miseries, and as a certain forerunner of a change in the constitution." "In republics," Montesquieu concludes, "women are free by the laws and restrained by manners; lust is banished thence, and with it corruption and vice.'' In Montesquieu's and in the pervasive discourse, the containment and amelioration of morality is viewed entirely as a problem of the control of disorders of female sexuality, and ancient precedents are invoked to justify this conception.

A concept of women as civic reward is cited approvingly by Montesquieu. Among the Samnites, opponents of Rome, all the youths would be assembled and their virtues openly assessed. "He that was declared the best of the whole assembly," he writes, "had leave given him to choose which girl he pleased for his wife." The second best had next pick, and so on. As *The Spirit of the Laws* sees it, "no nobler and grander recompense . . . more capable of influencing both sexes" could be imagined.[7]

Rousseau's "Letter to M. d'Alembert on Spectacles" unveils the tripartite gender politics the Revolution will espouse: the resentment of women's pervasive presence in society, seen as vitiating to its mores; the demand that women retreat to sexual modesty and pliancy; and the appeal to models from ancient history, to nature, or to both for exemplars of cleansing female regeneration. As to the first panel of the triptych, resentment of women's role in society, Rousseau writes that "people everywhere are convinced that in neglecting the manners of their sex [women] neglect its duties; everywhere, then, we see that in turning their insolence against men's firm male self-assurance, women vilify themselves by their odious imitation, thus simultaneously dishonoring both their own sex and ours." A woman's vulnerability must melt the hearts of men. After all, he reasons, "why give her a more feeling heart, less speed in running, a less robust body, a shorter stature, more delicate muscles, if [nature] had not destined her to let herself be vanquished?" Regarding the practices of republican Geneva in this letter, he turns chiefly to antiquity for his paradigm of society. "It is certain," he avers, "that where women were segregated and maintained as submissive members of a household" there reigned a domestic peace he could perceive nowhere in his own time. If Rousseau addresses women as *citoyennes*, he clearly conceives of them solely as citizen-consorts. For our present purposes, his most succinct formulation is this: "For a monarch to govern men or women must be a matter of indifference to him, so long as he is obeyed; but in a republic, we need men."[8]

We readily apprehend the relevance of the foregoing to the campaign for a neoclassical ethos that La Font de Saint-Yenne advocated in 1747 when he wrote that "the painter of history is the only painter of the soul."[9] Excoriating the rococo's preoccupation with the senses, La Font takes artists to task for pandering to the tastes of court women and makes himself the advocate of a manly art. His critique excludes the feminine, both as an aesthetic and as theme, from serious art forms, this to be achieved by reverting to the ancient history that relegated it to invisibility. For La Font, the male bond, as the prime mover of history, is alone a preoccupation worthy of art. It comes as no surprise to consider how completely David's *Oath of the Horatii*, *Brutus*, and *Tennis Court Oath* visually fulfill both La Font's prescriptions and Pateman's image of the male contract. As these works of David's display, however, women are not so much to be excluded as marginalized and privatized, integrated into a new separatist story that is invariably presented as an old one.

The Revolution's expulsion of women from the public scene as the focus of disorder will be effected by two means: First, the male populace at large will espouse, or at least not reject, the view that the freedoms of upper-class women are undermining national strength, equated with masculine potency. Second, Rousseauist prejudices, by no means his alone, of course, will become so popular and omnipresent in the discourse of the rising bourgeoisie that women will successfully internalize his pattern of femininity. We meet this phenomenon ad nauseam in the rhetoric of even the most militant women, who feel moved to make their pleas as *épouses et mères* or to disclaim their ambition in the very midst of sweeping pronouncements or demands. One example of this tendency can be found in Germaine de Staël's 1792 pamphlet appealing for the life of the queen, where she herself claims to be speaking only as a simple woman of sentiment and attempts to present the queen as a good, maternal woman, totally private and apolitical.[10] Even Olympe de Gouges, in her dedication of *The Rights of Woman* to the queen, in pleading with her not to traffic with France's enemies, reminds her, "Ah, Madame, songez que vous êtes mère et épouse."[11]

Restif de la Bretonne and Mercier, Rousseauists both, exploit their precursor for his authority. Robert Darnton has tellingly spoken of the smoldering resentment of such writers, in which misogyny played no minor role. In Restif's *gynographes*, he presents us with two women interlocutors, an example of pressuring women to internalize the dominant gender paradigm. One of them declares, "We women are a hundred times happier when we see in our husband a beloved Master rather than an equal, even were he cherished; what our hearts demand is a filial sentiment [for him]." Restif's simplicity is revealing of the temper of the contemporary quarrel: he grouses that "we must prove to women the necessity for subordination; things have gotten to the point where most of them believe that all must be, and remain equal. This is absolutely false."[12] His remark baldly conveys his perception that women were getting out of hand in their claims to equality.

For Mercier, classical culture provided less of a precedent than Jean-Jacques's Nature, which "has decreed that [a woman] should never raise herself above a man . . . without risk of becoming odious and ridiculous. Nothing excuses her from this eternal subordination, even were she to sit on the throne of the world. . . . It is not permitted her to be insolent to a man; that is, to scorn her master."[13]

P. D. Jimack has remarked on the rising tide in the quarrel over women that preceded the Revolution, in which both sexes were engaged. It is he who cites Mme de Miremont's cautious statement that "women are not born to command. Prejudice would constrain them to obey. Between these extremes, there is a mean which it depends on their skill to achieve."[14] Miremont concedes the whole show: women may not command, although she plainly identifies that it is prejudice (that is, regression to a past consensus of the norm) that decrees this, and forces women into postures of obedience. Her counsel to women is to develop tactical skills to circumvent being perceived as guilty of any extremes of behavior. She was far from alone in her rueful reaction to the wave of reductionism concerning women.[15] However, on the plane of influential discourse, Condorcet's would be the sole conceivably consequential dissenting voice to the chorus of denigration of women's capacities as other than mother-wives.

In 1788 and 1790, Condorcet was to raise the contractarians' own view, to press it home. All sentient beings have rights; women, being sentient beings, could not be denied them and must enter the social contract as partners, to become citizens in the full sense of the word. Yet even Condorcet walks with caution, proposing the limiting of women's franchise to propertied widows and unmarried women, thus resisting the fire of those who would accuse him of undermining the subordination of wives.[16] Condorcet's publications were virtually alone in resisting the prevailing repetition compulsion, as he averred that even if women had never, under any so-called free constitution, been granted rights, they ought still to gain them now. He finds his precedent neither in history nor biology, but in the attempt to carry contract reasoning to what he viewed as its logical conclusion.

Condorcet's pleas for something besides ridicule to meet his proposals seem mainly to have fallen into the void. One exception was Deputy Pierre Guyomar, in his *Partisan of Political Equality among Individuals*. Tellingly, Guyomar shares with Condorcet a rhetoric that excludes references to antiquity. Every day, he says, he hears people say that there are 25 million inhabitants in France, but no sooner do they speak of members of the sovereign nation than suddenly they subtract half the population. In fact he scolds the French for clinging to the feudal talisman of sexual prejudice. If women are granted no vote, says Guyomar, "elles n'ont point de cité," they remain outside the walls of the state, and, he claims, "the title of *citoyenne* is simply ridiculous and should be excised from our language."[17]

We recall the revolutionaries' ardor for mimicry of Plutarchian postures.[18] When Saint-Just failed to be elected to the Legislative Assembly, he sighed, "Dear God! Must Brutus languish far from Rome?"[19] Compare this confident assumption of Brutus's mantle with Claire Lacombe's labored negotiations with Roman heroism as she speaks before the National Assembly on July 25, 1792.

Born with the courage of a Roman woman and the hatred of tyrants, I should be happy to contribute to their destruction. Plotters, vile slaves of Neros and Caligulas, oh would that I could annihilate you! and you, mothers of families whom I would condemn for leaving your children to follow my example: while I do my duty in battling the enemies of the fatherland, you fulfill yours by inculcating in your children the feelings each Frenchman must have from birth, the love of freedom and the hatred of despots.[20]

Lacombe, while striving to find space for herself to play an active role as citizen, palpably needs to reassure her male associates that her civic act betokens no menace to their domestic peace.

As they did her male contemporaries, Plutarch's narratives inspired Manon Roland to love republican virtue. Her eventual and resentful transmutation of this cult into the more politic one of Roman matronism would in no way preserve her from the charge of comporting herself as a "public woman," even for activities carried on in private.[21] In André Amar's statement banishing women from the public space on October 30, 1793, among other political women, he cites Manon Roland as a corrupter of the Republic. "A wit with great ambition," she was "a monster in every way," who "wanted to rise above herself; her desire to be learned led her to forget the virtues of her sex, and that desire, always dangerous, ended by making her perish on the scaffold."[22]

Notice this same litany in the *Moniteur universel*'s denunciation of Olympe de Gouges, executed on November 3. "Olympe de Gouges, born with an exalted imagination, took her delirium for natural inspiration. She wished to be a statesman. . . . It is as though the law has punished this conspirator for having forgotten the virtues appropriate to her sex."[23] The law, rather than custom, as in Montesquieu's republican antiquity, is here explicitly invoked as a mechanism to police women's hubristic behavior.

Again, in the explosive climate created by her murder of Marat, the language of the *Répertoire du tribunal révolutionnaire*'s characterization of Charlotte Corday in July 1793 recapitulates the prevailing dread of and scorn for female actors on the political stage, berating her for affecting "pretensions to knowledge . . . strength of character and to the politics of nations." Finding her "heart empty for want of pleasure," it ends with this ultimate accusation: "She sought to end her life in the manner of Erostrates."[24] Erostrates burned down Diana's temple at Ephesus merely to make his name renowned. Corday, coupled with him as quintessentially uncivic, was equally impugned in her sex. In pursuit of confirmation of her sexual stain, a deputation of Jacobin officials, including David, went to examine her headless torso to ascertain whether or not she had died a virgin.[25] The terms of this revulsion by the Jacobins against her act reject not alone this specific political act, but those of all women. Her murder provided the pretext for a panicky restatement of women's intrinsic unworthiness to serve the state.

However a woman revolutionary might strive to modify the cultural repressiveness to her of the regnant imperatives, by assuming the prescribed postures and language of a Roman matron, as did Manon Roland, or by acting on a tacit assumption of her right to citizenship, like Olympe de Gouges, Etta Palm, Pauline Léon, or Théroigne de Méricourt, or by wresting for herself a role as hero, like Charlotte Corday, all were entrapped by the ambient masculine will to circumscribe and subdue them as actors.

Some women exhibited a consciousness of the nature of the repression, though like the men who saw it also, they were powerless to counter it. Mlle Jodin in her *Legislative Views for Women*, even as she panders somewhat to the moralism of the day, adopts a percipiently anticlassical approach. It would not be at all difficult, she warns men, to turn your logic around and debunk your great heroes of antiquity. We might "regard Horace as nothing more than an adroit and lucky soldier, who owed his triumph more to the overconfidence of his enemies than to his own courage; Brutus and Manlius, who sentenced their children to death against senatorial advice and despite the pleas of the populace, might appear to us simply as barbarians, rather than as ardent citizens."[26] Seeking, as a woman, to confront the present possibility for enlargement of women's rights, Jodin mocks outright the repressive imperative to cultural regression.

Staël too ridicules the slavishness of political argument to Greek and Roman precedents. "We are losing France through allusions to Roman history that many people come up with because they're so pleased with themselves for knowing them."[27] Like Jodin and the other social progressives, she observed how sweeping, inaccurate, and stultifying to germane confrontation with present circumstances the constant harping on ancient models had become.

Amar's proclamation provided the official seal of women's exile from the republic's workings. Conjuring up his own sex in all its neoclassical splendor, he decrees that only men possess the devotion, the impassivity, and the self-abnegation to govern, and asks this rhetorical question of his fellows, which he expects can be answered only by a chorus of "nos": "Do you wish women to be seen in the French Republic coming to the bar, to the tribune, to political assemblies like men, abandoning restraint, the source of all their sex's virtues, and the care of their families?"[28]

Chérieux's cartoon of a women's club meeting in a church captures an outrage like Amar's in a fiercely jocular way. Here we find the women in a contemporary scene, some of them sedate, natural, and unheroic, others gesticulating and orating, their breasts dangerously alienating all interest in their words. Unlike the affirmatively upthrust arms of David's *Horatii* or the pyramidal unity of the coveners of his *Tennis Court Oath*, conjoining in common purpose, the energies of the women's flailing arms meet only the empty air.

An appropriate pendant to Chérieux's representation of women engaged in Revolution is David's *Triumph of the French People*, an incomplete drawing for an opera curtain. The Hercules, whose figure Lynn Hunt has so fruitfully researched as being the result of a quest for a "distinctly virile representation of sovereignty," sits enthroned in his hugeness, leaning on his club, in the Roman chariot, the now minuscule goddesses of liberty and equality on his knees.[29] As armed citizens flay the fallen kings, the martyrs for freedom—Le Peletier, William Tell, Brutus, Chalier, and Marat—follow. The only human female presence allowed into this triumphant cortège is that of Cornelia with her Gracchi, a severely hooded figure bent to attend to the childish needs of future republican heroes. This image is clearly intended to represent the concretion not merely of the Jacobin Revolution, but France's continuing history, a history conceived of as a march in which muscular men slay tyrants.

Christine Fauré has observed that the *cahiers de doléances* of women's guilds and religious communities testify to "their disappointment at being deprived of representation in the Estates General in 1789."[30] Considered in a class with domestic servants and minors as passive citizens, those dependent upon the will and capacities of others, women saw themselves decisively excluded from consultative citizenship by the granting of civil rights to male domestic servants in 1793.[31] Even so, after Amar's speech in the Convention banning the Société de Républicaines Révolutionnaires and all other associations among women, the deputy Charlier spoke up on contractual grounds, to murmurs of derision. He affirmed that there was no ground for denying women the right of assembly without contesting women's membership in mankind, and that problems with this particular group should not impugn women's right to form groups. But Basire replied to his intervention that since women's societies had proven disruptive, "let no one speak to me of principles."[32]

The implacable silence that met women's efforts to be heard, even using the Revolution's own rhetoric, is a speaking one. It said that the men who made the Revolution needed only to close ranks and wait for women's activities to cease, for the engines of culture had long been set in place to render any dissent from a vision of the Republic as one of men only an absurdity.

Pateman emphasizes how powerfully an imperative to mothering sustains the patriarchal character of the modern state. For her, the importance lent to motherhood arises from the state's having constructed political difference as sexual difference, the difference that "naturally" subordinates women. Unspoken by the deputies as they refused to address issues of women's representation was that persons with female bodies may not be full members of the polis. Equally essential to the Republic's gender outcome is the issue of male sex-right, bound up as it is with male resentment of women's potential right of refusal of it. Women's vote and women's assembly represented only so many instances of their speaking up in ways threatening to one of the Revolution's implicit promises to its men: that they would be enthroned as heads of their own households, upheld by acquiescent and supportive women. Hence, they were deaf to Guyomar's plea: "What? at the birth of equality, we would also proclaim the slavery of half of humankind, whose happiness we claim to serve? The coming of a new order of things will leave women in the old, and they will reckon from this moment their assumption of the role of helots to the republic."

The naturally free and equal individual of the republican contract "must necessarily *agree* to be ruled by another."[33] From women, as Guyomar lamented, no such consent was solicited: their wills were subsumed under male right. And yet, whether the revolutionary world had the ability to recognize it or not, "gender is a system that divides power," as Catherine MacKinnon writes. "It is therefore a political system," under which women have been "economically exploited, relegated to domestic slavery, forced into motherhood, sexually objectified, physically abused, used in denigrating entertainment, deprived of a voice and authentic culture, and disenfranchised and excluded from political life."[34]

The Revolution's negative constitutional treatment of women seamlessly connects with the prerevolutionary discourse concerning them. Yet the antidote to female acquiescence lay dormant in the Revolution's conception of the free citizen, which women had patently responded to, despite all propaganda, much as did men. Staël, in 1799, reflects this as she remarks ruefully that "men, in France, will never be so republican as to be able to do without the natural independence and pride in women's nature" (*Litt.*, 362).

Even as the contagion of longing for individual salvation promised by the Reformation had slowly spread from men to women, the Revolution's promise of universal citizenship, once enunciated, could not ultimately be contained, only impeded and becalmed. Guyomar's sarcasm over the misleading title of *citoyenne* that the Revolution used to address its women proved to be excessively pessimistic: the French women's wait has been amazingly long, but rights are now theirs in principle. So savage was resistance to any alteration in the antique conception of the *citoyen* enshrined in the First Republic's visual constructs and in its discourse, that it forbade negotiation out of its rigid structures for more than a century. These structures proved powerful enough to exert still, as the twentieth century ends, some of their old exclusionary power.

NOTES

1. Germaine de Staël, *Oeuvres* (Paris: Lefevre, 1838), 3 vols., *De la littérature*, "Des femmes qui cultivent les lettres," 2:357. Subsequent references to this work, in parentheses in the text, are abbreviated: *Litt.*

2. For different styles of discussion of the structural dimorphisms of gender in eighteenth-century thought, see Paul Hoffmann, *La Femme dans la pensée des lumières* (Paris: Ophrys, 1977); L. Jordanova, "Natural Facts: A Historical Perspective on Science and Sexuality," in *Nature, Culture and Gender*, ed. C. MacCormack and M. Strathern (Cambridge: Cambridge University Press, 1980); and Joan B. Landes, *Women and the Public Sphere in the Age of the French Revolution* (Ithaca, N.Y.: Cornell University Press, 1988). Landes holds that the "Revolution was constructed against women, not just without them" (pp. 2–3).

3. Preface to the "Poème sur la loi naturelle" (1752), in Voltaire, *Mélanges* (Paris: Pléiade, 1961), 272, cited by Christine Fauré, *Democracy without Women*, tr. Claudia Gorbman and John Berk (Bloomington: Indiana University Press, 1985), 83.

4. Fauré, *Democracy*, 83, using Michèle Duchet's chapter on Voltaire's anthropology in *Anthropologie et histoire au siècle des lumières* (Paris: Maspéro, 1971), 306.

5. See Edmond and Jules de Goncourt, *La Femme au XVIIIe siècle* (Paris: 1877), 1; and Jean Starobinski, *L'Invention de la liberté* (Geneva: Skira, 1964), 55.

6. Carol Pateman, *The Sexual Contract* (Stanford, Calif.: Stanford University Press, 1988), 36, 2, 39, 100.

7. *The Spirit of the Laws*, tr. Thomas Nugent and Franz Neumann (New York: Hafner Press, 1949), 1: 101, 102, 107–108.

8. "Lettre à M. d'Alembert sur le spectacle" in *Du Contrat social* (Paris: Garnier, 1962), 193, 192, 204. I discuss this letter at length in my book *The Twilight of the Goddesses, Women and Representation in the French Revolutionary Era* (New Brunswick, N.J.: Rutgers University Press, 1992). All translations in the text are mine unless otherwise attributed.

9. *Réflexions sur quelques causes de l'état présent de la peinture en France* (The Hague: 1747), 8. Note Landes: "The early modern classical revival—with its political, linguistic and stylistic overtones—invested public action with a decidedly masculinist ethos" (Women and the Public Sphere, 3).

10. See my "Nature, cruauté et femmes immolées: Les Réflexions sur le procès de la reine," in *Le Groupe de Coppet et la Révolution française* (Lausanne: Institut Benjamin Constant, 1988), 121–40.

11. Olympe de Gouges, *Les Droits de la Femme* (Paris: 1791), quoted in *Les Femmes dans la Révolution française* (Paris: Edhis, 1982) 2, no. 36: 2.

12. *Les Gynographes* (The Hague: 1777), 1: 38, 21b. See also Robert Darnton, *The Literary Underground of the Old Régime* (Cambridge: Harvard University Press, 1980), 1–40.

13. Louis-Sébastien Mercier, *Paris pendant la Révolution ou le nouveau Paris 1789–1798* (Paris: Le Livre Club du Libraire, 1962), 2: 23–24.

14. Mme de Miremont, *Traité de l'éducation des femmes* (Paris: 1779, 1789), 1: 287, in Jimack, "The Paradox of Sophie and Julie: Contemporary Response to Rousseau's Ideal Wife and Mother," in *Women and Society in Eighteenth Century France*, ed. Eva Jacobs (London: Athlone, 1979), 152–65.

15. For other examples, see Nina Ratner Gelbart, "*Le Journal des dames* and its Female Editors: Censorship and Feminism in the Old Régime Press," in *Press and Politics in Eighteenth Century France*, eds. Jack R. Censer and Jeremy Popkin (Berkeley: University of California Press, 1987); Riballier, *De L'education physique et morale des femmes* (Brussels: 1779); and Marie-Armande Gacon-Dufour, *Mémoire pour le sexe féminin contre le sexe masculin* (Paris: 1787).

16. "Lettres d'un bourgeois de New-Haven," in Filippo Mazzei, *Recherches historiques et politiques sur les Etat-Unis de l'Amérique septentrionale par un citoyen de Virginie* (Paris: 1788); and "Sur l'admission des femmes au droit de cité, Société de 1789, 3 juillet 1790," in *Les Femmes dans la Révolution française*, 2, no. 25.

17. "Le Partisan de l'égalité politique entre les individus, ou problème important de l'égalité des droits et l'inégalité en fait," in *Les Femmes dans la Révolution française*, 2, no. 45, 10–11.

18. Dorinda Outram discusses the derivation of corporeal comportments from Graeco-Roman models in *The Body and the French Revolution* (New Haven: Yale University Press, 1989). See also Harold Parker, *The Cult of Antiquity and the French Revolution* (Chicago: University of Chicago Press, 1937).

19. *Oeuvres complètes de Saint-Just*, ed. Charles Vellay (Paris: 1908), 1: 347, letter of July 20, 1792.

20. "Discours prononcé à la Barre de l'Assemblée Nationale par Mme Lacombe, le 25 juillet 1792," in *Les Femmes dans la Révolution française*, 2, no. 43: 2.

21. See Gita May, *Madame Roland and the Age of Revolution* (New York: Columbia University Press, 1970), 184–85.

22. *L'Ancien Moniteur*, 18, 300.

23. Ibid., 450.

24. Charles-Aimé Dauban, *La Démagogie à Paris* (Paris: 1868), 277.

25. Jean Epois, *L'Affaire Corday-Marat prélude à la Terreur* (Paris: Cercle d'or, 1980), 207.

26. "Vues législatives pour les femmes adressées à l'Assemblée nationale," in *Les Femmes dans la Révolution française*, 1, no. 24: 18.

27. *Des Circonstances actuelles qui peuvent terminer la Révolution en France*, ed. Lucie Omacini (Paris: Droz, 1979), 300.

28. *L'Ancien Moniteur*, 18, 300.

29. See *Politics Culture and Class in the French Revolution* (Berkeley: University of California Press, 1984), 94–106.

30. Fauré, *Democracy*, 105–6.

31. Patrice Guéniffey, "Suffrage," in *Dictionnaire critique de la Révolution française* (Paris: Flammarion, 1988), 616.

32. *L'Ancien Moniteur*, 18, 300.

33. Pateman, *The Sexual Contract*, 40, 11, 40.

34. *Toward a Feminist Theory of the State* (Cambridge: Harvard University Press, 1989), 160.

3

THE NATIONAL ASSEMBLY AND THE INVENTION OF CITIZENSHIP

Michael P. Fitzsimmons

As with so many other facets of the French Revolution, the concept of citizenship had antecedents in the Old Regime, although Rousseau, in a note in Chapter 6 of *The Social Contract*, observed that the French had one of the most flawed notions of it.[1] Whether or not one agrees with his assessment, it is clear that the concept of citizen did begin to acquire greater clarity and definition between 1787 and 1789, as the fiscal and political crises demonstrated the deleterious effect of privilege on the polity. Ultimately, however, as is the case with so many elements of the Revolution, its realization was a particular achievement of the National Assembly.

Under the Old Regime there was no universal bond among Frenchmen apart from their common allegiance to the monarch, through whom all civic life was mediated. More than anything else the king was the supreme arbiter, a role recalling the medieval notion of the king as dispenser of justice, but now considerably enlarged. The position of the monarch as supreme arbiter under Old Regime society was most evident in the ubiquity of privilege, which the *Encyclopedia* defined without irony as rights belonging to some and not to others.[2] Privilege and civil rights were, in fact, synonymous—particular rather than universal and emanating exclusively from the monarch.[3]

The developing fiscal crisis of the 1780s, however, exposed the deficiencies of privilege as a principle or instrument of government. Calonne convened the Assembly of Notables to deal with the deteriorating finances of the crown, but the abdication of responsibility by the Notables—after three months of deliberations and negotiations, in the course of which the crown had acceded to most of their demands—led to a perception that privilege had prevailed over the interests of the state.[4]

The revelations made at the Assembly of Notables shocked most Frenchmen interested in public affairs, and the knowledge of the perilous state of the crown's finances, along with the failure of the Assembly of Notables, provided a greater focus for debate. In the polemic that followed, the idea of the nation initially emerged largely as the contraposition to privilege.[5] For that reason it was, in fact, somewhat amorphous; even after the opening of the Estates-General it could be used in reference to Provence or Brittany as easily as to France as a whole.[6]

Whereas the idea of the nation was indistinct, the concept of citizen, which was attached to it, had greater clarity. A definition put forward apparently by Guillaume-Joseph Saige, the author of the earlier *Catéchisme du citoyen, ou Eléments du droit public français, par demandes et par réponses,* which had appeared initially in 1775 in response to the Maupeou coup and was later reprinted,[7] is instructive. In a new pamphlet published in anticipation of the opening of the Estates-General, *Nouveau catéchisme du citoyen,* Saige defined a citizen as one "subject to the laws of nature, of reason and of his country, and who desires only the general well-being of the nation."[8] Of the various components of this definition, it was the last that was the most significant and the obvious practical touchstone in the period preceding the opening of the Estates-General—placing the welfare of the nation above the interests of one's order.[9]

The initial benchmarks for this elevation of the nation over personal or corporate interests were the relinquishment of fiscal privileges and the composition of the Estates-General.[10] The definition that Saige offered, as well as the issues that determined it, highlights another significant aspect of the idea of the citizen in the months preceding the opening of the Estates-General—there was no inherent social dimension to the concept of citizen. It did not in any way imply social equality; rather, it was a state of mind characterized by civic-minded disinterestedness and a primordial concern for the welfare of the nation. The absence of the idea of social equality is most evident in the fact that many *cahiers* advocated ennoblement on the basis of service to the nation.[11]

By the beginning of 1789, then, even after the doubling of the Third Estate and after the princes of the blood had agreed to yield fiscal privileges, the debate on procedure for the Estates-General continued to rage—much to the chagrin of the princes—but it was almost entirely political in nature. The objective of those who advocated vote by head was primarily to assure that privilege—the nemesis of the polity and embodied in vote by order—did not prevail over the interests of the nation. Neither the abolition of orders nor the extirpation of privilege was implicit in the idea of the nation or of the citizen.[12]

Indeed, at the Estates-General the Third Estate showed considerable respect and consideration for the clergy and nobility despite occasional vexatious incidents, beginning with the costume and protocol of the opening ceremony itself. Only after several weeks of attempted persuasion and repeated efforts at mediation and conciliation, through conferences again punctuated on occasion by imperious conduct on the part of the nobility, did the commons, as they now called themselves, take an independent initiative. Even at this juncture, however, the deputies avoided all social or quantitative definitions and gave primacy to the nation by adopting the title of National Assembly. As the assembly of the nation, it was open to all clerical or noble deputies concerned about the state. Those clerical and noble deputies who did cross over, in fact, were seated in separate sections designated for their order, underscoring once again that the quality of citizen was regard for the nation rather than a social category.

The victory of the commons in the formation of the National Assembly represented the triumph of a concept of the nation rooted in political equality and concern for the nation, but the conversion of that victory into a smoothly functioning institution proved elusive. Because a large plurality of deputies, including a majority of the nobility, were there not out of conviction but due to deference to the monarch, the National Assembly had difficulty achieving a sense of purpose or identity in its first few weeks of existence.[13]

The National Assembly dedicated itself to its stated goal of drafting a constitution and formed a Committee of the Constitution—the membership of which was carefully apportioned according to orders—to act as a virtual steering committee for the endeavor.[14] In a reflection of the state of affairs in the Assembly as a whole, the efforts of the committee were uncertain and tentative. This was particularly evident in the report offered by the committee on July 27, when it announced that it would use the *cahiers* as the basis for drawing up the constitution. This confused, sometimes conflicting, body of documents, from which the committee had extrapolated two sets of guidelines, did not offer a clear and compelling course of action. It is, in fact, indicative of how indistinct their mandate was that among the issues open for debate were whether sovereign courts would ratify laws or whether *lettres de cachet* would be merely reformed or abolished.[15]

Just over a week later, however, the night of August 4 completely transformed the situation at the National Assembly. In the aftermath of August 4, the hesitancy of the Assembly disappeared, to be replaced by a new boldness in constructing a polity that would, among other results, fundamentally redefine the concept of the citizen.

However contrived or premeditated the night of August 4 was in origin, and however limited the objectives of the initial motions offered that evening, the emotion generated launched the Assembly onto an independent course, consisting initially of an abandonment of privileges of every sort, which led, in turn, to a fraternal sense of unity through the nation. A large body of evidence leaves no doubt about the profound effect that the night of August 4 had on deputies,[16] and it subsequently had an equally profound impact on the nature of the French polity. Until recently, however, this aspect was less noticed, if not overlooked; the tendency was to focus instead on the degree to which the actions of that evening abolished feudalism, with particular attention paid to the undeniable regression on this issue, as well as a few others, that occurred in the following days.

The results of the night of August 4 were, in fact, profound and wide ranging, and one of them was to harmonize more fully the relationship between the nation and the citizen. Prior to August 4, a citizen had been conceived as one who would subordinate his own interests and the interests of his order to the greater good of the nation.[17] The elemental political equality attained in the formation of the National Assembly did not carry over into any type of social equality: orders had been maintained after the National Assembly had been fully formed, and there was an implicit recognition that the First and Second estates had particular viewpoints and concerns.[18]

The night of August 4, however, with its total suppression of privilege, destroyed in its entirety the political and social structure of the Old Regime, joining all in the nation and leaving no special issues with which to be concerned. The polity had to be built anew, and with the destruction of privilege each individual now had an equal role and place in it. Membership in the nation, rather than privilege mediated through the monarch, became the basis of rights in the polity. Indeed, the idea of citizenship, referring to rights accorded to members of a state, was realized on the night of August 4.[19] The nation became an all-encompassing entity and a source of deep unity and equity. It was as a result of the night of August 4 that the term "citizen" came to be invested with its connotations of equality and fraternity.[20]

With no special interests or privileges left to defend or consider, orders were superfluous, a fact the Assembly explicitly acknowledged on October 15, 1789. On that day, in the course of a discussion on how to replace those deputies who had left the Assembly during the October Days, it decreed the abolition of orders, the end of particular costumes for deputies, and the termination of designated places in the meeting hall. In a further indication of the link between this action and the sense of unity generated on August 4, the records of the meeting note that "the Assembly adopted this proposal appropriate to establish and to maintain a valued fellowship."[21]

The abolition of orders represented an effort by the National Assembly to reaffirm its sense of common purpose, and in the following months it went on to realize its new model of the polity not only in the nation at large, but in its own operations as well. In March 1790, the National Assembly offered a particularly striking assertion of its new ideal of citizenship when it elected Jean-Paul Rabaut de Saint-Etienne as president. The choice of a Protestant minister to preside over a body determining the destinies of France—a body containing a substantial number of priests and bishops—was a compelling demonstration that the Assembly itself elevated devotion to the nation over all other qualities. In fact, Rabaut de Saint-Etienne himself noted how extraordinary his election was and how the Assembly had fulfilled its own ideals.[22]

An additional demonstration of the new concept of citizenship by the National Assembly came in June 1790, when it abolished nobility. The motions offered that evening appear to have been prearranged in much the same manner as on the night of August 4, to which some compared it,[23] but the measure was at the same time a logical extension of the new ideal of the nation that the National Assembly was attempting to realize. The abolition of orders in October 1789 had been followed by the nationalization of Church lands in November 1789, thereby ending the independent corporate status of the Church and integrating it with the nation. In this respect, then, the nobility were an anomaly. Although some noble deputies saw the measure, and especially the manner in which it was proposed and passed, as theatrical, others, including at least one noble deputy apparently not involved in the motion, believed that it represented the complete fulfillment of the idea of citizenship promulgated on the night of August 4.[24]

The preceding actions reflected the loyalty of the Assembly to its own principles, but of much greater importance was the attempt by the Assembly to realize and institutionalize its new ideals in the nation at large. Ultimately, the Assembly focused on administration and the judiciary, which in their reorganization became the linchpin of the effort to transform France in accordance with the ideals of August 4.

The events of June and July 1789 had led to a de facto sovereignty of the Assembly, and the night of August 4, with the repudiation of privilege, completed the transfer of sovereignty from the monarch to the nation. The destruction of privilege thus left a vacuum in governance that came to be filled by law. Whereas privilege had depended upon royal dispensation and thereby highlighted the superiority of the king, law not only emphasized the sovereignty of the nation but also the unity and equality of all.[25] The Constitution of 1791, through which the Assembly ultimately transformed the polity, underscored its primacy.

After completing the Declaration of Rights and resolving the important issue of the royal veto, the first area in which the Assembly moved to realize its new ideal of the polity, for both practical and ideological reasons, was administration. The practical imperatives were evident in a speech delivered by Rabaut de Saint-Etienne in the Assembly in September 1789. Against a backdrop of the disintegration of authority as a result of the municipal revolutions throughout France, Rabaut de Saint-Etienne alluded to the irregular conglomeration of municipal entities in existence and warned the Assembly that its attempt to draft a constitution would be futile if it did not have a sound administrative base on which it could be built.[26]

But the new administration had a more profound purpose than correcting the unsettled condition of the municipalities: the predominant intention of the Assembly was to fulfill the new ideal of the nation that it had conceived on August 4.[27] It was to provide an administrative structure for the realization of that ideal that the Committee of the Constitution presented the Assembly with a report on September 29, 1789, proposing the creation of eighty departments of equal size, without regard for the physical contours of the former provinces.[28] Although the physical component of the plan was unrealistic and unworkable, the effort to bring about uniformity reflected the antipathy for privilege and its inequities that had taken hold of the Assembly on August 4.[29]

As a result of the October Days, the relocation of the Assembly to Paris, and other factors, debate on administration did not begin until early November. During this interval, much opposition to the plan of the committee developed, and the leading alternative to it became one offered by Mirabeau providing for 120 departments and no administrative structure between the municipal level and that of the department.[30]

The specifics of each plan are less important than the fact that one of the major points of contention between them concerned how quickly and effectively the new conception of the nation and citizenship could be realized. Critics of the project advanced by the committee believed that it was too sweeping in scope because it failed to respect former provincial boundaries or identities. They contended that inhabitants would only gradually come to identify themselves with the nation, and for the first few days of discussion these critics held sway in the Assembly.

After several days of desultory and inconclusive debate, however, two members of the committee intervened to justify its plan. On November 9 Jacques-Guillaume Thouret mounted a spirited defense of the plan of the committee against its competitors. Mirabeau asked for and received the right to reply, which he did the next day, after which the Assembly acceded to a request by Thouret to respond to Mirabeau.

On November 11, however, the initial speaker was not Thouret, but another member of the Committee of the Constitution, Guy-Jean-Baptiste Target, a formidable orator who had developed his considerable rhetorical skills as one of the leading barristers at the Parlement of Paris. In a forceful speech he showed great impatience with those deputies who favored preservation of vestiges of provinces in the new administrative structure. After remarks by other deputies Thouret spoke in defense of the plan of the committee, and his speech led to a demand that the issue be decided. In two critical votes the plan of the committee prevailed, and in the following days the elements of the new administration were rapidly defined.[31] The Assembly completed work on the project in early December 1789 and promulgated legislation on municipalities on December 14 and on departments on December 22.

Several deputies found the debate inspiring and considered the new administrative structure to be one of the most important achievements of the Assembly.[32] The objective of its members in ratifying the plan of the committee was evident: to realize as fully as possible the ideal of an undivided, united citizenry coming together in a sense of common purpose in the interest of the nation that had taken shape on August 4.[33] Indeed, the election of Rabaut de Saint-Etienne as president of the Assembly in March 1790, on the eve of the formation of departments, sent a powerful message to the electoral assemblies about to be convened for that purpose.

The National Assembly regarded the creation of a new judiciary as the other principal element in realizing its new ideal of the polity.[34] Due to the length of time required to determine the boundaries of the new departments, however, it did not begin consideration of the judiciary until March 24, 1790, when Thouret delivered a report for the Committee of the Constitution. As had been the case with administration, some deputies believed that the proposals put forward by the committee were too extensive and far-reaching. They were reluctant to break with centuries of legal tradition and wished merely to reform the existing system rather than destroy it altogether. After a heated exchange of opinions, the Assembly resolved the matter by voting to reconstitute the judicial system in its entirety.[35]

Discussion did not resume until March 29, and the committee once more faced opposition to its plan. As had previously been the situation with administration, several deputies offered alternative projects to that of the committee. Again, however, it is more useful to focus on the manner in which the National Assembly molded the new judiciary in order to achieve the new ideal of citizenship than to try to ascertain the authorship or genesis of the facets of the new judiciary.

Justice had traditionally been closely associated with the monarch, but this underscored the situation of the populace as subjects of the king; consequently, the transfer of sovereignty from the monarch to the nation obviously required a refashioning of his role. The Assembly accorded a continuing place to the king in the dispensation of justice through the office of *commissaire du roi*, but in virtually every other respect the judicial system reinforced or expressed the new notion of citizenship developed on the night of August 4.

The core of that ideal was an undivided, united citizenry joined together in the nation, which itself was benevolent and equitable, and the National Assembly formed the new judiciary in accordance with it. A critical institution was that of the justice of the peace, designed to promote harmony by settling quarrels at their point of origin at little cost.[36] This was, of course, in marked contrast to the Old Regime, where litigation had been costly, protracted, and therefore divisive; in contrast, the primordial intent of the Assembly was to unify citizens. The office of justice of the peace sustained the quality of fraternity intrinsic in the idea of citizen, resolving disputes before they could erode the concordance of citizens.

Indeed, in accordance with its view of the polity as a fraternal community of citizens, the National Assembly viewed litigation as a societal failure and consciously structured the judiciary in a manner designed to prevent it. Attached to each district tribunal was a bureau of peace and conciliation in which citizens were obligated to appear to attempt to arbitrate a settlement before it could proceed to litigation.

The institutions of justice of the peace and bureau of peace and conciliation represented mechanisms to reinforce the ideal of a fraternal community of citizens, but other aspects of the new judiciary highlighted the sovereignty of the people. One such element was the use of juries in criminal cases, vesting the citizenry with the right to judge. The National Assembly did not view the populace as an inert mass to be overawed or policed; instead, through the use of juries, the sovereign citizenry was to be the conscience of the nation and the bearer of its moral sense. Other indications of the judiciary manifesting the sovereignty of the people were the decisions by the Assembly that judges would be elected by the people and that the king could not refuse to recognize any judge so elected.[37]

In the final analysis, the National Assembly transformed altogether the ethos of the judiciary—just as privilege had emphasized the centrality of the monarch, and had meant that the rights of one generally came at the expense of another, and royal justice had stressed the authority of the king over society. In a fraternal community of sovereign citizens, however, in which rights were equal and universal rather than exclusive, justice would be administered in a rational and totally disinterested fashion.[38] Law and justice were so self-evident, in fact, that professional legal practitioners, whose existence in any case encouraged litigation, were superfluous. As a result, as one of its final acts in its discussion of the judiciary, the National Assembly abolished the profession of barrister.[39]

The completion of work on the judicial system led the Assembly to believe that it had largely realized its new vision of the polity.[40] It is indicative of how close the Assembly believed it was to completing its task that, shortly after it concluded work on the new judicial system, it elected a Committee of Revision to assist the Committee of the Constitution in preparing a final version of the constitution.

No discussion of the new polity created by the National Assembly or of its invention of citizenship would be complete without a consideration of what is unquestionably its most controversial aspect: the creation of active and passive citizens. The conventional view has held that it created a narrow band of political participation and has criticized the Assembly sharply for an ostensible betrayal of its principles.[41] Although R. R. Palmer long ago argued against such judgments, only more recently have scholars emphasized the degree of political change that the Constitution of 1791 produced.[42]

Keeping in mind that in both urban and rural areas almost two-thirds of males over twenty-five appear to have been active citizens,[43] two examples—one rural and one urban—should illustrate that the political and social transformation accomplished was much greater than is generally acknowledged in the harsh assessments of the Constitution of 1791. That the village of Sel in Brittany could convene an assembly of 650 active citizens to choose five electors to select the administrative authorities for the new Department of Ille-et-Vilaine was infinitely more immediate and equitable a political system than that of the remote and inaccessible Estates of Brittany, through which Sel had been ruled for centuries.[44] Similarly, in Toul, when the bishop, a captain in the royal artillery corps, the subdelegate, a captain of the infantry, and a captain in the engineering corps all participated on an equal footing as fellow citizens in primary assemblies with coopers, wig makers, vine growers, hat makers, booksellers, a cheese merchant, painters, wool spinners, and numerous day laborers, it was clear that the contours of civic life had been totally redrawn.

There was, in fact, nothing pernicious in the National Assembly's formulation of the electorate, for the intention of one of the chief architects of it, Sieyès, as well as the Assembly as a whole, was to encompass as many men as possible and to reduce the categories of exclusions to as few as possible.[46] The wage scale for a day's labor was almost invariably set low and, as Palmer noted, the Assembly reformed taxation in such a way that liability to direct taxation extended far down the social scale.[47] Indeed, as Norman Hampson has pointed out, the pool of active citizens included many on the poverty line.[48]

The National Assembly was not a calculating or disingenuous body, high-mindedness was one of its most distinguishing characteristics. Utterly devoted to the ideal of a fraternal community of citizens working together for the best interests of the nation, it did not want that ideal subverted. Ultimately, it sought to preclude the participation in political life only of those whom it legitimately believed might be susceptible to the influence of others with ulterior motives.[49] It is evident that contemporaries understood the operations of the Assembly in such terms, as a newly founded journal intended for administrators makes clear.[50]

While the electoral system devised by the National Assembly may have been flawed—and the imposition of a tax equivalent to ten days' wages of unskilled labor to qualify as an elector is usually cited, although Palmer has argued that approximately half of the male population twenty-five or older qualified as electors, and this estimate has been generally corroborated by subsequent studies[51]—whatever flaws there may have been should not obscure the larger significance of the structure it established. The National Assembly, basing the electorate on taxes rather than property and freeing it of any religious affiliation, brought into being one of the most participatory and democratic national communities in the world.[52] Furthermore, it extended complete legal equality and protection to every member of it, making each one a citizen. Indeed, there were few limitations on passive citizens aside from not being able to vote in primary assemblies, a restriction imposed only because of concern that they might not be independent participants; a passive citizen could, for example, be elected to a judgeship.[53] On the issue of passive citizens, it is perhaps time to shift our focus from the adjective to the noun.

If, by citizenship, one means the possession of equal rights and freedoms through membership in the nation, which is their guarantor, then the National Assembly did not simply redefine citizenship: it invented it. The National Assembly extended the full protection of the law to every single member of the polity to a degree unequaled anywhere else in the world. Furthermore, it also created the most participatory national political system in the world. Under the tutelage of the National Assembly, for example, France became the first national state to admit Jews on an equal footing. By comparison with the United States, where slavery existed in several states and where Catholics suffered disabilities in a majority of them, or England, where religious toleration was only customary and where Catholics similarly suffered civil disabilities, the polity created by the National Assembly was progressive and advanced. The boldness of its effort and the significance of its achievement deserve far greater recognition than they have received.

NOTES

The author gratefully acknowledges the assistance of the Newberry Library and the dean of the School of Liberal Arts of Auburn University at Montgomery. He also thanks Kenneth Margerison and Rochelle Ziskin for their helpful reading of this chapter.

1. See Jean-Jacques Rousseau, *Oeuvres complètes*, ed. Michel Launay (Paris, 1967–1971), 2: 523.
2. *Encyclopédie, ou Dictionnaire raisonné des sciences, des arts et des métiers, par une société des gens de lettres*, ed. Denis Diderot and Jean le Rond d'Alembert (Paris, 1751–1765), 13: 389.
3. See Michael Sonenscher, *Work and Wages: Natural Law, Politics and the Eighteenth-Century French Trades* (Cambridge, U.K., 1989), pp. 53–54.
4. Michael P. Fitzsimmons, "Privilege and the Polity in France, 1786–1791," *American Historical Review* 92 (1987): 269–95, especially 273–75. See also Gail Bossenga, *The Politics of Privilege: Old Regime and Revolution in Lille* (Cambridge, U.K., 1991), 96.
5. Fitzsimmons, "Privilege and the Polity," 277; Bossenga, *Politics of Privilege*, 102.
6. See Norman Hampson, "The Idea of the Nation in Revolutionary France," in *Reshaping France: Town, Country and Region during the French Revolution*, ed. Alan Forrest and Peter Jones (Manchester, 1991), 13–25.
7. See Keith Michael Baker, "A Classical Republican in Eighteenth-Century Bordeaux: Guillaume-Joseph Saige," in *Inventing the French Revolution: Essays on French Political Culture in the Eighteenth Century* (Cambridge, U.K., 1990), 128–52.
8. [Guillaume-Joseph Saige], *Nouveau catéchismen du citoyen* (n.p., n.d.), 1 [Newberry Library, Case FRC 5847].
9. Ibid., 3, 4, 5–6.
10. See, for example, [Joseph-Antoine Cérutti], *A la mémoire auguste de feu Monseigneur le Dauphin, père du Roi* (n.p., n.d.), xi.
11. See A.N., B^a 25^1, liasse 42, dossier 2, document 2; A.N. AB^{xix} 3258, *cahier* of combined orders of nobility and the Third Estate of Péronne, Montdidier, and Roye, 32.
12. [Saige], *Nouveau catéchisme*, 4–5; A. D. Côte d'Or C 2987^{6e}, *Requête au Roi, et délibération du Tiers Etat de la ville de Dijon, du 18 janvier 1789*.
13. Indeed, until the municipal revolution in Paris in July, the nobility continued to meet separately in the evenings in order to plan how to obstruct the work of the Assembly. See *Supplément au procès-verbal de l'ordre de la noblesse aux Etats-Généraux* (Paris, 1792), 365–76.
14. See Keith Michael Baker, "Fixing the French Constitution," in *Inventing the French Revolution*, 252–305; Michael P. Fitzsimmons, "The Committee of the Constitution and the Remaking of France, 1789–1791," *French History* 4 (1990): 23–47.
15. *Procès-verbal de l'Assemblée Nationale*, no. 33 (27 July 1789): 8; J. Mavidal and E. Laurent, eds., *Archives parlementaires de 1787 à 1860*, 1st ser. (Paris, 1862–1913), 8: 280–85.
16. Two published letters that convey its impact are Charles-Elie, marquis de Ferrières, *Correspondance inédite (1789, 1790, 1791)*, ed. Henri Carré (Paris, 1932), 113–17; and Francisque Mège, *Gaultier de Biauzat, député du tiers-état aux Etats-Généraux de 1789: sa vie et sa correspondance* (Clermont-Ferrand, 1890), 2: 224–228. See also Robert de

Crèvecoeur, ed. *Journal d'Adrien Duquesnoy, député du tiers-état de Bar-le-Duc sur l'Assemblée constituante 3 mai 1789–3 avril 1790* (Paris, 1894), 1: 267–68.

17. It was precisely for this reason that the first clerical and noble deputies had entered the chamber of the commons/National Assembly, but their sense of loyalty to their order was unquestioned. See Abbé Jacques Jallet, *Journal inédit de Jallet* (Fontenay-le-Comte, 1871), 52–53; Maurice Hutt, "The Role of the Curés in the Estates-General of 1789," *Journal of Ecclesiastical History* 6 (1955): 205–14; and *A Messieurs les citoyens nobles de la ville de Paris (n.p., n.d.)*. See also the speech by the duc d'Aiguillon in *Lettre de MM. les députés des communes de Lyon, à leur commettans* (n.p., n.d.) [Newberry Library, Case FRC 4841].

18. See A.N., KK 641, entry of 9 July 1789, and, although it does not refer specifically to orders but to special concerns, A.N., W 306, dossier 377, fols. 55–56.

19. My arguments on this have benefitted significantly from Bossenga, *Politics of Privilege*.

20. On contemporary understanding of the connection between August 4 and the idea of citizenship, see *Fête Nationale qui sera célébrée tous les ans le jour immortel du IV Août* (Paris, n.d.) [B.H.V.P. 12.272 (T.I, n°6)].

21. A.N. C 31^1, dossier 258, document 41. In some respects, the action only confirmed an already existing situation. See also *Courrier de Provence*, 14–15 October 1789; *Lettre d'un député de la sénéchaussée de Toulouse* (Paris, n.d.) [Newberry Library, Case FRC 4737]. B. M. Versailles Ms. F. 823, fol. 147, indicates that this only confirmed what was an already existing situation, but on the continuing division in the seating of orders in the Assembly at this time, see *Chronique de Paris*, 5 October 1789.

22. *Journal de Versailles*, 17 March 1790; *Courrier de la Patrie, ou Journal des Municipalités, assemblées administratives, districts, tribunaux et Garde nationale de France*, 18 March 1790 [Newberry Library, Case FRC 5289]; *Chronique de Paris*, 16 March 1790; Le Hodey de Saultchevreuil, *Journal des Etats-Généraux, aujourd'hui l'Assemblée nationale permanente* (Paris, 1789–1791), 9: 305–306.

23. See, for example, *Journal des décrets de l'Assemblée Nationale, pour les habitans des campagnes*, 19–25 June 1790. It should be noted that one of the authors of the motion, Alexandre de Lameth, denied that the measure had been planned in advance. See Alexandre de Lameth, *Histoire de l'Assemblée constituante* (Paris, 1828–1829), 2: 446.

24. For the perspective of the noble deputy who was apparently not involved, see Jean Baptiste Nompère Champagny, *Souvenirs de M. de Champagny, duc de Cadore* (Paris, 1846), 67. For the perspective of a noble deputy who was actively involved, see Lameth, *Histoire de l'Assemblée*, 2: 433–47, especially 433–34. See also A.N. KK 645, fols. 696–97; and Patrice Higonnet, *Class, Ideology and the Rights of Nobles during the French Revolution* (Oxford, 1981), especially 61–69.

25. That this was consciously understood by deputies in August 1789 is apparent in a letter by Gaultier de Biauzat. See Mège, *Gaultier de Biauzat*, 2: 241.

26. *Le Point du Jour*, 23 September 1789.

27. See Jean-Paul Rabaut de Saint-Etienne, *Réflexions sur la nouvelle division du royaume et sur les privileges et les assemblées des provinces d'Etats* (Paris, 1789).

28. *Procès-verbal de l'Assemblée Nationale*, no. 87 (29 September 1789): 2–3; Jacques-Guillaume Thouret, *Rapport du nouveau comité de constitution, fait à l'Assemblée Nationale le . . . 29 septembre 1789, sur l'établissement des bases de la représentation proportionelle* (Paris, 1789).

29. See A.N. CP NN 50/6 and 50/7 for the initial cartographic presentation by the

committee. Comments on the former indicate that the committee realized that this initial effort was too idealized.

30. For a detailed exposition of Mirabeau's differences with the plan of the committee, see *Courrier de Provence*, 3 November 1789. See also *Lettres de MM, les députés des communes de la ville de Marseille à l'Assemblée Nationale, à MM, les échevins et membres du comité de correspondance* (Marseille, 1789) [Newberry Library, Case FRC 4999]. In the interim between the presentation of its plan and the opening of the debate, the Committee of the Constitution amended its position and agreed to work within the contours of the provinces in creating the departments.

31. *Procès-verbal de l'Assemblée Nationale*, no. 122 (11 November 1789): 7–10; *Archives parlementaires*, 9: 744–59.

32. See B. M. Lyon Ms. 5430, no. 16, letter of 16 November 1789; A. D. Sarthe 10 J 122, letter of 8 December 1789; Duquesnoy, *Journal*, 2: 88.

33. On the way in which one deputy decided for the plan of the Committee of the Constitution, see Adam-Philippe, comte de Custine, *Cinquième compte rendu par le comte de Custine à ses commettans, de ses opinions dans les délibérations de l'Assemblée Nationale du 27 octobre jusqu'au 9 janvier 1790* (Paris, 1789 [sic]), 38.

34. See, for example, A. D. Sarthe 10 J 122, letter of 29 December 1789.

35. *Procès-verbal de l'Assemblée Nationale*, no. 239 (24 March 1790): 10; *Archives parlementaires*, 12: 349. See also B. N. Mss. Nouv. acq. fr. 4121, fols. 508–509.

36. See Richard M. Andrews, "The Justices of the Peace of Revolutionary Paris, September 1792–November 1794 (Frimaire Year III)," in *French Society and the Revolution*, ed. Douglas Johnson (Cambridge, 1976), 167–216, especially 169–73. I disagree, however, with his assertion that it was an instrument of social control, especially during the period of the National Assembly.

37. A.N. KK 645, fols. 644–45.

38. See, for example, Antoine-François Delandine, *De quelques changemens politiques, opérés ou projettés en France, pendant les années 1789, 1790 et 1791 ou Discours sur divers points importans de la Constitution et de la nouvelle Législation* (Paris, 1791), 166; and Jean Baptiste Joseph Innocent Philadelphie Regnault-Warin, *Mémoires pour servir à la vie du général Lafayette et à l'histoire de l'Assemblée constituante* (Paris, 1824), 2: 145–46.

39. See Lenard Berlanstein, *The Barristers of Toulouse in the Eighteenth Century (1740–1793)* (Baltimore, 1975), 168–70; and Michael P. Fitzsimmons, *The Parisian Order of Barristers and the French Revolution* (Cambridge, Mass., 1987), 62–64.

40. See *Courrier de Madon*, 23 September 1790.

41. A recent example is Barbara Luttrell, *Mirabeau* (Carbondale, 1991), 170.

42. See R. R. Palmer, *The Age of the Democratic Revolution* (Princeton, N.J.: 1959–1964), 1: 501, 522–28, especially the historical survey of the issue that comprises the latter section. More recent recognition includes Melvin Edelstein, "Vers une 'sociologie électorale' de la Révolution française: la participation des citadins et campagnards, 1789–1793," *Revue d'histoire moderne et contemporaine* 22 (1975): 508–29; "L'apprentissage de la citoyenneté: participation électorale des campagnards et citadins (1789–1793)," in *L'image de la Révolution française. Communications présentées lors du Congrès mondial pour le bicentenaire de la Révolution. Sorbonne, Paris, 6–12 juillet 1789*, ed. Michel Vovelle (Paris, 1989–1991), 1: 15–25; Melvin Edelstein, "Electoral Participation and Sociology of the Landes in 1790" (forthcoming); Malcolm Crook, "Aux Urnes, Citoyens! Urban and Rural Electoral Behavior during the French Revolution," in *Reshaping France*,

ed. Forrest and Jones, 152–67; "The People at the Polls: Electoral Behavior in Revolutionary Toulon, 1789–1799," *French History* 5 (1991): 164–79; and Patrice Gueniffey, "Elections" and "Suffrage" in *A Critical Dictionary of the French Revolution*, ed. François Furet and Mona Ozouf (Cambridge, Mass., 1989), 33–44, 571–81.

43. Philip Dawson estimated that 61 percent of males over twenty-five were active citizens, and estimates that there were approximately 2 million passive citizens as opposed to 4,298,360 active citizens. See Philip Dawson, "Active Citizen" and "Passive Citizen" in *Historical Dictionary of the French Revolution*, ed. Samuel Scott and Barry Rothaus (Westport, Conn., 1985), 1: 4; 2: 751.

44. A.D. Ille-et-Vilaine L 337, *procès-verbal* for nomination of electors in primary assembly held at Sel, 17 May 1790.

45. A.D. Meurthe-et-Moselle L 200, list of active citizens of municipality of Toul, 21 April 1790.

46. A.N. 284 AP 4, dossier 3.

47. Palmer, *Age of the Democratic Revolution*, 1: 523. The National Assembly encouraged a low figure for the calculation of a day's labor. See *Procès-verbal de l'Assemblée Nationale*, no. 175 (15 January 1790), 5–7.

48. Norman Hampson, *Prelude to Terror: The Constituent Assembly and the Failure of Consensus, 1789–1791* (Oxford, 1988), 90. Indeed, in the "economy of makeshifts" of which Olwen Hufton has written, it is entirely plausible that the poor—perhaps large elements of the poor—might have treated a vote as yet another economic asset, thereby making political assemblies vulnerable to manipulation.

49. Indeed, as Norman Hampson has noted, the *Comité de Mendicité* of the National Assembly classified those paying only two or three days of wages in taxation near the poverty level, and he pointed out that to enfranchise such people "was to invite them to sell their votes." Hampson, *Prelude to Terror*, 88–89.

50. *Journal des municipalités et assemblées administratives*, 3 May 1790.

51. Palmer, *Age of the Democratic Revolution*, 1: 501; Edelstein, "Electoral Participation." I would like to thank Professor Edelstein for sharing the results of his research with me in advance of its publication.

52. I would like to thank Melvin Edelstein and Elizabeth Dunn for helping me to clarify my arguments on this issue.

53. A.N. D* IV 2, p. 197.

4

CITIZENSHIP AND POLITICAL ALIGNMENT IN THE NATIONAL ASSEMBLY

Harriet B. Applewhite

The restructuring of the French state and nation required new definitions of citizenship from the National Assembly between 1789 and 1791. From the middle of the eighteenth century, the coercive power of the state had been gradually diminishing, while the size and power of the political nation expanded through institutions like provincial academies and Masonic lodges. Public opinion flowing through a lively book and pamphlet trade became a resource both for those opposing the government and for ministers and intendants seeking support for reforms.[1] After 1788, these developments converged around the convening of the Estates-General and its transformation into the National Assembly.

The research reported here is an inquiry into debates on citizenship, to see how deputies across the alignment spectrum defined themselves as representatives and their constituents as citizens. Deputies formed early and remarkably stable adversarial alignments. Although the National Assembly rejected the idea of legitimate political opposition, it established some important precedents for majoritarian politics that left a positive legacy for future French legislatures.

The National Assembly normally voted by voice or by sitting and standing; whenever an outcome was in doubt, a roll-call vote was held, but names of voters were not recorded.[2] Lacking such lists to establish alignment for all the deputies, I devised a ten-point scale with four categories on the right, three in the center, and three on the left.[3] Right-wing categories were determined by signatures on four protest lists circulated between April 19, 1790, and September 15, 1791; by the names on two contemporary attribution lists; and by evidence that a deputy resigned early from the National Assembly. For deputies in the center, information was either lacking or contradictory. Left-wing deputies were Feuillant and/or Jacobin members or those placed on the left by the author of a pamphlet published in December 1791 called *Le véritable portrait de nos lég-islateurs*.

These alignment categories, applicable to all deputies, are arbitrary but rigorous. When used in conjunction with the minutes of debates on various dimensions of citizenship, the scale reveals a persistent pattern of alignment established in the first days of the National Assembly.

On June 17, 1789, the deputies who declared themselves to be the National Assembly confronted the question of accountability to their electors. The text stated that since the assembly already included representatives sent by "ninety-six hundredths of the Nation," the deputies present were the only legitimate representatives of that nation. Representation was one and indivisible, and no deputies in any order or class had a right to exercise functions separately from the National Assembly.[4] This founding document of the National Assembly stated unequivocally the principle of unified national representation and denied the legitimacy of any effort that electors might make to hold their deputies accountable individually.

Controversy over accountability surfaced over the issue of mandates. Although a restrictive mandate could be considered a democratic mechanism to compel a deputy to carry out the will of his electors, it was in fact a vestige of the traditional form of the Estates-General in a society of orders.[5] A total of 232 mandates were imperative, and nearly two-thirds of those were assigned to deputies representing the first two estates: 112 to nobles and 38 to clergy. When the king acceded to the unified National Assembly on June 23, 1789, he permitted deputies to request their constituents to assign them new powers.

On June 26 the absent noble Lally Tolendal sent his colleagues an explanation that his mandate allowed him to support verification of powers in common, but his oath of office held him "unconquerably chained" to the vote by order. He personally wanted to join the new National Assembly but felt he had to return to his constituents for new powers. If he failed to get them he would resign, because he could no longer fulfill his mission fruitfully.[6] Lally Tolendal placed himself midway between the corporate notion of a deputy as a spokesman for his order and the contractual idea of an independent delegate empowered to vote according to his own judgment.

Clermont-Tonnerre tried to resolve the matter of imperative mandates, stating that the Estates-General [*sic*] was to prevent the veto of one order from stopping "the construction of laws which foster public well-being." The nobility sitting at Versailles had adopted the veto of any one order as a "constitutive principle" of the monarchy; that view contradicted the intentions of his deputation's own constituents, so he and his colleagues needed a clarification before they could vote.[7]

Early in July the clergy joined the debate. On July 7 the bishop of Autun, Talleyrand-Périgord, argued against binding mandates. An electoral circumscription (*bailliage*), he said, was not a single state like those in a federation, but a part of the whole nation that had the right to concur with the general will, while remaining subject to it. A deputy's mandate simply gave him his powers to represent the *bailliage* and the nation. Electors could set term limitations on a deputy's service, specify the order in which issues should be taken up, and limit the goals a deputy was to advance. However, if the Assembly got into areas beyond those specified goals, the deputy did not have the power to stop them. This argument effectively removed any controls that constituents might hold on their representative. Deputies, he said, came together to deliberate; if their opinions had been previously forced on them there could be no rational common deliberation. He proposed a decree nullifying all imperative mandates and ordering that any decree of the National Assembly was obligatory for all *bailliages*.[8]

After a long and inconclusive debate, the stormy session was adjourned without a vote. The next day, July 8, Le Franc de Pompignan proposed a compromise: the Assembly would decree that nothing could suspend its work, that it would receive new mandates or new or substitute deputies if electors sent them, and that it would establish a policy on imperative mandates when it formulated the structure of the [new] Estates-General. Sieyès proposed that the Assembly declare that the nation was always entirely legitimately represented by the plurality of its deputies. Its work could not be stopped nor its liberty altered—not by imperative mandates, not by the voluntary absence of some members, not by the protests of a minority (*AP*, 8: 207). There followed a tumultuous debate, resolved finally by a roll call vote, 700 to 28, that there was nothing to deliberate on the question of mandates (*AP*, 8: 208). Impassioned though this debate had been, an overwhelming majority preferred to avoid the question rather than vote on a substantive motion.

Behind this struggle lies a broader debate over the meaning of national sovereignty. Those in favor of binding mandates wanted to place some of the nation's power in the hands of electors chosen by estates, the largest elements in the corporate body of the state. The entire question should be considered in light of the deputies' Tennis Court Oath, sworn on June 20 to the whole nation, abstract and intangible. Any oaths that they had taken individually in their electoral assemblies were superseded by this new fraternal act of commitment binding them to write a constitution. When Lally Tolendal threatened to resign if his electors refused to release him from the obligation to support the vote by order, he was articulating a more democratic notion of accountability than that contained in the Tennis Court Oath. But because the electors who could claim that accountability remained attached to a corporate society of orders, their power to command their representatives was not admitted by the majority of the National Assembly.

Mandates, one of the earliest substantive questions before the National Assembly, divided the embryonic left from the embryonic right. A total of seventeen deputies participated in the debate. (See Table 1.) Seven spoke on the side of the left, against binding mandates; six favored compromise, allowing deputies with imperative mandates to return to their electoral committees for new powers;

Table 1.
Participation in Debate on Mandates by Alignment: Frequencies

ALIGNMENT CATEGORIES	% in DEBATE
Consistent right N=2	12
Moderate right N=5	29
Center right N=3	18
Resigning right N=0	0
Contradictory N=0	0
Unclassified N=0	0
Monarchical left N=4	23
Shifting left N=3	18
Jacobin left N=0	0

N=17

Totals: Leftwing debaters = 41%; Center = 0; Right = 49%

Table 2.
Categories of Opinion by Deputies' Alignment: Debate on Mandates

CATEGORIES IN DEBATE

Alignment Categories	Left: oppose binding mandates	Center: new powers	Right: binding mandates
	N=7	N=6	N=4
	%	%	%
Left	86	17	0
Center	0	33	0
Right	14	50	100

N=17 [total participants]
Gamma: .91

and four defended the right-wing position that imperative mandates were binding. These seventeen deputies aligned themselves in June 1789, very nearly in the same way that their behavior in 1791 indicates. (See Table 2). Six of the seven deputies who opposed imperative mandates in June 1789 ended up on the left of my alignment scale—one of them, Le Franc de Pompignan, on the center right. The six recommending compromise in 1789 became more divided, one (Joubert) ending up on the left, two in the center, and three on the right. The four who supported imperative mandates all ended up on the right. Although these data concern only a handful of deputies, they reveal a pattern of alignment that holds from the beginning of the National Assembly through to its end.

The alignment pattern was more permanent than the interpretation of mandates turned out to be. Mandates could be used by revolutionaries as well as by conservatives, as left-wing deputies rediscovered in the course of the debates on the royal veto. On September 1 Jean-Baptiste Salle defended the suspensive veto as a mechanism that would permit the nation to act as a judge between the king and its representatives. The general will could never be wrong, but an Assembly could; therefore, Salle recommended frequent elections, open and public surveillance over representatives, and a law allowing recall of deputies. Salle referred to "the necessity of imperative mandates" so that the people would always retain their sovereignty (*AP*, 8: 529–33). Others were edgy about using constituency pressures to limit royal power. The men of the left found mandates troublesome. They had difficulty reconciling the vesting of abstract sovereignty in the nation with the practical question of its exercise. If electors could restrict deputies, how could the National Assembly exercise sovereignty? And would not those electors inevitably act on the basis of a particular will rather than the general will or the public good? On the other hand, mandates could be a weapon of the left against the entrenched power of the Church, the nobility, and the ministers.

The question of deputies' powers actually turned on the relationship between citizens and their representatives in a constitutional monarchy. Le Chapelier claimed that their original mandates, followed by their oath not to disband until they had given France a constitution, were the two binding acts that gave deputies powers unlimited both by time constraints and content. At the moment of elections, citizens exercised the nation's sovereignty. Once sworn to produce a constitution, deputies alone were empowered to act on that sovereignty. The right-wing argument would place that active sovereignty initially in electoral assemblies; it did not carry the day when restrictive mandates were prohibited in April 1790.

I turn now to the debates on the Declaration of the Rights of Man and of the Citizen. In July, the abbé Sieyès had written that the object of any constitution was to guarantee, serve, and extend the rights of man; these rights had to come at the head of the constitution to instruct citizens, guide the authors of the constitution, and provide a standard for any reform.[9]

When debate began in August, the initial speakers argued for two days about whether a formal declaration should be produced and whether it should precede the constitution. On the morning of August 4, a new question was introduced; should there be a declaration of duties accompanying a declaration of rights? An inconclusive vote on a motion to include a declaration of duties required a roll call; the motion was rejected by a vote of 570 to 433. A second proposal to precede the constitution by a declaration of rights passed "nearly unanimously" (*AP*, 8: 341).

Between August 17 and 19, debate began on a draft of a declaration of rights. Controversy erupted over whether to include or imply duties and whether to invoke the "author of nature." On August 27 the Assembly completed a draft of the declaration that included an invocation of the Supreme Being and a strong formulation of the principle of separation of powers. On October 2 the Declaration was adopted and carried immediately to the king for his signature. Louis XVI hesitated, thus exacerbating confrontation during the October Days among the women marchers from Paris, the Parisian national guard, the king and ministers, and the deputies. The king granted his unequivocal acceptance of the declaration under the pressure of popular insurrection late in the afternoon of October 5.

By this date deputies had aligned themselves from right to left into fairly stable factions.[10] In order to examine the extent to which this early division paralleled later alignment, I tabulated the total number of participants in the long debates on the Declaration of Rights, classified their positions as left, center, or right, and compared this classification to that produced by my alignment scale based upon measures from 1791.

Holders of left-wing opinions were those who advocated a broadly drawn Declaration of Rights as the first step in making the constitution, favored open access to the National Assembly, took a strong free press stand, and wanted both deputies and ministers to be held accountable to the nation for their actions. Centrist views were held by those who favored compromise. They wanted all drafts of a Declaration of Rights to be voted on by the whole Assembly; they were willing to set up some restrictions on rights to a free press and to property; and they worked toward negotiation on religious freedom because they saw religion as necessary for social cohesion. Right-wing opinions were held by those who initially did not favor a Declaration of Rights and then wanted a narrowly drawn formulation, supported strict limits on public access to deputies, and favored a declaration of duties as part of the preamble to the constitution. According to the published records in the *Archives parlementaires*, a total of eighty-two deputies addressed the National Assembly at least once during the August debates on the Declaration of Rights. Twenty-nine of them articulated left-wing opinions (35.4 percent), eighteen center opinions (22 percent), and twenty-nine right-wing opinions (35.4 percent). A total of six remarks were too brief to use to classify the speaker (7 percent). The even representation of left and right was intentional. On August 3 the deputies voted to alternate supporting and opposing statements on the issue of whether to use a declaration as a preamble to the constitution.

I took these eighty-two debaters, all of those who spoke on the Declaration of Rights, and sorted them into the alignment categories drawn from their affiliations and protests of 1791. Table 3 presents the frequencies. Most of those who participated in the debate on the Declaration of Rights were not on either the extreme right or the extreme left; approximately a quarter of the debaters were moderate right, and an additional quarter were shifting left.

When categories are combined, the data show that 53 percent of the debaters were on the left, 40 percent on the right, and 7 percent in the center. Compared to the entire Assembly, the center was most underrepresented.

The alignment scale turned out to be a good predictor of alignment on this issue. Table 4 shows that 83 percent of those who ended up on the left articulated left-wing opinions in August 1789 during the debate on the declaration, while 76 percent of those on the right articulated right-wing views. The data also show how debates in the Assembly polarized left and right. Half of those who presented

Table 3.
Participation in Debate on Declaration of Rights by Alignment: Frequencies

ALIGNMENT CATEGORIES	% in DEBATE
Consistent right N=5	6
Moderate right N=20	24
Center right N=3	4
Resigning right N=5	6
Contradictory N=1	1
Unclassified N=5	6
Monarchical left N=15	18
Shifting left N=21	26
Jacobin left N=7	9

N = 82

Totals: Leftwing debaters = 53%; Center = 7%; Right = 40%.

Table 4.
Categories of Opinion by Deputies' Alignment: Debate on Declaration of Rights

CATEGORIES IN DEBATE

	Leftwing Views	Center Views	Right Views	Not clear
	N=29	N=18	N=29	N=6
	%	%	%	%
Deputies' Alignment				
Left N=43	8 3	5 0	2 1	6 6
Center N=5	7	6	3	1 7
Right N=34	1 0	4 4	7 6	1 7

N=82   [Total participants]
Gamma: .76

centrist views ended up on the left, 39 percent on the right, and only 11 percent in the center. Finally, Table 4 shows that just over a fifth of the right-wing spokesmen moved to the left according to the later measures, thus demonstrating that the pull toward the left was stronger than the pull toward the right.

By early fall 1789, the Assembly had continued to divide ideologically into a left whose members accepted sweeping principles of rights as the foundation of the constitution, and a right whose adherents had initially preferred to lay down constitutional structures rather than to declare rights and who were troubled by the absence of a declaration of duties. The deputies were pulling away from the center and into opposing blocs on issues of ideological substance. But, paradoxically, they were converging on matters of procedure. They seem to have been absolutely genuine in their convictions about majority rule as an operating principle, and they made every effort to design and uphold procedures to form and express a majority. Deputies yearned for a unified Assembly that would articulate the sovereign national will, and many of them reported how moved they were by the dramatic epiphanies they had experienced during the night of August 4. Sometimes speakers suggested recourse to the bureaus, as a way (probably) to avoid gallery pressure and give full consideration to all proposals and still avoid public visibility. Despite complaints about rudeness and impatience during speeches, they were careful to set up procedures that favored minorities, such as the August 3 decision to alternate speakers with conflicting viewpoints. Philosophically, they pulled toward a world view that valued the unity of a sovereign general will; practically, they laid down procedures that gave opponents of majorities their chance.[11]

In his July statement on the constitution, Sieyès had defined two different categories of citizenship, and this proposal was to become the basis for discussion when debate began on October 20. Civil rights, Sieyès had said, guaranteed the protection of one's person, property, and liberty and were enjoyed by all the inhabitants of a country, while political rights allowed one to contribute to the formation of public authority, a direct application of the political power that belonged only to property-owning white males above the age of majority.[12] On September 29 Thouret had calculated that, out of a population estimated at 26 million, 4.4 million men would be active citizens with the right to vote in primary assemblies to select 22,000 representatives to the next higher tier of communal assemblies (*AP*, 9: 203). The October Days and the move to Paris had intervened; now, on October 20, the Constitutional Committee proposed specific qualifications for active citizenship.

The most inflammatory part of the proposal was the tax qualification. To be an active citizen, a man would have to pay an annual tax equal to or above the value of ten days' labor in his region; in the final law, the value was reduced to three days' wages. If we follow Thouret's calculations of population totals, this rule made passive citizens out of 83 percent of the total population, including all women. An estimate made on the basis of 1791 population information says that 84.4 percent of the whole population were passive citizens, including 39 percent of the men over 25.[13] This denial of political rights to many domiciled and employed artisans and workers infuriated left-wing journalists but did not at this juncture occasion much discussion within the Assembly. (Political rights for women were advocated by the playwright Olympe de Gouges and by Condorcet, among others, but were not debated in the Assembly.) Only six speakers objected in principle to the distinction, and only two elaborated any argument: Grégoire insisting that to have political rights, it should "suffice to be a good citizen, [and] to have sound judgment and a French heart"; and Robespierre arguing for full citizenship for all men on the basis of the Declaration of Rights that granted sovereignty to the people as individuals equal in rights (*AP*, 9: 479).

Supporters of the active-passive distinction defended it on the grounds that productive labor earned a man property, giving him a stake in the society and its collective interests; those who were less productive did not have such a stake, were susceptible to the blandishments of aristocrats, and might sell their votes if they had the suffrage. Finally, the Assembly approved a restrictive set of qualifications for active citizenship.

The issue of eligibility generated more heated debate on December 3. Article 6 of a proposal on the structure of primary assemblies stated that qualifications to be an active citizen, an elector, and an office-holder would be considered filled by any male citizen who had voluntarily paid, for two consecutive years, a civic tribute equal to the value of the direct tax required by the earlier legislation. Opponents of this proposal focused on vote-buying and corruption, but Le Chapelier and Pétion argued that the civic tribute was a patriotic act that deserved recognition through the grant of political rights. After a voice vote, the president claimed that the article was rejected; but most doubted that outcome, and supporters of the proposal demanded a roll call. The results were 439 to reject the proposal on the civic tribute against 428 to accept it (*AP*, 10: 361).

The closeness of this vote raises the question whether active citizenship divided the left from the right along the same fault lines that had formed on the Declaration of Rights. (See Tables 5 and 6.) A total of fifty-five deputies spoke on this issue over a period of four nonconsecutive days, October 20, 22, and 27 and December 3. Only six (11 percent of the participants) took the extreme left position of opposing any property qualification for active citizenship; five of them were on the left according to my behavioral scale, and one was center right. The more centrist position I assigned to those twenty-five debaters (45 percent) who favored fewer rather than greater restrictions on qualifications—for example, including naturalized Frenchmen as well as native-born, or not excluding the sons of bankrupt men. Of those twenty-five, 84 percent were left wing on the alignment scale, 8 percent were center, and 8 percent right. Twenty debaters (37 percent) took right-wing positions, wanting tight restrictions on eligibility for active citizenship and office-holding. This group was more divided, with six of the twenty (30 percent) on the left, one in the center (5 percent), and thirteen on the right (65 percent). Finally, four deputies (7 percent of the speakers) made statements that could not be assigned to a category; three of them were on the left and one on the right.

The issue of citizenship qualifications divided the Assembly more nearly evenly than the vote on the Declaration of Rights. The extreme left-wing position, opposing any distinction between active and passive citizens, had very few supporters, while the true centrist position, favoring less restrictive qualifications

Table 5.
Participation in Debates on Citizenship by Alignment: Frequencies

ALIGNMENT CATEGORIES	% IN DEBATE
Consistent right N=5	9
Moderate right N=5	9
Center right N=6	11
Resigning right N=1	2
Contradictory N=1	2
Unclassified N=2	3
Monarchical left N=12	22
Shifting left N=16	29
Jacobin left N=7	13

N = 55

Totals: Leftwing debaters = 64%; Center = 5%; Right = 31%

Table 6.
Categories of Opinion by Deputies' Alignment: Debate on Citizenship

CATEGORIES IN DEBATE

	Extreme left	Center left	Right	Not determined
	N=6	N=25	N=20	N=4
	%	%	%	%
Deputies' Alignment				
Left N=35	8 3	8 4	3 0	7 5
Center N=3	0	8	5	0
Right N=17	1 7	8	6 5	2 5

N=55 [total participants]
Gamma: .76

for active citizenship, had the most adherents, 45 percent, against 37 percent for the right.

If we look at the December 3 debate only, twelve speakers for the right opposed making the civic tribute equivalent to the direct contribution, vigorously expressing their concern that wealthy men would pay the tribute on behalf of the poor in order to control votes. Nine of these twelve were classified as right-wing according to my alignment scale, two were ministerial left, and one (Dupont) was a Jacobin. The twelve speakers who favored the bill considered the tribute an act of patriotism that earned the right to active participation. One of these speakers, Milscent, resigned early; one, Garat, could not be aligned on my scale; and the remaining ten were all left-wing. The even division among these debaters and the sharp cleavage between the two sides anticipated the closeness of the actual vote on December 3, which the opponents of the bill won by 51 percent to 49 percent.

Those who took the centrist position in the citizenship debate in October assembled a majority to pass a law excluding a substantial minority of men from active citizenship; but they could not hold this majority when the issue came up in another form in December. Initially, most deputies had agreed that men of property were the foundation of the nation and the proper repositories of sovereignty. Very few radicals were ready to infer from the Declaration of Rights that equality implied the right to unrestricted participation in shaping political institutions and agendas. The proposed article on the civic tribute introduced the possibility of earning active citizenship through a direct monetary contribution as well as through work to acquire property. Had the bill passed, some citizens would have been defined by their property, others by a patriotic act. The possibility that one could be a patriot without being a man of property was a radical idea that bifurcated the Assembly at the end of 1789 and anticipated the republican movement of 1791.[14]

I turn now to another long and intense debate, on collective petitions, that shows the further erosion of the center and illustrates quite dramatically the dominance that the left had secured over the Assembly by the spring of 1791. The whole matter of petitions came to the attention of the Assembly as a result of the crowd action that virtually imprisoned the king and his family in their carriages in the Tuileries on April 18 and prevented their trip to St. Cloud. On April 26 a deputation came to the Assembly from the departmental and municipal government of Paris, requesting rapid passage of a penal code so that they could control agitators. They also requested a law on petitions, saying that their official pronouncements were not always distinguishable from communications from individuals or popular societies. Their request was forwarded to the Committee on the Constitution, which reported to the entire Assembly on May 9 a draft decree including the restriction of the right of petition to individual active citizens only. Anyone could complain, said Le Chapelier, and societies and collectivities could discuss political matters, but only active citizens were energetic and productive enough to be granted the right to petition individually (*AP*, 25: 678–81). Deputies on the left strongly opposed that reasoning, Pétion said that passive citizens would in effect be slaves if they could not make legal reclamations against repressive laws (*AP*, 25: 683). Grégoire claimed that the distinction between active and nonactive citizens (note that he did not use the term "passive") amounted to a restoration of a society of orders, which would be an even

Table 7.
Participation in Debate on the Right of Petition by Alignment: Frequencies

ALIGNMENT CATEGORIES	% IN DEBATE
Consistent right N=1	3.3
Moderate right N=0	0
Center right N=1	3.3
Resigning right N=2	7
Contradictory N=2	7
Unclassified N=1	3.3
Monarchical left N=9	30
Shifting left N=10	33.3
Jacobin left N=4	13.3

N = 30.

Totals: Leftwing debaters = 77%; Center = 10%; Right = 13%.

greater wrong if nonactive citizens were reduced to political nullity by lacking even the right to complain (*AP*, 25: 687). Buzot, also on the left, objected to the isolation of individual citizens who would figure that their individual petition would carry no weight (*AP*, 25: 690).

Centrist positions on the issue of the right of petition raised fears of insurrection and the potentially incendiary impact of petitions. (See Tables 7 and 8.) Provision should be made for those who could not write or who could not afford a notary's stamp for a poster, but municipal officials needed authority to control the effects of propaganda and to differentiate their legal documents from other kinds of communications.

Reactionary right-wing views were not expressed on the issue of collective petitions. The more conservative speeches stressed limits on petitions, favored their restriction to individual active citizens, and opposed any requirement that administrators be obliged to respond to petitions. No members of the consistent right intervened in this debate: those who remained in the Assembly were massively disaffected by the failure to declare a state religion, by the passage of the Civil Constitution of the Clergy, and by the erosion of monarchical authority. Furthermore, some deputies on the far right had committed themselves to sit silently in the Assembly as a protest.

The decree on petitions was passed on May 18, 1791, without distinguishing between active and passive citizens. It prohibited collective petitions, required individual signatures, mandated the municipal government to set up procedures

Table 8.
Categories of Opinion by Deputies' Alignment: Debate on the Right of Petition

CATEGORIES IN DEBATE

	Leftwing views	Center views	Rightwing views
	N=11	N=12	N=7
	%	%	%
Deputies'			
Alignment			
Left N=23	8 2	7 5	7 1
Center N=3	9	1 7	0
Right N=4	9	8	2 9

N=30 [Total participants]
Gamma: .22

to convoke the commune or section assemblies when petitions demanded them, and ordered that spaces be designated for the posting of official acts. A total of only thirty deputies participated in the debates on petitions. Eleven speakers took positions on the left, twelve in the moderate center, and only seven on the right. Again, as with earlier topics, there is a close match between the speakers' positions in this debate and their alignment on the scale of all deputies. Nine of the eleven speakers taking the left-wing position were classified as left, one in the center, and one surprise: the Abbé Maury, notorious for his position on the far right, spoke in support of collective petitions. Of the seven taking what I have labeled right-wing positions, five were classified as left and two as right. Finally, the twelve speakers with moderate positions were 75 percent left, 17 percent center, and 8 percent right. These numbers reflect a significant development: the center had become minuscule by May 1791. Only three deputies classified in the center of the scale participated in this debate, two of them taking a conciliatory position and one joining the left. In addition, the right had ceased to speak out on an issue that concerned direct relationships between deputies and their constituents.

This look at selected debates has established that the alignment scale based on behavior correlates reasonably closely with the positions that deputies articulated on citizenship. Such decisions as joining the Jacobin Club or protesting religious decrees were anticipated by opinions deputies expressed in the earliest debates. Furthermore, these alignment patterns remained consistent throughout the Assembly. Beginning with the dilemma of mandates, questions that directly connected deputies to their constituents tended to pull them away from the center rather than make them converge around any shared interests or common philosophical stance.

I now want to examine the larger significance of these consistent alignment patterns, coupled with the erosion of the center and the relative diminution of right-wing participation in debates. On questions of citizenship, what kind of legacy did the National Assembly bequeath concerning rights and limited government? What kind of new nation did they build on the foundation of an old state and an old society?

First, through specific definitions of the rights and powers of citizens, electors, and deputies, the decrees of the Assembly pushed the ordinary French person very far from the national legislature, during the time when that ordinary person was becoming extraordinarily engaged politically and gaining a political education that moved the private worlds of work and family into the public realm of assembly hall, gallery, popular society, and section. These political processes, which legislated exclusion parallel to and in contrast with popular empowerment, created one of the forces destabilizing constitutional monarchy. Deputies on the left played into this situation when, all the while condemning insurrections, they invoked popular support to rail against the category of passive citizens, to accept a civic tribute as equivalent to a tax qualification for active citizenship, and then finally to protest the exclusion of passive citizens from the right of petition.

The left-wing concept of citizenship was not radically democratic. Leftist deputies were not willing to set up channels of accountability between representatives and citizens; they distrusted collective forms of political participation and sought to prevent the reemergence of privilege as a medium of exchange between society and the state. All but a few radicals approved the idea of a property qualification for voters and a multilayered system of indirect elections for the national legislature. They toyed with the idea that a citizen could earn his right to political participation through a patriotic monetary contribution. For the left, a society operating according to the conventions of deference had to be replaced by new rules of fraternal patriotic conduct among equals in rights, although not in wealth.

If the left's understanding of citizenship was not radically democratic, neither was the right's radically reactionary. They too renounced privilege; reciprocal arrangements like mandates would bind their citizens to the state. They preferred to define rights after the completion of the constitution, not before, and they wanted a formal statement of duties to accompany these rights. To exercise political rights a man would have to have property; the right were convinced that a propertyless man would become a puppet of conspirators who would bribe him to manipulate his vote. The right-wing conception of citizenship still bound men unequal in wealth by rules of deference.

The political significance of the legislative dimension of the French Revolution is found both in constitutional texts and in deputy roles. When deputies are aligned left to right according to their behavior after the first revolutionary year, the lines that separate them fall along the same lines that divided them in debates all through the twenty-seven months of the National Assembly. There were many revolutionary moments; the political struggle over citizenship was multidimensional and adversarial conflicts formed along deeply etched and long-lasting fault lines.

During the debate on collective petitions, a concept of the political nation underlying the Constitution of 1791 was shaped by the struggle between left and right. The boundaries of that nation were not altogether what the left would have preferred yet were far more extensive than the right desired. Although most deputies yearned for unanimity, they understood that, practically speaking, the political nation was not one body, and popular sovereignty would require machinery to implement majority rule. Speaking against allowing the posting of notices by individuals or groups in the same place as official decrees, Barnave said it would be a kind of sacrilege to allow such postings, since laws must receive obedience and respect. Law was an emanation of the sacred general will. "[F]inally, it is essential that anything that demonstrates to all the character of the national will cannot be obscured by games, caprices, or by writing whatever one might want" (*AP*, 25: 699). This absolutist understanding of the general will was not the conviction of all the speakers. Dupont said that if a collective society could publicize its opinion without individual signatures, there would be no guarantee that the opinion in question was indeed held by a majority. A dozen people out of a society of 1,200 might broadcast a view about which 1,188 people had had no say. Briois de Beaumetz challenged this calculation, saying that it was possible to hold a society and its officers collectively responsible for their opinions. Regnaud denied that logic; a minority could not be held accountable to an act in which they refused to concur. As finally voted, the article allowed no posting of nonofficial notices.

This debate among deputies on the left seemed to turn on a technicality linked to the function of majority rule as an operating mechanism for popular sovereignty. All the deputies from left to right knew that the will of the nation was a sweeping abstraction. They believed politics to be about conflict and confrontation enclosed in a hierarchically tiered structure of electoral assemblies anchored by the 16 percent of the population who were active citizens. Only a few, like Robespierre and Regnaud, were willing to grant that a majority could be formed out of clashing opinions articulated throughout a whole nation by popular societies and other collectivities of citizens. Most people were excluded from the political nation, and those who were active citizens were to act only as isolated autonomous individuals empowered to elect the next higher assembly, with the national legislature at the pinnacle. Political conflict at this summit would be resolved in deliberation that would yield a majority, determined when necessary by roll-call votes, and the decisions taken would be in the name of the sovereign people but binding upon them. A new, fragmented nation of individuals, with its hierarchical political core in the legislature, replaced the old state bound through privilege to an organic society. The deputies who controlled the final two months of the National Assembly had crafted styles and structures for majoritarian politics, but they remained unable to accept the legitimacy of organized opposition.

NOTES

I would like to thank Douglas R. Applewhite for assistance with tables and statistics, Keith M. Baker for his thought-provoking commentary on a longer version of this chapter, and Arthur Paulson for his most helpful criticism of an earlier draft.

1. Keith M. Baker, "Public Opinion as Political Invention," in his *Inventing the French Revolution* (New York: Cambridge University Press, 1990), 185–90.

2. A proposal to keep voting registers was defeated on July 9, 1789. *Procès-verbal de l'Assemblée nationale* (Paris, 1789–1791), 1, no. 19 (July 9, 1789): 2, 3. (Henceforth cited as *Procès-verbal*.)

3. A detailed explanation of the alignment categories is in my *Political Alignment in the French National Assembly, 1789–1791* (Baton Rouge: Louisiana State University Press, 1993).

4. *Procès-verbal*, June 17, 1789, 2–4. Patrice Gueniffey, "Les assemblées et la représentation," in *The Political Culture of the French Revolution*, vol. 2 of *The French Revolution and the Creation of Modern Political Culture*, ed. Colin Lucas (New York: Pergamon, 1988), 105–23.

5. Norman Hampson, *Prelude to Terror: The Constituent Assembly and the Failure of Consensus, 1789–1791* (New York: Oxford University Press), 189.

6. *Procès-verbal*, June 26, 1789, 7–9.

7. Ibid., 13, 14.

8. *Archives parlementaires*, 1st ser., 8 (July 7, 1789): 200–203. (Hereafter cited as *AP* parenthetically in the text.)

9. *Procès-verbal*, July 27, 1789, 19, 36–38.

10. See Robert Howell Griffiths, *Le Centre perdu: Malouet et les "monarchiens" dans la Révolution française* (Grenoble, 1988), 10–16, 67, chap. 5.

11. Philippe Raynaud, "La déclaration des droits de l'homme," in *Political Culture of the French Revolution*, 139–49.

12. Sieyès, "Préliminaire de la Constitution française," printed in *Procès-verbal*, July 27, 1789, 36, 37.

13. Philip Dawson, "Active Citizen," in *Historical Dictionary of the French Revolution, 1789–99*, ed. Samuel F. Scott and Barry Rothaus (Westport, Conn.: Greenwood Press, 1985), 1: 4, 5.

14. William H. Sewell, "Le citoyen/la citoyenne: Activity, Passivity, and the Revolutionary Concept of Citizenship," in *Political Culture of the French Revolution*, 105–123.

5

THE CITIZEN IN CARICATURE: PAST AND PRESENT

Antoine de Baecque

Caricature is a form of representation that does not easily convey political acclaim. In it one finds many grotesque faces, ridiculously misshapen bodies, and dissolute characters, but few of those model citizens who were immortalized in the paintings and engravings that were produced as revolutionary propaganda. Its technique was still crude, and was used—often with virtuosity—for its "naive" effects, which, it was claimed, would appeal directly to the people through laughter or anecdote. Thus, caricature at the beginning of the Revolution would seem incapable of representing the complex idea of citizenship over which philosophers continue to argue even now. Because it aimed at ridiculing the other, the aristocrat, and was confined to a metaphorical interpretation of events, how could caricature of the revolutionary period represent the eminent citizen? What power did the image have when confronted with the citizenship that was being discussed in texts on political philosophy?

This initial question, indicative of a difficulty of representation is, however, a commitment to take a closer look at those bright-colored engravings and drawings of roughly sketched characters whose postures were hardly "philosophical." But this corpus of more than six hundred caricatures from the beginning of the Revolution constituted a "visual narrative of events" and was the product of a metaphorical language that was able to indicate the sources of historical rupture. By creating a series of standard characters, codified situations, conventional backgrounds, and symbols during the initial stages of the Revolution, caricature provided engravers with what amounted to a fictional canvas of political events. In this sense, just as the countless pamphlets that detailed the country's political evolution between the summer of 1788 and the spring of 1789, caricature played an essential role in the incarnation of political discourse, making ideas visible, supplying characters, gestures, and appearances for the political principles guiding contemporary thinking and writing. As a result of the network of metaphors provided in narrative and visual representation, concepts and processes such as sovereignty, liberty, the nation, the rights of man, bankruptcy, the relations among the three orders, the debates concerning privilege, and the discussions about the possible methods of convening the Estates-General found a correspondence in the words and images used to describe political society as a body. The pamphlets that narrated the Revolution and the caricatures that made it visible are two essential foundations for these representations.

It is within this logic of incarnation that caricature encountered citizenship, for caricature was able to relate the manner in which the French subject became a citizen. By the placement of figures in an engraving—by their appearances, garments, or gestures—caricature provided the same kind of demonstration as other forms of discourse within its specific representative space. The events of 1789 were experienced as a political enigma, for how could one suddenly change from being a subject (some people even said a "slave") to being a citizen? Caricature was able to represent this through the successive stages of a drawing: it reversed the "body-to-body" relationship, changed people's gestures, healed the sick, made fat people suddenly thin, and brought skeletons to life. At this moment representation took charge of the process of forming the citizen, his "transmutation," as it was called, and assumed the appropriate physiological register, displaying through its own metaphors just how the people of France— as they strode across the historical rupture then in progress—had changed their very appearance (at least in drawing). The goal of caricature was to provide a visual representation of citizenship through its depiction of the body; that is also the subject of this chapter.

This transmutation of the citizen was illustrated over a period of months, from July 1789 through January 1790, in a series of stylistically similar caricatures, signed "A.P." and accurately dated. There are three images, clearly related to one another, drawn by the same artist and engraved in the same workshop. They form a highly unusual series of prints, and for once the laws of loss and anonymity have been vanquished. These three images—and their order of appearance— form a perfectly coherent narrative. This narrative, however, conforms poorly to the process of the citizen's formation. There is a fundamental, and highly Manichaean, opposition between the "before" and "after" states in these prints. Figures and their positions materialize the temporal rupture characteristic of revolutionary upheavals. *A faut espérer qu'eus jeu-là finira bentôt* [Let's hope that this game will end soon] presents the "antisocial disease" that affected the French nation (Engraving 1). Two privileged and stately individuals are carried by the exhausted peasant of the Third Estate, his hoe "wet with tears," who is being prodded by the noble's "bloodstained" sword. In keeping with the reversal of social roles engendered by political events (the engraving is dated July 17, 1789) and symbolized by the tricolor cockade, the peasant in the second caricature now holds the noble's sword and has climbed onto the backs of the two formerly privileged orders (Engraving 2). Consistent with the symbolism of the image,

1. "Let's hope that this game will end soon."

2. "I knew our turn would come."

3. "I swear, they'll never get over this one!"

the hare and the partridges who were devouring the cabbage and pecking at the grain in the first image have been rendered harmless once and for all: the hare can be seen hanging from the peasant's sword and the partridges lie motionless on the ground. Historical rupture, the sign and condition of renewal, is here dynamically transcribed in a reversal of the social order that was a product of the carnival tradition. But this reversal was also integrated into the process of the social transfer of wealth, and commentators generally associate this image with the night of August 4. An antisocial disease and the healing of France through a more just distribution of social roles provide the oral focus of this double-acting image, one of the most frequently reproduced in the collections of the Bibliothèque Nationale and the Musée Carnavalet.

This physical metaphor of social change required a sequel, however. A few months later the same engraver continued the series, in a sense completing the citizen's transformation and concluding the metamorphosis: the earlier exhausted peasant, the "slave," having raised himself up, has now become an active spectator in a political scene or, rather, playlet, from which the two privileged individuals have been brutally excluded, relegated to a debased oblivion (Engraving 3). This third image is frequently overlooked and even separated from the two earlier images. It is essential, though, for it confers upon the peasant, symbol of the Third Estate, the power to struggle effectively against the previous social order. In the second image the citizen has been born, thereby weakening the Ancien Régime; in the third, this citizen-peasant has established himself permanently: historical rupture found a means to keep a new organization alive, consolidated the gains of the summer of 1789, and succeeded in its struggle against the privileged classes by effacing them from the image. In its description of the different weapons that constituted the power of the citizen, representation turned citizenship into a spectacle.

But how could the old order be destroyed? This third caricature, in which the figures from the two earlier images reappear, illustrates the means—realistic or symbolic—then available to the French patriot to frustrate the intrigues of the privileged classes. The image introduces a new social type, who alone embodies the representation of the citizen: the French Guard, the hard core responsible for the defense of the capital during the summer of 1789 and the armed branch of Parisian citizenship. This caricature can be read on several levels. As is frequently the case, a symbolic activity occupies the center of the image, draws our eye, and functions as the metaphoric expression of the image's key idea, while individual details throughout the document help explain its overall organization. Here, the French Guard performs its functions symbolically by covering the two members of the privileged orders with excrement, to the great joy of the hero of the Third Estate, who, the lone spectator, applauds while laughing. To the right, half hidden, a different and more suspicious character looks on questioningly as dark clouds gather overhead. The new power of the people of Paris, embodied in the drawing's considerable scatological power, seems to intimidate him. The reference is to one of the masked and hypocritical plotters (he is even wearing the cockade) who were so often denounced in caricatures and pamphlets. Around the foreground action a number of pictorial elements refer to revolutionary events that had occurred since July 1789, when the first two engravings appeared. This third caricature is a response to the first two and offers a summary of events, six months into the new order. It illustrates the contemporary obsession with plots and the mobilization of the citizenry against the enemy: in the "dead end of the aristocrats" leading to the "Hôtel de Lambesc" (Lambesc was one of the leaders of the counterrevolution of mid-July 1789), the privileged orders, repeated in the same drawing, sharpen their swords and castigate the patriots. Clouds gather above them, exposing the ill intentions that dominate their clandestine meetings. The lantern, however, symbolizes the enveloping light that will allow the citizens to undo these plots and investigate the "dead end of the aristocrats," which would otherwise remain in conspiratorial shadow. This lantern, the "fearful restorer" indicated in the sign over the inn, is also a symbol of chastisement. In the image it speaks as clearly as the severed heads and posters, which remind everyone of the power of an angry populace (the hanging of Bertier, the faces of de Launay and Foullon, the profile of the marquis de Favras, instigator of the most recent plot, who was executed at the beginning of 1790). The sign "House for Sale," suspended from the porch of the Hôtel de Lambesc, completes this canvas of popular vigilance; the aristocrats who have escaped the vengeance of the Parisian people have fled shamefully. The Revolution, however, is more than simply a punitive campaign. The citizenry demands that surveillance be carried out at every moment but makes preparations for important victories and ensures the advancement of the new values. The signs indicating "Liberty Street" and "Clerical Property for Sale" remind us, just as do the dead game lying at the feet of the Third Estate, of the initial gains of the Revolution: the conquest of certain rights, the sale of national property, and the abolition of privileges. In spite of the apparent naïveté of the image, it remains one of the most suggestive caricatures of the period. It reverses the old order, punishes then eliminates the privileged orders, and promotes the gains of 1789, making it a decisive representation of the process of the citizen's formation. This transformation is embodied in three successive moments, three stages represented by the three engravings: the disease afflicting France, worn out by privilege; the radical cure that heals the body by reversing earlier values; and the emancipation of the new France, now an active spectator in an unfamiliar political event—citizenship—during which the privileged orders are removed from power and new values on which to found society are promoted.

This narrative of revolution was a common theme in several forms of political representation. From texts by Sieyès to anonymous pamphlets of political commentary, from caricatures to folk songs, we find the same emphasis on the decisive rupture. This was visualized by the reversal of physical posture, the use of identical descriptions of the disease of privilege afflicting pre-revolutionary France, and in a shared idea of the citizen's vigilance as the first line of defense for the new regime born in 1789. In this sense the entire *Essai sur les privilèges* by Sieyès can be read as a clinical description of the corporal vice introduced through privilege into the body of the citizen.

Thus was born in the heart of privilege the desire to overcome, an insatiable desire for domination. This desire, unfortunately too much at home in the human constitution, is a true antisocial disease. Try to enter for a moment into the feelings of a member of the privileged class. He considers himself and his colleagues to be part of a separate order, a chosen nation within the Nation. This is no longer the body of citizens, to which he once belonged, it is only a people, a people that will soon become, in its language as well as in its heart, an assembly of inconsequential beings, a class of men created expressively to serve, whereas he himself has been made to command and consume. Yes, members of the privileged orders have really come to regard themselves as a different species of humanity. As a body they are unique to certain races. In their heart of hearts, they reproach Nature for not having placed their fellow citizens among the inferior species, destined solely to serve. In this sense, there exists an inveterate superstition that displaces reason and even takes offence at any sign of doubt. Certain savage peoples take pleasure in deformity, and honor it as they would other natural charms. In our hyperborean nations we shower our stupid praise on political excrescences, which are much more deformed and far more harmful, for they eat away and destroy the social body. But superstition passes, and the body it degrades reappears in all its strength and natural beauty.[1]

malheureux comme tu etoit rongé de tous les cotés .

Le François d'autre - fois

4. The Frenchman of yesteryear.

Sieyès's text could be a commentary for our first engraving: the different
"species of men," the privileged orders who, having become "political excrescences," erode and fatigue the Third Estate, which has been "made sub-
servient." The writing of the philosopher-priest is imagistic, sarcastic,
metaphoric, representational, and very similar to the pamphlets of his time and
the drawings of the caricaturists in its efforts to hunt down and describe the
"disease of deformity" that afflicts the body of the nation, dividing and degrading
it. Engravers had been illustrating this theme of the diseased body of "old
France" for quite some time; it was the first, essential stage, primitive and
negative, in the description of the "transformation of the citizens." This incomplete stage took the form of a sluggish France, still held in the shackles of
infancy, an immature people concerned with its rattle, weak and afraid, laughing
at its own misfortune, incapable of standing without the help of a walker, and
"eaten away on all sides" by squabbling (Engraving 4). But this condition can

Le Tems présent

Le Tiers Etat   *La Noblesse*   *le Clergé*
C'est ici que les premiers sont les derniers.

5. Present time.

easily change, leading to the exhaustion of the body and a people of "frightened old men," as Sieyès called them, a decomposed body as revealed in *Le temps présent*, where the Third Estate is represented as a "walking skeleton" (Engraving 5). A spectacular image, which transcribed the language of politics into the realm of the organic, this skeleton became a part of the important corpus of physical metaphors concerning the decay of Ancien Régime France. Skeleton, slave, cripple, dwarf, child, creature in rags, bedridden old man—the figures of degeneration abound, crossing all levels of political discourse. It was as a result of this process of multiple representations of revolutionary events, due to these different levels of complementary and intertwined discourse, that certain metaphors provided unexpected resonance. I feel it would be reductive to read Sieyès without the pamphlets that accompanied his writings, impossible to understand his echo without looking at the caricatures that transcribed his words into the body of imagery.

Similar encounters accompanied the entire process of the citizen's transformation. The antisocial disease known as the Ancien Régime, which had been diagnosed by all the political doctors, was followed by a period of death (the final crisis) and regeneration. It was an extraordinary time marked by a decisive break with the past, which Sieyès, to follow through with my comparison, announced in these words: "The political body is disorganized; it is dead."[2] This theme was immediately transferred to the world of images. The death of the old body is one of the favorite metaphors of caricaturists, who buried in their funereal and derisive "funeral processions" "social injustice," and "clergy," and the "nobility" (Engraving 6) (before counterrevolutionary satire turned the idea against them; in 1791 it was the "dying constitution" and the members of the Jacobin Club who were led to their graves). The autopsy of the old body, conducted with mockery, is equally revealing. "I can't find a heart," exclaims the doctor peevishly, after having opened the chest cavity of the "aristocratic monster."

The announcement of this death is a blessing, a salutary catharsis, relieving the healthy part of the nation from the dead weight of privilege. Sieyès expresses the idea quite clearly: "We owe our cure to the excess of sickness. The excess of sickness will do it all," suggesting a radical and violent cure, which most frequently involved amputating the older growth, the

separation from the body of the oppressors, a separation that is extremely desirable. . . . It is impossible to say which place the body of privilege should occupy in the social order. That would mean asking where in the patient's body we want to place the malignant tumor that ravages and torments him. We must neutralize it. We must reestablish the health and functioning of all the organs so that these morbid conditions never occur again, for they have the power to vitiate the most basic principles of life.[3]

The language of metaphor is filled with violent and occasionally bloody imagery, capable of impressing the reader, arousing the imagination. The historical break became a radical medical operation, a beneficial trauma, a comparison that was often present in the pamphlets of political commentary and could be found in the meetings of the Estates-General, as this extract from the *Cahier céleste* would indicate: "Imagine a capable doctor, having in his care a patient whose limbs are covered with sores. The doctor doesn't waste time in applying different salves on every sore; he is only concerned with destroying the cause of illness. But where is it? In the blood. He bleeds the patient and purifies him; the sores heal."[4] A similar idea is expressed in *Margot, la vielle bonne femme de 102 ans, à Messieurs des états généraux*:

Strip yourselves of all enthusiasm. Focus only on the need to simplify everything that ignorance and greed have allowed to proliferate. Take a close look, Gentlemen of the Estates, spare nothing; cut to the core; let the patient cry out. Once the incision is made he will thank you. If you leave behind any gangrened or rotting tissue, the patient will die, and everyone will cry out. Bring twenty-four million gout inflicted and paralyzed arms back to life, and cut out the stomachs that consume everything and digest nothing, with their biscuits, their consommés, and their sugar. Make a clean cut of those stomachs, which are only good in the kitchen.[5]

Caricature played an important role in constructing an imaginary world that reflected the radical change the French populace was undergoing. Like the pamphlets I discussed earlier, it helped popularize characters such as the "patriotic doctor," "the national surgeon," the dentist, and other healers by emphasizing

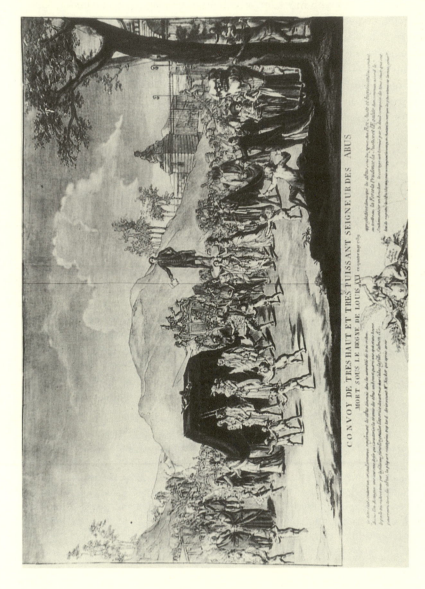

CONVOY DE TRES HAUT ET TRES PUISSANT SEIGNEUR DES ABUS
MORT SOUS LE REGNE DE LOUIS XVI ce quatre may 1789

6. A convoy of the most esteemed and most powerful lords of abuse.

7. The national unguent.

the excess of evil present in the social order. The trauma experienced by the liberating body of France was frequently portrayed in caricature. There was the symbolic figure of "Cornu," for example, the patriot pharmacist who discovered the "Calembourg," or "national unguent," that "destroyed corns and prevented them from recurring" (Engraving 7). The remedy was represented by a caricature[6] in which two "citizen soldiers" are busy "grinding the fat of a canon and the brains of a noble" and an abbot "is cooking over a fire" that is being tended by the pharmacist, while on the right side of the composition a "very fat priest" uneasily watches the preparation of the potion. The captain carefully details the ingredients of the recipe:

Take two pounds of saddle of canon; three ounces of gall from a parliamentary president; four ounces of skull from an investigating magistrate, court clerk, and state counsel; two drams of brain from a duke, a baron, and a marquis; four thighs of financier; a grenadier's heart; two ounces of aristocrat's bile; and six chunks of precipitate; mix carefully and cook until done over a fire made of orders, bulls, and privileges; shape into logs the length of the Abbé Maury's nose or Déprémesnil's tongue, and wrap them in the *Actes des apôtres*; use as needed on corns that appear on the feet or anywhere else, which it is time to remove.

The fragmentation and dismemberment of the old corporative privileges involved the radical elimination of corns, excrescences, warts, and tumors; caricature had never before used drawing, bodily posture, and captions to represent the transformation of the citizen with so much cruelty and malevolent laughter. The imagery based on this model often represents a teeming humanity bent on amputating the former body politic, an unwieldy machine designed to generate a political fantasy of the citizen's transformation: the new body, freed of its previous degradation, would be ushered into existence, by force if necessary. This physiological element, formed and deformed by contemporary drawing, was used to manage a political discourse that was as consistent (and occasionally just as inconsistent) as the pamphlets of the period and metaphorically diffused the ideal mechanisms that had been constructed by men such as Sieyès, Rabaut Saint-Etienne, and Mirabeau. A similar mechanism was at work establishing norms to which everyone was made to conform: patriot surgeons, armed with large saws, lopped off anything that exceeded the standard dimensions (Engraving 8). There were machines to remove the grease from the privileged orders (Engraving 9), dentists to tear out the rapacious jaws of an earlier age, and apothecaries who administered enemas and bled bodies that were too well fed (Engraving 10). "Abbots who held too many titles and were too fat" were given purgatives that made them regurgitate their ecclesiastical benefits and incomes.

The transformation of the citizen reached the third stage of its development: following the diagnosis of the subject-slave's illness and the radical operation, performed with all the suddenness and violence of historical rupture, a new body politic appeared. The initial vision was of a new union among the three traditional orders, based on a return to equality, the dream of a new golden age. It was reflected in a number of images celebrating the union of the three orders. Three symbolic men collectively and equally bear the burden of taxes; three Frenchmen dip their "crusts" of bread, which are all the same size, into the "national egg" (Engravings 11–12); three musicians play together in perfect harmony (Engraving 13). It is always three individuals who come up to the same mark when measured by the "national standard." While endless variations on this "comedy of the three orders" were being played throughout the lively debate concerning the convocation of the Estates-General, other, more radical proposals sprang up, which were visually represented by contemporary caricaturists. Supported by the weight of Justice, the social balance could then be shown to teeter clearly in the direction of the Third Estate, hurling into the air the ridiculous puppets representing the two privileged orders (Engraving 14). As I described in the beginning of this chapter, the arrangement of the various figures could easily be reversed. From now on it is the Third Estate that climbs on the back of those it was once forced to support. This same dynamic of reversal occurs in *Le Réveil du tiers état*, where the character of the commoner, awakened from a "bad nightmare" by the storming of the Bastille, breaks his chains and prepares to rise up and terrorize the "fears of the past" (Engraving 15). In the following engraving the patriot drives the privileged away and crushes the monster of the

8. The national level.

9. The patriotic degreaser.

Je t'avais bien dit mon ami,
Qu'ils nous feraient tout rendre.

10. "I told you, friend, that they would make us give it all back."

L'ŒUF A LA COQUE.

11. The soft-boiled egg (time past).

13. "Well! Now we agree!"

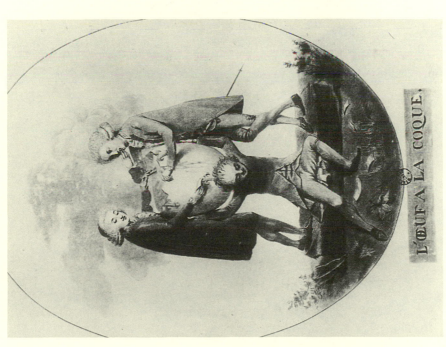

12. The soft-boiled egg (time present).

14. "This time, justice is on the side of the strongest."

15. The Third Estate awakens.

16. Destruction of the Bastille after vanquishing the enemies of liberty on July 14, 1789.

ADIEU BASTILLE

17. Goodbye, Bastille.

Bastille (Engraving 16). In the third image the patriot, representing the new political man, manipulates the puppets of two members of the privileged orders (Engraving 17). The transformation is now completely out in the open. A single image collapses time and, through the use of what eighteenth-century artists referred to as a *repentir* (several successive stages of a figure in the same drawing), displays the gestures and appearances of a character "before" and "after," clearly indicating the radical transformation of the French populace (Engraving 18).

The final possibility for the new, "great national body of citizens," as Sieyès wrote, was the incorporation of all the signs of political legitimacy in a single character. The union of the three orders gave way to a unique body. The philosopher-priest described this process as the creation, resulting from the transformation of the citizen, of an indivisible "National Assembly" that would replace the hierarchical and divided Estates-General, a process that caricature displayed with its own tools of representation: the warm and intimate "embrace" of the three old orders that finally give birth to a single body (*Le Souhait accompli*) (Engraving 19), or the "gentleman of the three estates," a single figure provided with all the symbols of the attire and labor of the different orders (Engraving 20).

This phenomenon of incorporation reached its conclusion when all references to the orders themselves disappeared from the images. The comedy of the social orders was followed by the era of the citizen. This temporal and political swing was never given a more concrete manifestation than in the engraving entitled *Le Francais d' autrefois, Le Francais d' aujourd' hui* (Engraving 21). Here, through the benefits of political regeneration, a man exchanges the frail constitution of the powdered fop, mannered and effeminate (he has the hands of a courtier), for the colossal stature of the giant clothed in the uniform of the Paris National Guard, wearing the cockade in his hat, holding on the end of his bayonet the political symbol of citizenship, the red cap engraved with the name of liberty, with the cannon in the background magnifying a reconquered virility. Uncomfortable with victory, caricature left the triumphant celebration of this conquest to other forms of representation, shifting the terrain of praise toward ribaldry. The rights of the citizen, having cast off once and for all the fragmentation and weakness of the old, diseased body, became the symbol of sovereign power. Through the use of metaphor, licentious imagery provided the "droit de l'homme"—symbol of the newly acquired citizenship—with a sublime cortège where the allegories dance around the new virility while carrying the spoils of the ancient world (Engraving 22). Thus, the transformation of the citizen was completed in caricature, which turned its attention to other subjects, violently attacking the clergy, the counterrevolutionaries, and, finally, the king himself.

Translated by Robert Bononno

18. Memorable scenes from the Revolution.

Monsieur des trois Etats.

20. The gentleman of the Three Estates.

Le souhait accompli.
I'a comme javons toujours desiré que ça suts.

19. A dream come true.

Le Francois d'autrefois. | Le Francais d'aujourd'hui

21. The Frenchman then, The Frenchman today.

NOTES

1. *Essai sur les privilèges* (Paris, 1788), 17–18.

2. *Vues sur les moyens d'exécution dont les représentants de la France pourront disposer en 1789* (Paris, 1789), 117.

3. *Qu'est-ce que le tiers état?* (Paris, 1789), 127.

4. *Le Cahier céleste* [1789]. (B.N., 8° Lb^{39}. 1603.)

5. *Margot, la vieille bonne femme de 102 ans, soeur du curé de 97 ans, à Messieurs les Etats-Généraux*, 1789. (B.N., 8° Lb^{39}. 1733.)

6. *L'Onguent national*, Cabinet des estampes de la Bibliothèque Nationale, de Vinck collection, no. 3061.

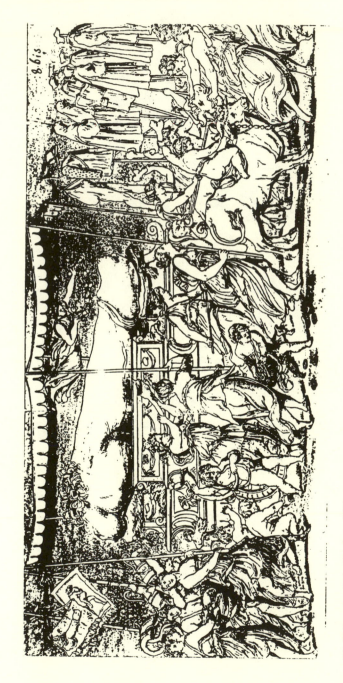

22. Triumph of the Rights of Man.

6

THE CITIZEN IN THE THEATER

Marvin A. Carlson

The period of the French Revolution was the period of the most extensive and intense theater activity Paris has seen before or since. Literally hundreds of theaters operated in the city during the 1790s, attracting thousands of spectators, most of whom had never attended theater before this time. What they found on these stages provided both commentary upon and escape from the concerns of these turbulent days, and both positive and negative examples of behavior in a society in the most rapid evolution, where all previous models and established ideas were being challenged.

The new concept of citizen had particular importance for those who made theater their profession. Until this time, largely due to opposition from the Church, actors in France had led a marginal social existence, excluded not only from the rites of the Church, such as baptism and burial, but often from more clearly secular privileges as well, such as holding or inheriting property. The statement of the Declaration of the Rights of Man and of the Citizen, symbolically perhaps the foremost document produced by the Revolution, was drawn up by the new National Assembly in August of 1789 and at least on its surface seemed to guarantee such "natural rights" as liberty, property, and security to the entire population of France. Protests were made, especially by delegates from the Catholic Church, against extending rights to such previously excluded groups as Protestants, Jews, and actors, but all of these groups were, after heated debate, accepted as citizens in the new order. Among the revolutionary leaders who specifically championed the cause of the actors were such distinguished figures as Mirabeau and Robespierre.

In addition to granting the rights and privileges of citizenship to actors, the National Assembly vastly enlarged their opportunities to pursue their profession by officially ending the ancient royal monopoly granted to *opéra*, *comédie*, and *comédie italienne*. Although this monopoly had in fact been eroding steadily for a number of years, it still placed all manner of serious restrictions upon any new theatrical enterprise in Paris in terms of size, repertoire, and even manner of presentation. Both the monopoly and the close ties of the old theaters to the court gave them an aura of privilege and bias that gained them little sympathy from members of the new Assembly. After July of 1790, however, any citizen had the right to establish a public theater and to present in it plays of any kind, including works by any authors dead more than five years.

The enormous boom in theatrical production that followed may not have made the theater a school of virtue and patriotism, but it certainly exposed a vastly larger section of the public to theater than had ever been the case before. Before the liberation of the theater in 1791, Paris had ten theaters. Twenty-three more opened within a few months after this decree, with a total seating capacity of about sixty thousand for a city whose population at this time was about sixty-five thousand. Theaters appeared in every district for audiences of every taste. In the desperate competition for audiences, these ventures offered almost every conceivable type of entertainment, but not surprisingly a great majority of the plays reflected in some manner or other the concerns of the day. The great public events—battles, festivals, assassinations—were almost instantly reproduced on stage, along with intimate scenes of contemporary family life. Even the classics, which continued to be presented, were consciously interpreted by both actors and audience in the light of contemporary events.

For a public struggling with such new questions of self-definition as what it meant to be a citizen or a republican, the theater naturally offered positive and negative models for consideration, even before the National Assembly, early in 1792, began to work through its Committee of Public Instruction to encourage the theater to offer works designed to further the goals of the Revolution. Perhaps the most striking symbolic event attempting to crystallize the new national consciousness in the early years of the Revolution was the Festival of Federation, held on July 14, 1790, with the participation of citizen-soldiers from all over the nation. In addition to the ceremony itself, the preparation of the field where it was held became symbolic of the new order. Citizens of all classes, ages, and both sexes joined in the common labor. Various trades wore identifying ensignia as they worked, and prominent among these were the actors of Paris, who brought with them the orchestra from their theaters to provide music to accompany the labors.

In preparing for the great festival the new citizen had for the first time the tangible experience of working with his fellows for a common goal in which previous social distinctions were forgotten. The activity provided a model, not only for social interaction, but for a new concept of family life based upon patriotic fervor. The federation in turn served to inspire a wide variety of theatrical productions that reinforced these images. One of the most popular of these was Collet d'Herbois's *La famille patriote ou la Fédération*, opening just three days after the festival. In it M. Gaspard, inspired by the new order, embraces his servant as an equal and schedules his daughter's wedding for July 14, to tie his family happiness to that great day. Even Gaspard's brother, an aristocrat, is inspired by the federation events to declare, "I forswear my prejudices forever. I have become a citizen. All other titles are chimerical. I sacrifice them on the altar of the nation."

In the popular culture of the period, the role of citizen was continually opposed to that of aristocrat, so that any supporter of the old order and of privilege came to be styled an aristocrat, whatever their former social position, while those who had actually been aristocrats were expected, like Gaspard's brother, to cast off this role in order to be able to embrace the new one of citizen. Not infrequently, the aristocrat appeared in dramatic structures recalling Molière's comedies, as in Hyacinthe Dorvo's *Patriote du dix août* (November 1792), with the aristocrat as a blocking agent preventing the marriage of his enlightened daughter to a patriotic citizen, despite the pleas of his liberal brother.

Rivaling aristocrats in the popular imagination as determined enemies of the new order were the priests, and it is hardly surprising that the theater, which had so long suffered under the suspicion and condemnation of the Church, should take particular pleasure in anti-clerical drama. Exciting tales of innocent maidens incarcerated in convents against their will and rescued at last by republican lovers were so common as to form essentially a special subgenre of revolutionary theater, and the convent provided a simulacrum of the Bastille in the popular imagination as a symbol of oppression and tyranny, here with a titillating erotic edge. Priests, like aristocrats, were expected to renounce their title to embrace the more honored one of citizen, and many plays made this a pivotal moment. This trope became particularly popular after November of 1793 when Gobel, the bishop of Paris and a member of the Constituent Assembly, publicly abdicated his post to join the ranks of citizens. As usual, theatrical commentary appeared on this event almost as soon as it occurred, resulting in such plays as Radet and Desfontaines's *Encore un curé*, which celebrated a simple country curate who renounces the church to marry a republican wife and enlist in the army to defend the nation, and *A bas la calotte ou les déprêtrisés* by Pierre Rousseau, himself a former abbot, which shows a vicar who gives up his calling to marry a liberal young woman. This example encourages the girl's father, himself a Protestant minister, to exclaim: "My friend, your example inspires me to do likewise. From this moment I renounce my ministry; let us unite in the abjuration of all cults and preach to all citizens the gospel of the rights of man!"

In the early years of the Revolution and in the spirit of the great federation, such theatrical illusions of priests and aristocrats becoming good citizens and the founders of happy republican families were frequent, but in the darker period of the Terror, such conversion and reconciliation was rarely seen. The aristocrat and priest became the inveterate enemy of the citizen, to be denounced and rejected, even at the loss of friendly and familial ties. Pierre Duplessis's spectacle *Les Peuples et les rois ou le tribunal de la raison* in the spring of 1794 showed the banner of Liberty being saluted by the allegorical figure of Citizenship, surrounded by such companions as Fraternal Love, Conjugal Love, Filial Love, Modesty, Charity, Maternity, and Paternity, but the previous and highly successful production at this same theater Citizen Pompigny's *L'epoux républicain*, glorified family betrayal in the name of citizenship. The hero, a former Leroi who has renamed himself Franklin, has married a former prioress. When he discovers that his wife and son are planning to flee the country, he promptly denounces them to the authorities. A priest who was conspiring with them asks Franklin, "Can you desire the death of your wife? Of your son?" The good citizen replies: "It is nothing to me, since they deserve it. Long live the Republic!"

Not all theaters were, of course, this extreme in their interpretation of a citizen's responsibilities, but by mid–1793 the authorities became much more demanding that all theaters actively support the new order. Confidential reports were submitted by secret police officers to the Committee of Public Safety, not only on the plays presented, but on the reactions of audiences to them. It is clear from these reports that many theaters had a fairly predictable political orientation. As one police observer reported, the smaller theaters, frequented by the less well-to-do citizens, generally showed "in the spectators and in those who entertain them a spirit of patriotism pleasant indeed to the true republican," while the more elegant houses, "excluding all but the rich by their high prices, receive only the enemies of liberty or those indifferent to it." Clearly the former remained committed to providing models of good citizenship, while the latter ignored this responsibility or worse, as this same report notes, even made light of it. At the aristocratic Théâtre Feydeau, says the report,

the light, bantering tone of the actors whenever they touched upon a Revolutionary ideal made them no better than the spectators. The glorious and sacred title of citizen was to them an object of comedy; and this abuse of so respectable a title was all the more unpardonable as it was committed in a play whose subject and details came from an era long before our new age. It was therefore a clear attempt on the part of these gentlemen to render this title vile in the eyes of the spectators rather than using it to elevate their spirits. They were well aware of what their audience wanted.[1]

The conversion of all theater personnel and indeed of all dramatic characters into citizens was demanded by a police ruling in April of 1794 that required that all such titles as duke, count, marquis, baron, monsieur, and madame be banned from the stage, replaced by citizen and citizeness, regardless of rhyme, meter, or content. Nor was this merely a matter of title. Greeks, Romans, Venetians, and Gauls appeared now in the national colors, and the tragic heroines of Racine suffered their agonies with large patriotic cockades pinned to the breasts.

These extreme conditions, however, were short-lived, and although police continued to watch the theaters very carefully, closing them and arresting actors and directors whose patriotism was suspect, Robespierre himself intervened after a few months to remove some of the more extreme of the police regulations. "Without doubt," observed Robespierre's spokesman Claude Payan, it is as ridiculous to say Citizen Cataline as it is to see Jupiter or Armide in a tricolored cap. Therefore, the police have today informed all directors that they may leave intact all tragedies written before the Revolution, or later ones dealing with non-Revolutionary subjects. The titles "Monsieur," "Seigneur," etc. need not be changed. . . . In short, we ask only that new plays use the words "citizen" and "citizeness," and that in them "Monsieur" and "Madame" be used ony as an insult or to distinguish an enemy of the Revolution.[2]

After the Thermidorian reaction, those dramas most obviously concerned with commentary on the contemporary social and political scene were almost all devoted to condemning the excesses of the terror, and bloodthirsty Jacobins replaced priests and aristocrats as the source of evil in the state, abusing their new political power to pursue private ends of revenge, lust, or, most often, financial gain. The most popular play in Paris in the spring of 1795 was Ducancel's *L'intérieur des comités révolutionnaires,* which showed a revolutionary committee in Dijon plotting against an honest patriot, Dufour, and his soldier son to gain his possessions. As their schemes are about to succeed, an officer arrives, like the messenger in *Tartuffe,* to announce the fall of Robespierre and to arrest the members of the committee. "Generous Dufour," announces the officer, "the reign of the brigands is over. Justice and humanity will rule in their place." He urges Dufour to join in the work of ridding society of such vampires, so that "posterity, weeping over the ashes of innocent citizens, will bless their avengers." In such plays the role of the citizen shifted from that of active contributor to the success of the Revolution (and, indeed, sometimes even a member of the Jacobins) to that of passive and innocent victim of revolutionary excess and corruption.

The various factions that had come to power during the rapidly changing political situation of the revolutionary years had each recognized the theater as a powerful tool for providing examples and civic guidance to the citizens of the new state. Sometimes by conviction, sometimes by coercion, most of the theaters in Paris had accepted this role, but it was a very difficult one. After the generous enthusiasm of the federation period passed, the various political factions that struggled for power in the new state utilized the theater as one of the weapons in their conflict, and the models of citizenship and of civic responsibility depicted on stage often reflected less a thoughtful attempt to explore these questions in light of the new social order than an attempt to further the agenda of a particular party.

The various governments of the Revolution abetted this process, regarding the theater as a branch of public education and controlling and censoring its productions accordingly. The arrival of the Consulate in 1799 provided a major change, since Napoléon's concern from the beginning was to put behind the factionalism of recent years and to reinstitute a spirit of national unity like that of the federation. He too saw the theaters as instruments of public instruction, but he prohibited the sort of specific political topics so characteristic of the revolutionary drama and encouraged a search for more positive and conciliatory themes. Scarcely a week after the Directory was dissolved, the new government issued a general directive to all theaters stating:

In the succession of parties which have in turn come to power, the theater has usually resounded with unnecessary insults for the vanquished and idle flattery for the victor. The present government scorns and disdains the support of factions; it desires nothing from them, and is concerned only with the Republic. Let all Frenchmen rally to the same concern, and all theaters promulgate it. Let feelings of harmony, maxims of moderation and wisdom, the expression of noble and generous sentiments alone be represented on our stages. Let nothing of that which divides spirits, encourages hatred, prolongs unhappy memories, be tolerated there. It is time at last that only Frenchmen dwell in the French nation.[3]

The process of protecting the new citizens and their new republic by what Simon Schama calls "the rooting out of Uncitizens" was thus officially ended, and the Napoleonic era began its program of stressing dedication of all citizens to mutual support and to support of the state. Although the new government officially "scorned and disdained" the spirit of factionalism it saw as characterizing its predecessors, it pursued its own agenda with equal determination, and like its predecessors, it looked to the theater, the most public of the arts, to provide inspiration, examples, and instruction to the citizenry.

NOTES

1. Henri Welschinger, *Le Théâtre de la Révolution* (Paris, 1880), 155–58.
2. Ibid., 149–50.
3. L.-Henry Lecomte, *Napoléon et le monde dramatique* (Paris, 1912), 34–35.

PART II

Citizenship in Action

7

REVOLUTIONARY DEMOCRACY AND THE ELECTIONS

Patrice Gueniffey

In studying the elections of the revolutionary period, we must guard against what might be referred to as the "illusion of transparency." This illusion is based on the spontaneous association of suffrage with a political system whose legitimacy is founded on popular sovereignty, and the notion that elections are self-evident within a democracy. The logic is simple: if there can be no democracy without elections, and if the French Revolution established the foundations of modern democracy, then the Revolution must also have established the outlines of the modern doctrine of suffrage along with an electoral system characterized by the democratic conception of the vote. Elections were subsequently regarded as the basis of a political system in which governmental authority resided in the people to whom it was responsible, while the system itself was assigned a variety of separate functions: choosing the method of selecting its leaders, providing an opportunity for citizens to express their confidence or their defiance, and acting as the instrument for adjusting the relationship between society and power.

The lack of thought about the specificity of the revolutionary system of suffrage, and whether it is possible to apply to it analytical techniques of modern electoral science drawn from contemporary voting experience, has resulted in a misunderstanding of the act of voting itself, the moment when a collective decision is made. Election studies, of which in fact there were few, concentrate on two principal topics: voter participation and the results of elections. The emphasis given to the beginning and the outcome of the election provides a method of creating the continuity and transparency that are essential in order to look at voting from a contemporary point of view. Perceived as the basis of partisan rivalries, suffrage could then be used to project existing social divisions onto the political order. Conversely, this continuity could also make it possible to reconstruct the geographic and social basis of these divisions.

In reality, this transparency or continuity is nonexistent, as shown by the fact that some elections cannot be reduced to sociological or political forms. Because this approach requires a minimum of political "consistency," which the majority of elections of the revolutionary period lacked, the same elections are invariably referred to: those of 1789 and 1792, and those of 1797 and 1798, when new members were elected to the Directory councils—the latter because of their obvious relationship to the immediate political context, the former because they were accompanied by open deliberation. The lack of interest in other elections is a result of their problematical relationship to the political situation. The choice of municipal officers, administrators, or representatives to the 1791 Legislative Assembly exhibits a selection process dissociated from any expression of a political intention or even debate concerning contemporary opinions or issues— that is, precisely, what elections were intended for.

THE VOTE IN 1789

The decrees voted by the Constituent Assembly at the end of 1789 called upon the citizens to vote in two kinds of assemblies: the communal assemblies, responsible for the direct election of municipal officers, and the primary cantonal assemblies, which were to choose justices of the peace and second-stage electors at the ratio of 1 percent of the registered electors who, together within the electoral assembly of the *département*, would fill the various public offices. These included legislative and administrative bodies, tribunals, high-court juries, magistrates for the Court of Cassation, and, eventually, bishops, priests, postmasters, etc.

In all these voting assemblies the process was the same. First of all, voting took place in an assembly, and theoretically all the electors were to remain in the same location until the announcement of the results of the last ballot for the last office. In this situation everyone could participate in checking the credentials of those who were present and also elect a *bureau*, consisting of a president, a secretary, and three polling officers responsible for counting the ballots. There were to be three rounds of voting by majority vote. The first two rounds required an absolute majority, the last a relative majority or run-off vote, depending on whether a plurinominal or uninominal system was used. The plurinominal system, dual in 1790, single after 1791,[1] was used primarily to nominate second-stage electors, local functionaries, and municipal counsellors, whereas the uninominal system governed the choice of deputies, mayors, and the public prosecutor for the *département*'s criminal court. The votes were taken by roll call. The secretary called the names of each of the citizens registered on the lists supplied by the mayors of the different communes of the canton for first-stage elections, and from the list of electors nominated by the primary assemblies for second-stage elections. Once called, each citizen would go to the *bureau*, where, after having sworn the oath, he would fill out his ballot or, if he was unable to read and write, have it filled out for him by one of the polling officers, before depositing it in an urn.

Methods of voting such as these, which required a considerable amount of time, might seem archaic today. In 1789, however, they were developed in response to the modernization of political participation. To understand the change that so deeply affected voting after 1789, we have to go back to the spring of 1789 and the elections to the Estates-General. Voting traditionally occurred within the parish or the local guilds, the customary universe of social existence, where each individual was related to everyone else by a solidarity and dependence, and in which voice voting reinforced influence. There were two distinct aspects to this form of voting: the group came to a decision that resulted in the preparation of the grievances, or *doléances*, and the formulation of a political intention, and a second-stage election took place, during which a delegate was chosen who was responsible for presenting and defending the will of his constituents.

The arrival of the principles of national sovereignty and citizenship had serious repercussions for this system. The first sign of change was the break with the tradition of the strict mandate. The end result of voting was no longer the formulation of a common will but the designation of representatives who, unfettered by any form of dependence on the desires of their constituency, were responsible for expressing the common intention. The consequences of this were most fully expressed in the decrees establishing the electoral system, which were voted on in December 1789. They carefully separated the election proper—which belonged to the electors gathered within their voting districts—and deliberation, reserved for the nation as a whole in the form of an assembly of its representatives.

The second change involved the primary agent in this event—no longer a community but an individual; no longer social man, whose right of participation resulted from his belonging to a community or his personal status in the hierarchy of elements that constituted an organic society, but the individual citizen, an abstract entity defined by universal rights and a numerical unity reduced to his will alone: one man, one vote. This individualization of participation was made concrete by the substitution of cantonal for parish districts and the increasing use of the secret ballot, both of which aimed at increasing the voter's independence. The enlargement of election districts to the cantonal level was intended to free citizens from the influence of their day-to-day relationships by requiring the inhabitants of different communes to mix with one another. In this way the break with a familiar environment and the increase in the number of participants would help weaken personal influence.

Along with these modernizing tendencies, however, the new electoral system preserved two features that were characteristic of earlier practices: the vote in an assembly and the lack of either an electoral candidacy or public debates concerning the issues being voted on. These features clearly contradicted the new principles. The first created an obstacle to the individualization of participation, and the second was incompatible with the gradual evolution from deliberation to election. The electoral system of the revolutionary period was, in a sense, an amalgam of old and new, archaic and modern, illustrating the ambiguity of its political culture. This resulted in low numbers of voters and an almost total absence of real elections. The modern elements within this system came into conflict with a society that was still very much steeped in tradition; the archaic elements led directly to a negation of the vote.

THE NEGATION OF THE VOTE

The absence of meaningful elections was a result of elements inherited from the past—the vote in assembly and the lack of public candidacies—that offset individual participation and the substitution of a majority decision for the characteristic deliberations of traditional political practices.

The organic concept of representation—that of the Estates-General—possessed none of the elements required for making a real choice, such as clearly identified candidates and publicly debated issues. According to this traditional approach to elections, there really was no question of choice; candidates were elected even before the electors met. They were considered natural leaders, whose authority was simply recognized or confirmed by the voters. The situation was quite different after 1789, when authority was no longer an inherent right but resulted from the free and voluntary support of individuals. When called on to provide a real choice, the vote had to be effective, which meant it would need publicly named candidates and issues.

With the exception of the events of Year V (1797), there was nothing in the elections of the revolutionary period that resembled a candidacy prior to the actual election. There were no electoral campaigns, no avowed candidates, no platforms. The results of this situation can be summarized under three main categories. Following each round of voting, it was common to collect a large number of ballots "containing names without sufficient information to know what they stood for."[2] Because of frequent similarities among the voters' names, these ballots often led to confusion and argument. Unaccepted nominations were just another symptom of the political vacuum in which the elections took place. The lack of candidates often produced irrational results, as when a citizen who had no intention of seeking public office received a majority of the votes. And the number who declined election was not negligible: there were twenty-two during the election of deputies for the Legislative Assembly in 1791 and twenty-eight one year later, during the elections to the Convention,[3] giving as their reasons, generally, lack of ability, the material impossibility of abandoning one's family and business, or some undisclosed "infirmity."

But the primary result of the lack of candidacies was the dispersal of votes since every eligible citizen from a circumscription could be a candidate. Many voters were genuinely at a loss, unable to find guidelines and produce a valid vote that would not be wasted on some obscure citizen who lacked all chance of support from more than a handful of voters.

This phenomenon was very important during the primary assemblies. In the three sections that formed the canton of Carpentras in August 1792, where the voters—72, 76, and 48—were far from numerous, the number of votes scattered during the first round was respectively 59 percent, 72 percent, and 54 percent.[4] The percentages increase with the number of voters: in 1792 it was close to 91 percent in St.-Jean de Valence (Drôme), where 231 citizens were present,[5] and 98 percent in Angers, where 951 citizens assembled to nominate 51 electors.[6] The second round of elections did not result in any appreciable concentration of votes. The number of votes lost was above 91 percent at Angers and rose from 59 percent to 81 percent during the primary assembly in Carpentras. The method of voting used also had an effect on these results. There was less scattering of votes during the second-stage assemblies, when the elections for each position called for a majority in the ballot. It was still high, however, and the records indicated ''a large number of insignificant ballots.'' These varied (in 1791) from 23 percent to 58 percent in Indre-et-Loire, from less than 20 percent to 63 percent in Loiret, from 13 percent to 52 percent in the Oise, and from 21 percent to 68 percent in Deux-Sèvres.

In the absence of any arrangement that would limit the voters' preferences, it was often necessary to hold a third round of voting, which was either a majority or a relative vote, in order to come to some decision. From this point of view, the revolutionary elections cannot be interpreted with modern analytical methods that demonstrate how several rounds of voting enable voters to express the diversity of their individual opinions before sacrificing initial disagreements during the final vote in order to arrive at a decision that somehow still conforms to the wishes of the majority of the electorate.[7] During the revolutionary period, however, the first two rounds of voting certainly allowed the citizens to express their preferences, but to such an extent that the results of the third round could not possibly represent the majority will, only the victory (during a run-off vote) of those whom chance had placed in the lead at the end of the second round. It is obvious, as Condorcet had noted, that the first two rounds indicated not the ''attitude'' of the overall assembly but that of ''a few parties'' formed during the assembly, whose candidate, notwithstanding his lack of support, received enough votes to be a front runner at the beginning of the final round of voting.[8] Because of the very absence of the limitation of choice, we can't speak of real freedom of choice in this situation. In the absence of a limited set of candidates the electors were unable to take advantage of a freedom that was tempered by the possibility of several successive rounds of voting: during the first round, each elector designated the individual he felt most qualified; during the third, without having modified his initial opinion (and on what basis?), each elector was required to choose between two competitors, neither of whom might represent his own position, and both of whom had arrived at the top either by luck or through the support of a minority bloc. During the revolutionary period, the only possibility of arriving at a decision was through the use of third round of voting, which cannot be understood from the perspective of current practice, but as an arbitrary mechanism destined to cut through the irreducible diversity of individual preferences.

Because nature abhors a vacuum (even political), there were unofficial candidacies. To show that this is so, we need only look at the number of deputies to the Legislative Assembly and the Convention who were elected during the first round of voting: 240 out of 715 (33.6 percent) in 1791, 318 out of 729 (43.6 percent) the following year. The large number of candidates elected during first-round voting was especially significant during the 1791 elections because, in conformity with the law, all the assemblies had used secret ballots, and since the members of the Constituent Assembly could not be reelected, there were no legally sanctioned candidates. The higher number of deputies elected during first-round voting in 1792 can be attributed to two main factors: the eligibility of the members of the two previous assemblies, who formed a de facto electoral slate, and the use of a voice vote by thirteen electoral assemblies, which favored the quick formation of a majority.

We know little concerning the way in which the majority of elected officials were nominated and supported during the elections. One revolutionary indicated in his *Souvenirs* that "a citizen's prominence was sufficient to recommend him, and all the propaganda was created by his friends during private caucuses,"[9] an electoral method that left few written traces. Though they did no actual campaigning, candidates relied on the zeal of influential friends. Condorcet's wife was able to write with assurance to Etienne Dumont on September 3, 1792, less than a day after the elections had begun, that "Monsieur Condorcet was nominated in five *départements*."[10] And he was, in fact, elected by five assemblies.

Meetings were held before an election, and these were continued during the assembly by negotiations among influential electors from different districts. This in no way prevented the majority of voters from being excluded from the proceedings, as indicated by the significant scattering of votes. A letter written a few days before the electors' meeting by a man named Nérac to a merchant at La Rochelle, who was a member of the Electoral Assembly of Charente-Inférieure in 1791, gives us some idea of the nature of these preliminary caucuses. "That would be a very bad idea, my dear friend," wrote Nérac, "to throw my name in with those who are supposed to renew the legislature. Not only do I lack both strength and talent, but my position does not allow me to accept this honor. If, contrary to my wishes, a few well-inclined individuals should decide to elect me, I ask you, as a mark of friendship, to dissuade them." When the electors of Charente-Inférieure insisted on voting in favor of Nérac, his correspondent made the letter public.[11] Because the actual list of candidates was in no way legal, the assembly was divided between a minority of electors who had access to the unofficial list and the unorganized mass of voters, deprived of the information necessary to make an informed choice. It was, therefore, essential to form a compact group of voters, no matter how small, to serve as a rallying point for the undecided and unleash a majority or, if all else failed, to hold a third round of voting under the most favorable conditions possible. There was one unchangeable reality, however. In every assembly there were two groups of voters: those whose tactics and decisions were prepared well in advance, and those who came to the polls undecided, possessing neither the means nor the time to do anything about it.

Was some form of corruption involved in the transformation of this minority into the majority? We have nothing that would prove this, and there was, in fact, little overt fraud. This would include the distribution of ready-made lists, ballots surreptitiously dropped into the voting urn, false ballot counts by polling officers, falsification of the minutes, the use of false papers to gain access to second-stage assemblies, etc. Responsibility for such fraud most often lay with isolated individuals who did not have any genuine support in the assembly and lacked either the means or the patronage that would have enabled them to win over the unorganized majority of voters. Anyone guilty of fraud was excluded from the assembly. The small number of frauds is easily explained: manipulation was already an inherent part of the voting process. The lack of information or a limited and predetermined group of candidates handed the electoral process over to active minorities directly involved in the elections. This misappropriation of the suffrage resulted from the absence of any system that would guarantee open competition among different opinions and interests. The flaws in the electoral system favored this inappropriate outcome. By refusing to regulate competition, by wrongly assuming common interests, and by blocking the legitimate ambitions and appetites that had been set free by the political openness of 1789, the electoral laws turned the political environment over to brutal and unregulated competition, the results of which were subordinated less to the decisions of an electoral body than to the ability of organized minorities to manipulate the assemblies. This was true for any public candidacy that was felt to compromise freedom of choice, any confrontation between the opinions and proposals of those who claimed popular support. In a system where the candidate's resourcefulness was paramount, the elector's wishes counted for little.

A second factor that encouraged the spread of voter manipulation was the vote in assembly. Electors voted in succession in the presence of the members of the *bureau*, so the two conditions indispensable to a free vote were lacking: simultaneity and secrecy. The secret ballot was a purely theoretical construct at this time, as each elector had to write his ballot in public or, if he was unable to write, have it written by one of the polling officers. Because of the time it took for the roll call, there was ample opportunity to put pressure on the electors. It is easy to imagine the private caucuses, the insistent urging that could have swayed those who were undecided or supplied any remaining candidates for the lists of those who were unable to provide the required number of names.

More important, and easier to verify, was the influence exercised by the *bureau*, which was responsible for ensuring that voting went smoothly and for maintaining order. Apart from the acknowledged powers of the president, the reasons for this influence are easy to understand. When his name was called, each citizen had to go up to the *bureau* to fill out his ballot or have it filled out for him. In this situation he was forced to rely on the honesty of the official without ever being sure that the ballot slipped into the urn expressed his own choice. Of course, the polling officers had to swear that they would fulfill their duties with care and preserve secrecy, but there was no way of monitoring their activities, and some were quite willing to impose their own choice on undecided or illiterate voters, whose large numbers made this kind of manipulation easy. For them, the freedom and secrecy of voting was largely fictional; their inability to complete their ballots made them the ideal prey for anyone who was trying to obtain additional votes. Within the primary assemblies, election to the position of president served as a stepping stone to the electoral assembly. The *bureau* held a strategic position, and its control was often sufficient to guarantee success. It is easy to understand why so many decisive confrontations occurred during the election of the president and his aides. The results of this struggle foreshadowed those of the elections, where the defeated parties often abandoned the battlefield to their adversaries. Those who were defeated in their quest for the presidency voluntarily withdrew, as if the final result had been determined during this initial stage. A careful study of the figures shows a marked decrease in the number of voters after the election of the *bureau*, whereas the main purpose of the meeting was to choose the second-stage electors.

The important role played by the *bureau* simply illustrates the ease with which minority groups could impose their will in the assemblies, where voting was not really secret and lacked any means for helping voters make an informed choice. Whether the result of chance or, more frequently, the tactics of minority blocs, elections during the revolutionary period remained a mixture of irrationality and manipulation.

RATIONALIZING THE ELECTIONS

The ban on public candidacy during the revolutionary period was part of a cultural, and primarily religious, tradition.[12] A public display of ambition was a sufficient reason to be rejected, for it demonstrated that the presumptuous candidate lacked enough humility to hold public office. The rejection of a system of public campaigning was also supported by historical example: republican Rome, where the candidates, clothed in white togas, rounded up their supporters and bought votes, and eighteenth-century England, where notoriously corrupt elections resulted in confrontations between the supporters of different factions. By banning public campaigning, their counterparts in France were convinced that they could prevent any form of confrontation between factions and thus avoid corrupting the elections. In one sense, the Frenchmen of 1789 idealized the vote. When elections were held, social man would give way to the citizen, society would divide itself into a number of autonomous individual wills—each a numerical unit freed from the system of need—and with passions silenced, the citizen would be called upon to decide. The ban on public campaigning and the secret vote were intended to undo social solidarity and subjection and to destroy the influence of wealth and culture on popular opinion. The political vacuum surrounding elections appeared to guarantee the freedom of the vote and equality among voters. But the isolation and political vacuum in which voters found themselves in no way resulted from some abnormality in the system. In order to solidify the fundamental principle of political democracy—one man, one vote—the revolutionaries felt it was necessary to separate the electors from one another and allow them to make their decision in a context of total liberty, both of which were essential if voting was to be truly equal. In doing so the members of the Constituent Assembly would have demonstrated their theoretical clairvoyance and pragmatism if the continuation of the vote in assembly had not negated their efforts to individualize the exercise of the citizen's rights.

Brissot was the most influential proponent of this conception of voting.[13] While his contemporaries excluded public competition between divergent opinions, interests, and ambitions in the name of a morally superior concept of voting, Brissot showed that the effective moralization of electoral practice could take place only by accepting the inherent immorality of elections. It was preferable to have "broad daylight rather than night" and recognize that there were some things it was pointless to try to prevent. Moreover, according to Brissot, with publicly declared candidates it would be possible to discredit ambitious individuals who lacked virtue and talent, by making each and every elector the true judge of the competition. Only complete publicity, "through frank and open discussion," could restore equality among voters within the framework of a competitive environment that now made sense for everyone, and enable them to make a rational decision.

In 1790 Brissot founded the Society of Patriotic Electors to debate the candidates. It served as a model for the electoral clubs in several *départements* in 1791[14] and 1792. The results were limited and ambiguous. If these societies had been open to all electors, if they had been satisfied with organizing the debates and allowing the electoral body to decide matters, they would have had a decisive effect. But access to the clubs was not open to all. "We realized in advance," wrote Brissot, "that to indiscriminately admit people who did not have this character [of patriotism], would have meant reversing the principal goal of the Society, which met to evaluate to their proper place men who had distinguished themselves by their patriotism." This was accomplished not by favoring the rational expression of the electors' wishes in open discussion but, rather, by creating within the society a unity of opinion and will that would sway the vote of anyone who was undecided on the day of the election. It wasn't the discussion of the candidates that was made public, but its result. The debate, itself inherently contradictory, was followed by a vote of censure intended to select the candidates who would receive the public support of the society. This vote, as Brissot admitted, was supposed to reflect the "general opinion of the Society." In spite of Brissot's embarrassed denials, this purificatory vote was a form of preelection that took place before the electoral process and without the participation of all the electors. Brissot agreed that ''the majority of the Society were guided by the same principle; during the first vote [on the day of the election] there were . . . an impressive number of votes, which swayed the undecided, of whom there are always so many.'' The intention was to gather an initial concentration of votes, which would be a decisive factor given the isolation of the majority of voters. The decision was, therefore, made well in advance of the election. The club stated its choice; the assembly sanctioned it.

The movement in favor of public debates shifted the decision-making process to before the election. Although there was a genuine desire to rationalize the vote, this only helped spread a condition the societies initially wanted to reform, and further strengthened the use of voter manipulation as the only means of forming an otherwise unattainable majority. Could it have been different? Each group of electors was free to define its own procedures and fix the conditions of introducing the candidates and orchestrating debates. Competition was not regulated by law or monitored by any administrative body. There could be no real guarantee of what might happen. The electoral clubs did not owe their existence to law but to the initiative of citizens who had actively competed with one another. According to Kersaint, a Jacobin candidate in 1791, whose election was prevented by the Jacobin Club in 1792, ''public debate . . . could only take place when the candidates had been recognized legally.''[15] A law was required that would create the conditions for an electoral candidacy that was limited, public, diversified enough to allow real choice, recorded by an administrative body separate from the decision-making body, able to provide the candidates identical means to conduct their campaigns, and introduced before voting took place in order to ensure equality among the electors. Except for the first requirement, however, none of the systems that had been tried contributed to organizing an open competition in which the electors' vote was the deciding factor.

REVOLUTIONARY DEMOCRACY AND THE ELECTIONS

The legalization of public candidacies depended on two preconditions: admitting that a plurality of opinion and interests was legitimate, and conceiving the decision-making process as a way of choosing between preexisting views by means of majority rule. This meant accepting that there were legitimate divisions of interest and acknowledging the ''truth'' in the arithmetic of voting, both of which were foreign to the revolutionary political universe.

Concerning the first point, one can begin with a written statement published by Quatremère de Quincy in 1797.[16] Without denying the drawbacks of the political vacuum surrounding the elections after 1789, Quatremère wanted to show that a system based on declared candidacies was incompatible with the principles of representative government and could not maintain the foundations of political order. Following many other writers, he repeated that France could not be a (pure) democracy. Because it considered the nation as an assembly of equals and representation as a deliberating body responsible for disclosing the common will, the Constituent Assembly had, in dissolving the subordinate relationship between the elected and their electors, broken with the traditional doctrine of representation, which turned deputies into proxies without autonomy and the assembly into an accurate copy of the existing plurality of interests. The element of revolutionary representation, however, did not reside in a collection of separate bodies, but in the shared character of citizenship. Representation no longer aimed at bringing about a compromise between opposing interests but in defining the unified interest of a unified nation through a common process of deliberation.

The radical exclusion of conflicting interests from the public sphere helped establish representation as the substitute for a "Rousseauist" people who, in reality, did not exist.[17] The assembly did not "represent" anything but, on the contrary, gave existence to a nation that was one and indivisible, in whose name it was supposed to speak. The establishment of this "absolute" representative system cannot be separated from its historical context. As Quatremère noted, the introduction of such a system was the price that had to be paid for putting an end to the division among corporative interests. In contrast, it substituted the legitimacy of a common interest that transcended individual interests, but this doctrine was far too absolute. By absolving the representatives of any form of accountability, it created an obstacle to the development of a more democratic political system, in which citizens could have participated in the formation of a collective will, and in which the exercise of citizenship would not have been circumscribed by relinquishing one's rights. The limitations of the struggle against a society of separate orders had led to a different conclusion. The independence of those elected and the postulate of an identity of will between the nation and its representatives meant proscribing anything that might foster the idea that the nation was in any way antecedent to the act of representation, as well as anything that might favor the development of a political debate earlier than the meeting of the National Assembly and outside the representative system.

This would have meant jettisoning even the possibility of a system of public candidacies. By strengthening the bonds between elected officials and individual electors, the organization of competition within each district would weaken the legal fiction that each deputy represented the entire nation that had chosen him. On the other hand, a system of public candidacies would give a political dimension to individual choice. Competition was inseparable from public debate involving local or national voting issues, and in order to gather votes, competitors would be forced to make certain concessions to their constituents, limiting their freedom of decision in any legislative body. The legalization of public candidacies would give national representation an unwanted representative character that it ought not to have and whose absence was the proof of its ability to speak for the general will in open debate. Public candidacies were especially undesirable because of the uncertainty surrounding the legitimacy of collective decision making.

When the constitution was revised in August 1791, the members of the Constituent Assembly debated the question of constituent power. The Feuillants wanted to subject the summoning of a convention to representative formalities (the repeated vote of several legislatures). The leftist deputies, however, asked that the constitution provide an option for the people to convoke an assembly for constitutional revision, using their right of petition.

In his speech of August 31, 1791, in support of the "representative" position, Barnave[18] presented to the partisans of direct convocation an argument that had been used by Sieyès in 1789. He claimed that the general will did not consist of the arithmetic sum of preexisting individual wills whose representatives were responsible for nothing more than publishing the results. The general will, he said, must result from deliberation. Here, Barnave was echoing the words that Frochot had spoken shortly before him: "The act of convening the National Convention or its members is an act of the general will. But there can be no act of the general will except when all the parties have deliberated, and there can be no deliberation except when the meeting is effective"[19]—that is, through representation, which in 1789 the nation had recognized, in Frochot's words, as "the effective gift of the general will." Representation was even more necessary because it offered the possibility of a (mediated) assembly of all wills and created the conditions for an informed discussion, which was indispensable to the expression of the true wishes of those present. This was a means of resolving any initial differences through an enlightened comparison, free of prejudice and self-interest. In this way a common standard could be created to which each participant had to submit as he would to the expression of his own will. The logic of an aggregate of individual wills did nothing to alter any initial disagreements. Barnave, however, suggested a different approach to decision making based on open discussion, whose validity depended less on the number of votes than on the ability of those present to resolve and extinguish the diversity of initial divisions through the use of a single standard.

The notion of the general will was widely shared, as shown by the debates concerning suffrage. With few exceptions, the revolutionaries were quite indifferent to the "technology" of the vote—the methods of assembling votes and forming majorities—and were content to make use of the procedures that had been employed during the convocation of the Estates-General. Before and after the Jacobin period, however, they paid a great deal of attention to determining the qualifications to vote and eligibility to be elected, in the hope of guaranteeing that those elected would be able to form judgments that expressed the general will. It is true that in 1792–1793 the members of the Convention avoided this issue, but as the basis of the ability to form a judgment, they substituted the need for virtue in place of the complex blend of self-interest and "enlightenment," which was simply another way of looking at collective decisions. Their notion of decision making, which rejected the identification of the general will with the arithmetical number of votes, was marked with the imprint of rationalism of that century. The Revolution itself, however, had little to do with pure rationalism. While the democratic elaboration of the law was inescapable in 1789, it became harder and harder to reconcile with the need to hold informed discussions, so necessary for a valid decision. After 1789 this tension was central to the debates on suffrage. By restricting eligibility and creating a two-stage electoral system, the members of the Constituent Assembly went to great lengths to neutralize the influence of numbers alone, to which they refused to submit.

The electoral system, a mixture of contradictory attitudes that tended both to individualize and restrict participation, provided another means of managing the decision-making process, which, if left to the effective and equal actions of individuals, would have become a product of ignorance and corruption (any "bad" decision would, of course, have been identified as such by the dominant faction). The electoral system of the revolutionary period can be defined as a mechanism for the deliberate production of a "political class." Did this result from a lack of forethought or reflect the "innocence of new beginnings?" Although there is nothing to show that this kind of participatory equality—a mechanism that contradicted its own premises—was consciously elaborated, its effects were soon felt. The system did not lack lucid defenders, but once they had come to power, none of them—including Brissot—brought up the question of reform. . . . and for good reason. The system had been responsible for their success.

A cynical explanation alone is certainly insufficient for the prolonged absence of any form of change. The electoral system of the revolutionary period possessed two remarkable properties: it produced elected officials without holding real elections; and though it provided no assurance for true participation, at least it guaranteed good results. A significant event occurred at the beginning of Year III (the end of 1794), when J.-Y. Delacroix, the publisher of the *Spectateur Français*, suggested a mechanism that would enable citizens to express their true opinions about the form government should take, monarchy or republic. He suggested they abandon the vote in assembly. "Each citizen . . . will go into a private room divided into several booths, where he can write without being seen." Once he has made his decision, "he will fold the paper, stamp it with the national seal, and deposit his ballot in a closed box." The genuine individualization of the vote through the use of voting booths was not without its drawbacks. In his article, written in the form of a dialogue, Delacroix introduces a Thermidorian who states, "I understand your plan, but it seems to me that, in spite of its simplicity, it possesses some severe flaws. . . . What if the nation's wish is somehow contrary to the republic! What if it were necessary to restore the constitution of 1791, which we abolished!"[20] The results of such a plan were so obvious that Delacroix was immediately denounced at the Convention, arrested, and sent before the revolutionary tribunal, which had fortunately become rather merciful. The dangers of a reform that would guarantee effective electoral participation were certainly quite real and reflected the situation of a national power required to govern a hostile population to which the end of the Terror had given a voice. The reelection of a third of the legislative councils in 1797 confirmed these fears.

The campaign led by Brissot, Condorcet, and their friends at the outbreak of the Revolution in favor of legalizing public candidacies and reforming the electoral system resulted, on September 11, 1795, in a vote on an important law that completely transformed earlier conditions of voter participation. Although it did not overturn the principle of vote in assembly, the Convention established a procedure for registering candidacies. They would be received two months prior to the election by the municipalities, which were required to record them. The list of candidates would be published in the month before the electors met, displayed and read in the assemblies before voting began. This meant that a limited number of candidates, declared prior to voting and recorded by an official administrative body, would not be subject to prior censure of any sort that might replace the final vote. The physiognomy of the elections would change. The legalization of candidacies favored the development of public competition among candidates who were now clearly identifiable and would no longer emerge from the shadows solely through the efforts of a few devoted friends. Subject to public scrutiny, they could be discussed and compared by voters. And it was now possible for candidates to campaign openly for an office.

It was a democratic reform but an illogical one. By allowing electors to have a real say in the choice of their representatives, it inevitably led to the fall of the Thermidorians from power. It was already visible in 1795, notwithstanding the decree requiring the continuation of two-thirds of the deputies in office. The elections of 1797 had, from the Directory's point of view, and even because of their openness, turned out very "badly." The coup d'état initiated by the government on 18 Fructidor (September 4, 1797) against parliamentary representation allowed it to undo what had been done by the free and democratic development of the vote earlier that year, and the system of public candidacies was abandoned (decree of 24 Pluviose, Year VI, February 12, 1798).

The return to the situation that had been in effect since 1789—voting in assembly and the political vacuum—was, in fact, a recognition of this system's effectiveness. With the exception of the unfortunate experience of 1797, the electoral system of the revolutionary period provided a relatively sure degree of protection against the consequences of equal and individual political participation implied by its principles. It supplied the means to control the decision-making process in a world that had been turned upside down by the increased number of electors, who were theoretically freed of any personal allegiance. And finally it reduced the growing uncertainty in political matters, which was associated with the arrival of democracy. The uncommon spectacle of the elections of the revolutionary period was a counterpart to the invention of citizenship.

Translated by Robert Bononno

NOTES

1. This was not a list but, rather, a plurinominal system, because there were no declared candidates. Each elector drew up his own list by indicating on his ballot either an equal number or twice the number of names as there were available offices, the names

being chosen from among those eligible in the canton or the *département*, depending on the voting district. There was, therefore, nothing that even remotely resembled the list system, modified or unmodified, with which we are familiar in France.

2. A.N. C 138 no. 80.

3. A.N. C 135-C 138 [1791]; A.N. C 178-C 181 [1792].

4. A.D. Drôme L 161.

5. A.D. Drôme L 160 bis.

6. A.D. Maine-et-Loire 1 L 324.

7. See, for example, Maurice Duverger, ed., *L'influence des systèmes électoraux sur la vie politique* (Paris, 1950), 21–22, 75.

8. Jean-Antoine-Nicolas Caritat, marquis de Condorcet, "Sur la forme des élections" (1789), in *Sur les élections et autres textes*, ed. O. de Bernon (Paris, 1986), 449–50.

9. Albert de Rochas, *Journal d'un bourgeois de Valence* (Grenoble, 1891), 189.

10. Quoted in Elisabeth and Robert Badinter, *Condorcet. Un intellectuel en politique* (Paris, 1988), 492.

11. A.N. C 135 no. 16.

12. See, for example, Leo Moulin, "Les origines religieuses des techniques électorales et délibératives modernes," *Revue internationale d'histoire politique et constitutionnelle*, 1953, 106–48.

13. Jacques-Pierre Brissot, *Réflexions sur l'état de la Société des électeurs patriotes.* . . . (Paris, 1790).

14. Concerning the clubs founded by the Jacobins, see Michael L. Kennedy, *The Jacobin Clubs in the French Revolution: The First Years* (Princeton, N.J.: Princeton University Press, 1982), 210–23.

15. A.-G. Kersaint, *De la Constitution et du Gouvernement qui pourraient convenir à la République française* (Paris, 1792), 16–17.

16. Antoine-Chrysostome Quatremère de Quincy, *La Véritable liste de Candidats, Précédé d'Observations sur la nature de l'institution des Candidats, et son application au Gouvernement représentatif*, 2nd ed. (Paris, 1797).

17. See, for example, Marcel Gauchet, *La Révolution des droits de l'homme* (Paris, Gallimard, 1989).

18. *Archives parlementaires de 1787 à 1860. Première série, de 1787 à 1799* 30: 113–15.

19. Ibid., 99.

20. Jacques-V. Delacroix, *Le Spectateur Français pendant le Gouvernement révolutionnaire,* . . . (Paris, 1795), 232–38.

8

ELECTORAL BEHAVIOR DURING THE CONSTITUTIONAL MONARCHY (1790–1791): A "COMMUNITY" INTERPRETATION

Melvin Edelstein

French scholars were pioneers in the study of electoral behavior, but until recently they have largely ignored the subject of voting during the French Revolution. Explanations of electoral behavior remain untested by France's first experience with mass electoral politics. Recently, René Rémond and François Furet have called attention to the failure of historians to study revolutionary elections.[1]

The study of elections is a contribution to our understanding of the meaning of citizenship. Embodied in the concept of citizenship is political participation. Where the people are sovereign, elections are needed to legitimize authority, select public officials, and hold them accountable. During the Revolution, however, political rights were unequal; only "active citizens" could vote, an estimated 60 to 70 percent of males twenty-five and older. The active citizens could vote only for "electors," who named the administrators and legislators from among the eligible citizens. I estimate that 60 percent of the active citizens and about 40 percent of adult males were eligible, but only a small percentage qualified to be deputies.[2] Although hardly democratic, the electorate was inclusive enough so that the Revolution marked the beginning of mass electoral politics. This chapter contributes to our knowledge of the origin of democracy.

The study of electoral behavior in 1790–1791, when the new institutions were established, addresses important questions about the nature and consequences of the Revolution. Part of the controversy over the meaning of the Revolution is based on conclusions drawn from the history of ideas, not institutions and how they functioned. We know very little about voting. Analyzing voter behavior will enable us to evaluate the degree to which the Revolution succeeded in mobilizing the citizenry politically.

The study of voting is pertinent to several assertions that have been made by interpreters of the French Revolution. Some, like François Mitterrand, see in the Revolution the ancestor of modern democracy. Others maintain that it was inherently flawed and unable to put down durable roots,[3] that it failed to mobilize the voters,[4] or that the elections were dominated by a minority of militants.[5] Insurrection was a form of political participation, but not the only form. Perhaps historians have been misled by a distorted image of intense urban political participation, based on the popular movement and the clubs. The differences between urban and rural electoral behavior, as well as urban influence on rural voters, need to be investigated.

The timing of peasant engagement in politics raises still another set of questions. It has been argued that high levels of voter participation were first attained in 1870–1914 in the "underdeveloped" rural regions of the west, center, and south, and that peasants were politicized by a process of urban acculturation akin to colonization.[6] However, several historians propose that the peasants became politically aware and involved during the Second Republic.[7] I have argued that the Revolution initiated France's apprenticeship in citizenship.[8] Related to any debate on the chronology of politicization, there is the question whether recent theories designed to explain electoral participation and abstention are applicable to electoral behavior two centuries ago. How should we explain voter behavior during the Revolution?

The few existing studies of revolutionary elections provide some localized conclusions. Paul Bois discovered that rural turnout in the Sarthe in the "national" elections of June 1791 was only 10 to 12 percent, whereas it exceeded 50 percent in the "administrative" elections of May 1790. He concluded that the peasants were more interested in local issues than in national politics.[9] Since the *citadins* voted in larger numbers than the rustics in 1791, they were more interested in national elections.[10] Bois concluded that the peasants lacked any political consciousness, but I have argued that Bois's conclusions do not apply elsewhere. The *citadins* did not always vote more assiduously than the *campagnards* in national elections, nor do I accept his arguments that the peasants were politically immature and that the Revolution failed to politicize them.[11]

Recently, when Jean-Louis Ormières tested Bois's conclusions about electoral behavior in the western departments of the Mayenne and Maine-et-Loire, he came to different conclusions. Rather than massive absenteeism, he found the peasants of Maine-et-Loire voting in large numbers in June 1791.[12] Since Ormières found electoral documents for the Mayenne only for 1790, while those for Maine-et-Loire are only for 1791, his study is not strictly comparable to Bois's.

Roland Marx came to very different conclusions than Bois. He did not find any significant difference between rural and urban voter behavior in Alsace. He concluded that everywhere the turnout was the highest in municipal elections.[13] Malcolm Crook challenged both Bois's distinction between urban and rural voter behavior and my critique of it, comparing the capital of the department either with the rural cantons in its district or in the department. Although he agrees with me that in 1790 the *campagnards* generally outvoted the *citadins*, he insists that the pattern is less clear-cut in June 1791. Thereafter, he found a growing tendency for rural voting to decline more precipitously than urban turnout or for urban participation to be greater than the rural vote.[14]

As for the voter turnout in general, I made the following estimates: a *median* of 40 percent for the elections to the Estates-General, 65 percent for the municipal elections of January-February 1790, and 24 percent for June 1791.[15] Recently, I estimated an *average* of 50 percent in the first municipal elections of 1790, 40 to 50 percent in the administrative elections of May 1790, falling to 20 to 25 percent in June 1791.[16] As for regional differences, Crook concludes that the highest participation was in the northeast.[17] He attributes this to a high level of economic development, a superior road network, extensive literacy, and a greater incidence of revolutionary journalism.

These divergences call for empirical data. The explanation of revolutionary electoral behavior requires a more comprehensive approach. I will try to discover correlations between voter participation and a number of variables. Thanks to political scientists, there is a large body of literature about political and electoral participation. Although using these works is problematical, they are suggestive. I will test the validity of their general conclusions for 1790–1791.

American political scientists provide us with two alternative models to explain voter behavior, one that predicts higher turnout in the cities and metropolitan centers and another that predicts the opposite. The first, which is referred to as the "mobilization" model, assumes higher political participation in cities as a result of extensive communication networks, numerous voluntary associations, and social integration. The second, which I call the "community" model, explains higher rural participation as a result of a tradition of village autonomy, communal solidarity, and tight-knit social integration.

Advocates of the "mobilization" model argue that city dwellers participate in politics more than rural residents, and that farmers are less likely to vote than urbanites. Persons with higher educational and socio-occupational status are more likely to vote than those with less education and status. According to Seymour Martin Lipset, "Men vote more than women; the better educated, more than the less educated; urban residents, more than rural; those between 35 and 55, more than younger or older voters; married persons, more than unmarried; higher-status persons, more than lower; members of organizations, more than nonmembers."[18]

Lester Milbrath found a correlation between political participation and the size of the community. Metropolitan areas have the highest participation, smaller cities and towns are next, and rural areas have the lowest rates.[19] He also argues that *"persons near the center of society are more likely to participate in politics than persons near the periphery* [emphasis in original]."[20] Stein Rokkan concluded that in Norway the peripheral communes had a markedly lower turnout in national elections than the central ones. By "peripheral," he meant those communes with economic activity in the primary sector—small farms, low income, and relative isolation in terms of the existing transport network.[21] Applying these generalizations to the Revolution, we would expect Paris to have the highest turnout, followed by such metropolitan centers as Lyon and Marseille. Manufacturing cities, ports, market towns, and administrative centers should have higher turnout than smaller towns and rural areas. Turnout in regions with high literacy and intensive communication networks should be higher than in isolated areas and those of high illiteracy. The north, east, and Paris basin should outvote the west, center, and south.

In opposition to the "mobilization" model, Sidney Verba, Norman Nie, and Jae-on Kim proposed a "decline-of-community" model, which predicts higher participation in rural communities than in cities.[22] They found no consistent correlation between community size and voter turnout.[23] A small, tight-knit community explains high rural turnout. These conclusions are supported by the "exceptions" cited by Milbrath and Herbert McClosky. Milbrath acknowledges that, in Sweden, farmers outvote persons employed in many other industries. He comments that "rural voting is also high in France and Italy."[24] In Japan since World War II, turnout is higher in rural areas than in the cities. The explanation is that "rural areas have higher community integration."[25] McClosky points out that "in some countries that have long traditions of communal leadership or cooperative forms of agricultural organizations, participation is greater in rural than in urban areas—e.g., Japan, France, . . . and parts of Scandinavia."[26] Applied to the Revolution, this observation would lead us to expect higher turnout in rural areas than in cities. Regions with a tradition of village autonomy, vigorous communal life, and strong solidarity based on the management of communal property should have a high turnout.

French political scientists also explain voter behavior by social integration, but they support the "mobilization" model. The more the citizen is socially integrated, the more the community is integrated into the larger society, the higher the political participation. The regions with the highest turnout are those where socialization is the most developed.[27] French voter behavior is also explained in terms of geography and habitat. Isolated, mountainous regions, those with poor roads of dispersed habitation, are poorly integrated into the larger society, so they have lower turnout. Jean Meynaud and Alain Lancelot argue that "participation is higher in the plains and the regions of easy communication than in the mountains and territories with difficult access. . . . Even in the plains, we must take account of the type of habitat: dispersed, it favors abstention."[28] Accordingly, in the Revolution, we would expect higher turnout in Paris and other cities than in the rural areas. We would also expect higher turnout in regions with good roads—the plains—and areas of agglomerated habitation— the north, east, and Paris basin. Since the region with the highest road density was north of an imaginary line dividing France from Saint-Malo to Lyon, the turnout should be higher there than in the west, center, and south.[29] We would expect lower turnout in the Alps than in Normandy. Turnout in the regions of dispersed habitation in the west and center should be lower than in the areas of nucleated villages and wheat-farming in the north and east.[30]

Recent studies that cite higher abstention in Paris and other big cities make it questionable whether there is a relationship between high abstention and a low level of social integration. Abstention increases with the size of the commune, and it is higher in cities than in the countryside. It is an urban phenomenon.[31] During the Revolution, turnout in the rural areas and small towns should have been higher than in the big cities. We would expect very high abstention in Paris.

Lancelot discovered a "geography of abstention." During the period 1876–1914, he found three big zones: the Ouest Maritime, including Brittany; the center; and the Midi Méditerranéen. The Seine *département* is also an area of high abstention. The four zones with the highest turnout are the north, the east, the Ouest Intérieur and the Loire Moyenne, and the Sud-Ouest Aquitain. After 1936, Lancelot divides France into a "voting" north and an "abstentionist" south, based on a line running from La Rochelle to Geneva.[32] In modern France, turnout is highest in national elections, next in municipal elections, lowest in cantonal voting. If voting in the Revolution corresponded to the geography of abstention later, in the early Third Republic, we would expect higher abstention along the west coast, in the center, along the Mediterranean—and in the Seine region.

The division of France into a voting North and an abstaining South roughly corresponds to the "Maggiolo line," which divides eighteenth-century France into the north and east, with more schools, and the west, center, and south, with higher illiteracy (the Hautes-Alpes is an exception).[33] This line corresponds to the division of France based on communication networks and is also the line Weber uses to divide France. The convergence of all these lines fits the "mobilization" model and Lancelot's "integration" theory. Accordingly, in the Revolution, we would expect the highest voter turnout in the north and east. This is what Crook found.

Which of the theories of political participation, the "mobilization" model or the "community" model, best explains electoral behavior during the Revolution? The former predicts higher turnout in the cities and the north and east; the latter predicts higher rural turnout. The first explains peasant politicization as a response to urban influence, which is Weber's argument; the second assumes that the peasants were capable of independent political action, which is my argument.[34] This assumption has roots in revolutionary historiography, since it fits Georges Lefebvre's argument that there was an "autonomous peasant revolution."[35] The "community" model is also supported by Theda Skocpol, who stresses the role of autonomous peasant communities and strong rural solidarity in initiating revolutionary peasant mobilizations.[36] Perhaps no one model can adequately explain all revolutionary electoral behavior.

Using data for participation in the municipal and cantonal elections of 1790

and the legislative elections of 1791, I shall try to answer these questions about
voter behavior provisionally for the constitutional monarchy. Although the elections to the Estates-General serve as a reference point, there is no synthesis of
voter turnout. Since the data are very disparate, the conclusions that historians
have reached are contradictory.[37] Unlike conditions in 1848, the first elections
of the Revolution were local, the municipal elections of January-February 1790,
the only direct elections held in the commune itself. We would expect high
turnout. I have argued that, on an average, they attracted the highest turnout of
the revolutionary decade and that the *campagnards* generally outvoted the *citadins*. Crook, who studied nine big cities from 1790 to 1792, concluded that
turnout rarely surpassed 30 percent, especially after 1790.[38] This is contrary to
the "mobilization" model and the Weber thesis, but it fits the "community"
model.

Using a sample of twenty-seven cities, I will test Crook's conclusion and the
assumptions of Weber and the "mobilization" model. The largest cities, those
with 100,000 or more inhabitants, ranked among the lowest in turnout. Turnout
in Paris was only 18 percent, while it was 37 percent in Lyon and 33 percent
in Marseille. Among cities with over 50,000 inhabitants, turnout in Toulouse
was 31 percent, 33 percent in Lille. Turnout in ten of the twenty-seven cities
was 50 percent or higher, with a median of 37 percent. In fact, eighteen had 30
percent or higher, which is different from Crook's conclusion. Since turnout in
the medium-sized cities like Colmar and Dijon was higher than in the metropolitan
centers, this is contrary to the "mobilization" model. Regionally, turnout was
highest in the north and east, but Paris and two northern cities had turnout of
only 16 to 18 percent. Participation was high in the Finistère in Brittany, while
the ports of Marseille and Toulon had low turnout. While there is some support
for the "mobilization" model, it is hardly conclusive.

Studies of participation in the "underdeveloped" regions of the Limousin,
Languedoc, Franche Comté, and Brittany support the "community" model. In
the Haute-Vienne, turnout was in inverse proportion to population size.[39] Similar
conclusions were reached for Languedoc.[40] In the Jura also, rural turnout was
massive, with participation inversely proportionate to the size of the community.
In the Breton department of Ille-et-Vilaine, rural turnout averaged 67 percent.[41]
The data overwhelmingly fit the "community" model. Even in the north and
east, rural turnout was generally higher than in the cities. In Artois, turnout
averaged 64 percent in twenty-six communes, whereas it was only 17 percent
in Saint-Omer. In Burgundy, turnout was 65 percent in Dijon and 50 percent in
Beaune, but it was 83 percent, 82 percent, and 59 percent in three rural communes. In the Seine, it was 38 percent in Suresnes, which is more than double
the 18 percent in Paris.[42] The data do not support the "mobilization" model or
the Weber thesis.

How do we explain the fact that the *campagnards* outvoted the *citadins*? Why
was turnout inversely proportionate to the size of the community? How do we
explain the high turnout in the underdeveloped regions? According to the authors

of the study of the Jura, "The smaller the population, the stronger the cohesion of the village community."[43] In Languedoc, participation was highest in the small villages, which usually inherited the "democratic" tradition of the general council. Georges Fournier's explanation is that "the community reflex remains the most determining emotional element."[44] In Artois, the peasants were very interested in self-government. Communal solidarity, combined with a tradition of self-government or a keen desire for it, explains high rural turnout. An institutional rupture may have exacerbated low urban turnout. In 1789, voting was by corporation, which the revolutionaries prohibited. Thereafter, voting in the cities was by section. Social integration explains high rural turnout, while the lack of social cohesion explains low urban turnout. An institutional rupture in the cities, which did not occur in the rural parishes, aggravated the situation. This explanation is similar to the "community" model, while it does not contradict Lancelot's theory of social integration.

The second elections were the cantonal administrative elections of May 1790, which took place from March through August and even in October in the Seine. Voting took place in the capital of the canton, requiring villagers to travel several miles to a town. Long and complicated electoral procedures caused the balloting to last for days or even a week. The active citizens voted for electors, who named the administrators from those eligible. In spite of all these obstacles, plus the absence of political parties and declared candidates, turnout was high. Patrice Gueniffey calculated that turnout in ten departments averaged 31 percent, whereas I estimated that turnout in eighteen departments was 40 to 50 percent.[45] I calculate an average turnout of 48 percent for twenty-six departments, or nearly one third of the eighty-three. In a sample of twenty-eight departments for which I have a percentage, but not the raw numbers, the median is 50 percent. This confirms the soundness of my earlier estimate.

A map of electoral participation seems to fit the "mobilization" model and the Weber thesis. Five of the seven departments with the highest turnout are in the north and east, while four of the six departments with the lowest turnout are in the west and southeast. The Aube and the Côte-d'Or had the highest turnout, 73 percent and 71 percent respectively. The Meuse, the Marne, and the Seine-et-Oise had turnouts of 63 to 65 percent. In Brittany, the Loire-Inférieure and the Ille-et-Vilaine had turnouts of 24 percent and 32 percent. Turnout in the Basses-Alpes was only 32 percent, while it was 35 percent in the Drôme.

Doubts about the validity of the "mobilization" model arise because two departments with the lowest turnout were in the north. The Seine had the lowest, 16 percent. Two Norman departments had lower turnout than two "underdeveloped" Breton departments; turnouts in the Eure and Calvados were 43 percent and 30 percent, while 49 percent and 46 percent were the results in the Finistère and the Morbihan. The biggest problem for the "mobilization" model is the "underdeveloped" south, center, and west. Two of the seven departments with the highest turnout were in the south. Turnout in the Hautes-Alpes was 64 percent, while it was 61 percent in the Landes. In the center and south, seven departments had a turnout of 50 to 57 percent, as compared to only two in the northeast. Turnout in the Aveyron was 51 percent, which is higher than the 41 percent in the Rhône-et-Loire. In the west, turnout in the Sarthe was 57 percent, the eighth highest.

How do we explain voter behavior? What correlations can explain the high turnout of 61 to 73 percent? At first sight, it might seem that the "mobilization" model fits best. Considering that five of the seven departments with the highest turnout were in the north and east, there seem to be correlations with urbanization, market penetration, literacy, good communication networks, and administrative centralization. The fact that these departments were integrated into the global society fits Lancelot's theory and Weber's thesis. Although the Hautes-Alpes was isolated, it was one of the few literate regions outside the northeast, which tends to tie it to the "mobilization" model. But the fact that John Markoff did not find any correlation between literacy and rural revolt raises doubts.[46] The Landes, one of the most backward, isolated, and illiterate departments, is an anomaly. The low turnout in Paris and Normandy makes us skeptical. The fact that the Basses-Alpes, with its Provençal sociability and "urbanized" villages, had half the turnout of the Hautes-Alpes in Dauphiny raises problems for the "mobilization" model.

I maintain that the "community" model offers a more plausible explanation of voter behavior. The argument that communal solidarity explains high rural turnout in municipal elections is valid for the cantonal elections of 1790. A tradition of autonomous villages, elected village officials, and the management of communal property can explain high rural turnout in the north and east as well as in the "underdeveloped" regions. Before it was a political entity, the rural community was an economic community. Burgundy had vigorous rural communities that freely elected their village officials.[47] In the Landes, the rural communities elected *jurats* and syndics. In the Briançonnais in the Hautes-Alpes, politics were organized around annual elections of two consuls by a village assembly of all male household heads.[48] Although Provence and Languedoc had *conseils politiques* with municipal functions, they did not produce high rural turnout in Provence. The traditional communal mentalities and practices of the Old Regime persisted in the Revolution. The active citizens of many rural communities went as a group to vote in the primary assemblies, where voting was by roll call by municipality.

Another proof that the "community" model explains voter behavior better than the "mobilization" model is the lack of a strong correlation between turnout and habitation. We would expect low turnout in the center and west, regions of dispersed population. While this is true in the Ille-et-Vilaine, it is not valid in the Finistère, Sarthe, Vienne, and Haute-Vienne, nor is it true in the Landes and Aveyron in the south. The Aube, Côte-d'Or, and Haute-Garonne, departments with agglomerated villages, had high turnout, but the Eure and the Drôme did not.[49]

Are there any continuities between a "geography of abstention" in 1790 and the one Lancelot discovered in 1876–1914? In both periods, abstention was high in parts of Brittany and Normandy, Provence, and the Seine, while turnout was high in the north, east, and in the Landes in the southwest. But just as the "Maggiolo line" does not explain voter behavior in 1790, it is impossible to discern a voting north and an abstaining south.

Contrary to what we would expect from the "mobilization" model and the Weber thesis, the *campagnards* generally outvoted the *citadins*. In a sample of a dozen apartments in which I compare turnout in the capital city with the vote in its district and the whole department, the *campagnards* always outvoted the *citadins*. Turnout in the biggest cities was very low: 13 percent in Paris, 14 percent in Nantes, 21 percent in Lyon and Caen, and 27 percent in Toulouse. It exceeded 40 percent in only three cities: Troyes and Dijon, 41 percent; and Quimper, 45 percent. In May 1790, there is no correlation between urbanization, size of community, centrality, and participation. The "community" model best explains voter behavior.

Although historians agree that, after an initial enthusiasm, voters became disenchanted, they disagree about the timing and causes of high abstention. Using fragmentary data for the elections to renew half of the municipal officers and notables in November 1790 and the much-neglected elections of the *juges de paix* in October–December, I will try to estimate participation at the end of 1790. That there was a general and substantial decline in urban and rural voting is clear. In the Haute-Vienne, turnout fell from 50 percent in twenty-five municipalities to only 24 percent in nineteen communes in November. But it was still inversely proportionate to the population. It remained high, 78 percent, in the smallest communes, whereas it was only 16 percent in Limoges.[50] In Burgundy, turnout was higher in the villages of Ruffey and Larrey, 65 percent and 45 percent, than in Dijon, 41 percent. Turnout in the cities was low: 5 percent in Toulon, 16 percent in Limoges, 23 percent in Lyon, 37 percent in Colmar, and 41 percent in Dijon.[51] Turnout plummeted in Colmar from 81 percent to 37 percent. The fact that participation was higher in the rural communes than in the cities, and highest in the smallest villages, is similar to January–February 1790. This fits the "community" model better than the "mobilization" model.

Although turnout plummeted in the elections for the municipalities in November, it was still high in the elections for the *juges de paix* in October–December. It was 60 percent in the Côte-d'Or and 65 percent in the Haute-Vienne, averaging 62 percent.[52] In the Côte-d'Or, turnout fell from 71 percent in April–May, while in the Haute-Vienne, it increased from 55 percent. The fact that turnout in Dijon was only 22 percent while it was 60 percent in its district does not support the "mobilization" model, nor does the fact that turnout was higher in the Haute-Vienne in the center than in the Côte-d'Or in the northeast.

Is Marx's conclusion that everywhere and always municipal elections attracted the highest turnout generally true? If so, it would seem to indicate that both the *campagnards* and *citadins* lacked any political consciousness beyond their narrowest horizons. It would also confirm Weber's argument that national issues did not mobilize the peasants before 1870–1914. The Revolution would have failed to politicize the peasants in terms of elections. But Marx's conclusions cannot be generalized. According to Fournier, "rural participation in the Haute-Garonne is clearly higher in the primary assemblies of 1790 than in the municipal elections of February."[53] In the Haute-Vienne, the *campagnards* were more interested in the elections for the *juges de paix* than in the municipal elections. Considering that seven departments had a turnout of 61 to 73 percent in May 1790, it is possible that participation was higher in these administrative elections than in the municipal elections. On the other hand, in eight of eleven cities, turnout was highest in the municipal elections and the same in Toulouse. Turnout in Paris, however, was higher in 1789 than in 1790. The preference of the *citadins* for municipal voting does not support the "mobilization" model or the Weber thesis.

The vote for the Legislative Assembly in June 1791 was the first national election since 1789. It was also local in that half the administrators were renewed. There were no political parties or declared candidates; balloting was by assembly, not individual. Voting took place in the capital of the canton to name electors. It is not surprising that turnout was low. All historians speak of a "collapse" of voting. Gueniffey calculated that turnout in thirteen departments averaged 17 percent, but I estimated that it was 20 to 25 percent.[54] Based on a sample of nineteen departments, or nearly one quarter, I calculate an average of 23 percent. The median for a somewhat different sample of nineteen departments is also 23 percent. Turnout declined from 48 percent in May 1790 to 23 percent in June 1791, which confirms my estimate. The fact that participation in these national elections was only about 25 percent and that it declined by half seems to support Bois's conclusion that the *campagnards* were more interested in local elections than in national votes, as well as the Weber thesis that the peasants lacked any awareness of national issues before 1870–1914.

A map of electoral participation seems to support the "mobilization" model and the Weber thesis, but the "community" model explains the exceptions as well as the leaders. Four of the six departments with the highest turnout, including the top two, are in the northeast. As in 1790, the Aube, Marne, Côte-d'Or, and Meuse are among the leaders. Among the departments with the lowest turnout, the Loire-Inférieure, the lowest, is in the west, and the Aube is in the southwest. But two of the top departments, the Finistère and the Haute-Vienne, are in the west and the center. Among the departments with low turnout, the Eure and the Seine are in the north. As for habitation, the Aube, Marne, and Côte-d'Or, with high turnout, had agglomerated villages; so did the Eure, but it had low turnout. The Finistère and Haute-Vienne with high turnout had dispersed habitation. There does not seem to be any correlation between turnout and habitation.

If the "mobilization" model and the Weber thesis can explain voter behavior, we would expect higher urban than rural turnout in these national elections. Crook provides some support when he argues that, in 1791, the pattern of the *campagnards* outvoting the *citadins* is less clear-cut. In 1791, in two of six departments, turnout in the capital was higher than in the rural cantons, while in one other it was virtually identical.[55] But in my sample of eight departments, turnout in the capital city was higher than in the rural cantons in only two, virtually identical in one, and lower in five. Although Crook is correct that the pattern of the *campagnards* outvoting the *citadins* is less clear-cut in 1791, the evidence supports the "community" model more than the "mobilization" model or the Weber thesis. It also calls into question the universality of Bois's conclusions.

If Bois's conclusion that the *citadins* outvoted the *campagnards* in these national elections can be generalized, it would support the "mobilization" model and the Weber thesis. But no one has done a comparable study. Using data from three departments in the northeast, I compared turnout in the capital of the district with the vote in the whole district in 1791 and 1790. This is supplemented by data from three departments in Languedoc. In the Côte-d'Or, turnout in the capital was higher than in the district in only one of seven districts. The *campagnards* outvoted Dijon, the capital of the department. In the Marne, turnout in the capital was higher than in the district in only one of six districts. The *campagnards* outvoted Châlons, the capital. In the Aube, however, turnout in the capital was higher than in the district in three of six districts. But the *campagnards* outvoted Troyes, the capital. The fact that the capital of the district outvoted the rural cantons in only five of nineteen districts in three northeastern departments does not support Bois, the "mobilization" model, or the Weber thesis. In three departments in Languedoc, only one supports Bois's conclusion. In the Aube, the *citadins* outvoted the *campagnards* by 27 percent to 13 percent. In the Hérault, urban and rural voting were virtually identical. In the Haute-Garonne, turnout in Toulouse was 14 percent, whereas rural turnout in its district was 24 percent.[56]

How do we explain the fact that about three-quarters of the voters abstained in June 1791? The main reason for the decline was a sharp drop in rural turnout. Why did the *campagnards* abstain massively? One explanation is that the peasants quickly tired of frequent elections.[57] I am not convinced. In 1790, there were only two cantonal elections and two municipal elections. The vote in June 1791 was only the third cantonal vote and the fifth vote in a year and a half.

Ormières and others insist that the religious controversy over the Civil Constitution of the Clergy explains high rural abstention,[58] but I am unable to find any consistent correlation between a map of electoral participation and one of clerical oath taking. There is a stronger correlation between high turnout and oath taking than there is for low turnout and high proportions of refractory clergy. A comparison of the districts with the highest and lowest turnout in five departments with the highest participation reveals a close correlation between turnout and oath taking in three, the Côte-d'Or, Marne, and Meuse, but not in two others, the Aube and Finistère. Religious controversy alone does not explain electoral behavior.

Is there any correlation between voter turnout in June 1791 and the distribution of political clubs? Using a map of the Jacobin clubs in 1791, it is impossible to discover any correlation in the six departments with the highest turnout. None of these departments is located in the three zones with the most clubs in Year II: the southeast, southwest, and northwest.[59] The clubs may have mobilized the voters in 1792–1793, when they were more numerous. Since the clubs were largely urban, these seems to be a political sociability expressed in them that differed from electoral behavior.

The political situation may have had an effect on voter turnout, but it is hard to prove. The royal family fled Paris on the night of June 20, in the midst of the elections. Although the Côte-d'Or, where voting started on June 13, had high turnout, so did the Aube, which voted on June 21. Other departments with relatively high turnout voted on June 24 or 26. In the Marne, voting in Vitry-le-François was suspended for several days because the National Guard was sent to Châlons to guard the king. Does that explain why its turnout was only 23 percent, compared to 39 percent for the district?[60]

Historians may have overlooked the role of membership in the National Guard in reducing electoral turnout. A law of June 18, 1790, stipulated that to be an active citizen, one had to be inscribed in the National Guard. In the Côte-d'Or, when several sections in Dijon and Nuits insisted that the number of their electors be based on the number of active citizens in April 1790, rather than the members of the guard, the departmental directory agreed. While this increased the electors, it lowered the participation rate. In the section of Saint-Benigne in Dijon, there were 323 guardsman, yielding three electors, whereas there were 455 active citizens in 1790, yielding five electors. Using the latter figure lowers the turnout from 26 percent to 18 percent. In Nuits, it lowered it from 21 percent to 15 percent.[61] Did the administrators use membership in the guard or the active citizens of 1790 in June 1791? How many citizens were disenfranchised? Since the guard was largely urban, the requirement would have lowered urban turnout more than rural voting.

Does the fact that these were legislative elections explain the high abstention in June 1791? When he discovered that turnout in Languedoc rose from 20 percent in June 1791 to 35 percent in November, when the municipalities were renewed, Fournier concluded, "The fact that it is a question of the only legislative elections of the period seems to be the main explanation."[62] This is similar to Bois's conclusion that the *campagnards* were more interested in local elections than in national votes. Borrowing from the Tillys, I would rather argue that the peasants had not yet recognized that "the locus of relevant politics" was shifting to the national level.[63] While centralized state power had been shattered in 1789, a new form of state power had not yet become manifest. Therefore, the peasants continued to regard local conflicts as more important, since local power affected their lives more than the national government. In 1793 and under Napoléon, when state power became more intrusive, there was an increase in voter turnout.

Since the main reason for the collapse of voting in June 1791 was a larger decline in rural than in urban voting, we must seek the explanation for rural abstention. We should not assume that low rural turnout means that the *campagnards* were indifferent to national affairs or that the Revolution failed to politicize the peasants. The explanation for high rural abstention in June 1791, after a high initial turnout in 1790, may be that the peasants were disappointed with the results of the Revolution. This has been my opinion, as well as that of Charles Tilly, Crook, and Audevart. Although Bois interpreted high rural abstention as political apathy, Tilly argued that it was a protest. He commented that the peasants in southern Anjou withdrew from voting only after they were defeated in the contest for political office.[64] I argued that the *campagnards* were interested in political issues, and that rural aspirations for self-government took the form of demands for greater representation in the district and departmental administrations. Recent studies of the *chouannerie* argue that peasant resistance was motivated by frustrated expectations.[65] The *campagnards* believed that the *citadins* received most of the benefits of the Revolution. The peasants, who abstained in 1791, resorted to agrarian insurrections in 1792–1793, showing that they were not politically apathetic. Although my explanation for high rural abstention is difficult to prove, it is plausible.

Although it is also unprovable, peasant abstention may have resulted from the dislocation of the rural community. We have seen that rural communal solidarity explained high turnout in 1790. Since Lefebvre and Albert Soboul insist that it was opposition to the feudal lord and outside agents that cemented that solidarity, the Revolution may have weakened it, thereby reducing turnout in 1791.[66]

Although it is impossible to find a consistent relation between a community's electoral participation and its curé's taking the constitutional oath, it is hard to believe that religious conflict did not reduce rural voting. In the Revolution, as under the Old Regime, the Church was the locus of political life. In 1790, the priests read the announcement of elections after Sunday mass, voting took place in the Church, and priests were elected president or secretary of the primary assembly. By dislocating the electoral mechanisms, the religious schism may have contributed to rural abstention in some places.

A study of voter behavior during the constitutional monarchy shows that initially the Revolution mobilized large numbers of voters. The data on electoral participation do not support the revisionists' argument that the Revolution was inherently flawed and incapable of putting down durable roots. In 1790, half or more of all active citizens voted in the first municipal and cantonal elections. If this is the final national average, it would mean that over 2 million adult males voted in these elections. This is more than the 1.8 million who voted in the constitutional plebiscite of July 1793. Proportionally, turnout was even greater than in the Napoleonic plebiscites.[67] Although turnout fell sharply in June 1791 to roughly 25 percent, nevertheless, over 1 million men may have voted. Despite complicated procedures and lengthy votes, many peasants left their villages to vote in the capital of their canton. That these high levels of voting in 1790 were achieved without political parties or declared candidates is remarkable.

The fact that 60 to 70 percent of adult males qualified as active citizens and that about half of them voted in 1790 shows that the Revolution contributed greatly to the origin of mass electoral politics. Even in the mountainous Hautes-Alpes or the backward Landes, over 60 percent of the active citizens voted in 1790. In 1790–1791, the Revolution was not the work of a minority of militants; voter participation was broad. Mitterrand is correct to insist that the French Revolution is the ancestor of modern democracy.

Although it is sometimes argued that the French Revolution failed to put down durable political roots, whereas the American Revolution was a success, this is not evident from voting statistics. When participation during the French Revolution is compared to voting in postrevolutionary America, one is struck by the fact that the French equaled or surpassed American turnout. Turnout in gubernatorial and congressional elections in the United States in the 1790s rarely exceeded 40 percent and was sometimes as low as 10 percent. Only 27 percent of voters participated in the presidential election of 1824. When the United States first achieved high turnout in presidential elections in 1828 or even 1840, it was with political parties and opposing candidates, neither of which existed during the French Revolution.[68]

Studies of the urban popular movement and the clubs have seduced historians into thinking that political participation in the cities was intense. It was not, as measured by voting. This study of voter behavior confirms my argument that the *campagnards* generally outvoted the *citadins* during the constitutional monarchy. Although Crook is correct that the pattern is less clear-cut in 1791, it was not until 1792 or 1793 that the disparity was reversed. This was mainly due to the withdrawal of the *campagnards*, who were dissatisfied with the results they obtained from the Revolution. The fact that the *campagnards* often outvoted the *citadins* in 1790–1791 calls into question the conclusions of Bois, the Weber thesis, and the "mobilization" model.

Voter behavior during the constitutional monarchy cannot be explained by the "mobilization" model. There are no strong correlations between turnout and urbanization, market penetration, state centralization, literacy, good communication networks, or habitation. The "Maggiolo line" did not divide France into a voting north and an abstaining south. I conclude that the "community" model best explains voter behavior during the constitutional monarchy. Rural communal solidarity explains voter behavior in the "underdeveloped" west, center, and south, as well as in the north and east. Crook also explains high initial rural turnout by rural solidarity, while the *citadins* had difficulty adapting to voting in neighborhood assemblies.[69] Peter Jones's explanation of peasant politicization in the southern Massif Central is based on a "cultural" community with its locus in the parish.[70] The "community" model is consistent with explanations of peasant politicization in premodern societies. Skocpol cites the role of autonomous villages and rural solidarity in initiating peasant revolutions. Peasant politicization and electoral behavior cannot be explained by ideology or Weber's model of acculturation by the cities. Lefebvre is correct that there was an autonomous peasant revolution.

The French Revolution initiated France's apprenticeship in citizenship, a long and protracted process that was not completed until the nineteenth century. Although the Revolution politicized the peasants, it did not achieve modern forms of voter behavior. Participation under the constitutional monarchy was higher in local than in national elections, unlike today. This incomplete modernization may be due more to timing—local elections in 1790 preceding national elections—the absence of political parties, and the lack of state mobilization of voters than to political immaturity. When these conditions were reversed and the peasants realized that the locus of relevant political power had shifted, they voted massively in national elections. Even in 1848, however, there is little evidence that the "mobilization" model explains voter behavior.[71]

NOTES

1. René Rémond, "L'Apport des historiens aux études électorales," in *Explication du Vote*, ed. Daniel Gaxie (Paris, 1985), 46; François Furet, "La monarchie et le règlement électoral de 1789," in *The French Revolution and the Creation of Modern Political Culture*, ed. Keith Baker, François Furet, Mona Ozouf, and Colin Lucas (Oxford, 1987–1989), 1: 375.

2. Melvin Edelstein, "Participation et sociologie électorale de Landes en 1790," *Bulletin de la Commission d'Histoire Economique et Sociale de la Révolution Française* (forthcoming).

3. François Furet and Denis Richet, *La Révolution* (Paris, 1965); Furet, *Penser la Révolution française* (Paris, 1978); Furet and Mona Ozouf, eds. *Dictionnaire critique de la Révolution française* (Paris, 1988); Keith Baker, ed., *The Political Culture of the Old Regime* (Oxford, 1987); Baker, *Inventing the French Revolution* (Cambridge, 1990).

4. Peter McPhee, "Electoral Democracy and Direct Democracy in France, 1789–1851," *European History Quarterly*, 16 (1986), 77.

5. Augustin Cochin, *L'Esprit du Jacobinisme* (Paris, 1979), 79–93.

6. Eugen Weber, *Peasants into Frenchmen* (Stanford, Calif.: 1976); Weber, "The Second Republic, Politics and the Peasant," *French Historical Review*, 11 (1980), 521–50; Weber, "*Comment la Politique Vint aux Paysans*: A Second Look at Peasant Politicization," *American Historical Review*, 87 (1982), 357–89.

7. Maurice Agulhon, *La République au Village* (Paris, 1970); John Merriman, *The Agony of the Republic* (New Haven, Conn., 1978); Ted Margadant, *French Peasants in Revolt* (Princeton, N.J., 1979).

8. Melvin Edelstein, "L'Apprentissage de la citoyenneté: participation électorale des campagnards et citadins (1789–93)," in *L'Image de la Révolution Française*, dir. Michel Vovelle (Oxford, 1989–1990), 1: 15–25.

9. Paul Bois, *Paysans de l'Ouest* (Paris, 1960), 261–66.

10. Ibid., p. 266.

11. Melvin Edelstein, "Vers un 'sociologie électorale' de la Révolution française: citadins et campagnards (1789–1793)," *Revue d'Histoire Moderne et Contemporaine*, 22 (1975), 526–27.

12. Jean-Louis Ormières, "Politique et Religion dans l'Ouest," *Annales: ESC*, 40 (1985), 1041–66; Ormières, "Les Scrutins de 1790 et 1791 et le soulèvement de 1793:

interprétation du comportement électoral," in *Les Résistances à la Révolution*, ed. François Lebrun and Roger Dupuy (Paris, 1987), 82–86.

13. Roland Marx, *Recherches sur la vie politique de l'Alsace prérévolutionnaire et révolutionnaire. Publications de la Société Savante d'Alsace et des Régions de l'Est. Collection "Recherches et Document"* (Strasbourg, 1966), 4: 58.

14. Malcolm Crook, *"Aux urnes, citoyens!* Urban and Rural Electoral Behavior during the French Revolution," in *Reshaping France*, ed. Alan Forrest and Peter Jones (Manchester, U.K., 1991), 161.

15. Edelstein, "Vers une 'sociologie électorale,' " 515, 521.

16. Melvin Edelstein, "Integrating the French Peasants into the Nation-State: The Transformation of Electoral Participation (1789–1870)," *History of European Ideas*, 15, no. 1–3 (1992), 319–26.

17. Crook, *"Aux urnes, citoyens!,"* 162.

18. Seymour Martin Lipset, *Political Man* (Garden City, N.Y., 1963), 187.

19. Lester Milbrath, *Political Participation* (Chicago, 1965), 130.

20. Ibid., 113.

21. Stein Rokkan, *Citizens, Elections, Parties* (Oslo, 1970), 183–91; Rokkan and Henry Valen, "The Mobilization of the Periphery: Data on Turnout, Party Membership and Candidate Recruitment in Norway," in *Approaches to the Study of Political Participation*, ed. Stein Rokkan (Bergen, Norway, 1962).

22. Sidney Verba, Norman Nie, and Jae-on Kim, *Participation and Political Equality: A Seven-Nation Comparison* (Cambridge, U.K., 1978), 281.

23. Ibid., 271.

24. Milbrath, *Political Participation*, 129.

25. Ibid.

26. Herbert McClosky, "Political Participation," in *International Encyclopedia of the Social Sciences* (New York, 1968), 12: 256.

27. Alain Lancelot, *L'abstentionnisme électoral en France* (Paris, 1968), 216, 226, 249.

28. Jean Meynaud and Alain Lancelot, *La Participation des Français à la politique* (Paris, 1965), 52.

29. Guy Arbellot, Bernard Lepetit, and Jacques Bertrand, *Atlas de la Révolution française: Routes et communications* (Paris, 1987), 14–16.

30. Isser Woloch, "The State and the Villages in Revolutionary France," in Forrest and Jones, eds., *Reshaping France*, 222 and Table 1, 237–42.

31. Françoise Subileau and Marie-France Toinet, "L'abstentionisme en France et aux Etats-Unis: Méthodes et Interprétations," in Gaxie, ed., *Explication du Vote*, 187.

32. Lancelot, *L'abstentionnisme électoral en France*, 74–75.

33. Michel Fleury and Pierre Valmary, "Les progrès de l'instruction élémentaire de Louis XIV à Napoléon III d'après l'enquête de Louis Maggiolo," *Population*, 12 (1957), 74–89.

34. Melvin Edelstein, "La Place de la Révolution française dans la politisation des paysans," *AHRF*, no. 280 (1990), 135–49.

35. Georges Lefebvre, "La Révolution française et les paysans," in his *Etudes sur la Révolution Française* (Paris, 1954), 249.

36. Theda Skocpol, *States and Social Revolutions* (Cambridge, U.K., 1979), 112–26.

37. Ran Halévi, "La Monarchie et les élections: position des problèmes," in Baker

et al., eds., *The French Revolution and the Creation of Modern Political Culture*, 1: 387–402; Edelstein, "L'Apprentissage de la citoyenneté," 1: 16–17.

38. Edelstein, "Vers une 'sociologie électorale' ", 521–22; Malcolm Crook, "Les Français devant le vote: participation et pratique électorale à l'époque de la Révolution," in *Les Pratiques Politiques en Province à l'Epoque de la Révolution Française* (Montpellier, 1988), 28.

39. Olivier Audevart, "Les Elections en Haute-Vienne pendant la Révolution," in *Limousin en Révolution*, ed. Jean Boutier, Michel Cassan, Paul d'Hollander, and Bernard Pommaret (Treignac, 1989), 133.

40. Georges Fournier, "La Participation électorale en Haute-Garonne pendant la Révolution," *Annales du Midi*, 101 (1989), 51; Georges Fournier and Michel Perronet, *La Révolution dans l'Aude* (Le Coteau, 1989), 99.

41. Catherine Grandadam and Henri Hours, "Les Elections municipales du début de l'année 1790 dans le Jura," *Travaux de la Société d'Emulation du Jura*, 1990, 215; Jean Bricaud, *L'Administration du département d'Ille-et-Vilaine au début de la Révolution (1790–91)* (Rennes, 1965), 53.

42. Jean-Pierre Jessenne, "Continuités et ruptures dans la détention des fonctions locales en Artois (1789–1800)," in *La Révolution Française et le Monde Rural* (Paris, 1989), 400; Michel Lancelin, *La Révolution en Province* (Saint-Omer, 1972–1988), 1: 125; for Dijon and Beaune, see A. D. Côte d'Or, L 254 and L 258; Marcel Fossier, Nathalie Kozlowski, and Suzanne Vienne, *Pouvoir municipal et communauté rurale à l'époque révolutionnaire en Côte-d'Or (1789–An IV)* (Dijon, 1981), 19–20; Maurice Genty, *Paris, 1789–1795* (Paris, 1987), 152; Raymonde Monnier, "La politisation des paroisses rurales de la banlieue parisienne," in *La Révolution Française et le Monde Rural*, 430.

43. Grandadam and Hours, "Les Elections municipales," 215.

44. Georges Fournier, "Démocratie et vie municipale en Languedoc. Du milieu du XVIIIe au début du XIXe Siècle" (unpublished doctoral thesis, University of Toulouse–Le Mirail, 1991), 2: 562; Jean-Pierre Jessenne, *Pouvoir au Village et Révolution* (Lille, 1987).

45. Patrice Gueniffey, "La Révolution française et les elections: Suffrage, participation et élections pendant la période constitutionnelle (1790–1792)" (unpublished doctoral thesis, Ecole des Hautes Etudes en Sciences Sociales, Paris, 1989), chap. 7; Edelstein, "La Place de la Révolution française," 140.

46. John Markoff, "The Social Geography of Rural Revolt at the Beginning of the French Revolution," *American Sociological Review*, 50 (1985), 773.

47. Daniel Ligou, "Quelques caractères des municipalités bourguignonnes au XVIIIe Siècle," *Annales de la Faculté des Lettres et Sciences Humaines de Nice*, 9–10 (1969), 146; Pierre de Saint-Jacob, *Documents relatifs à la communauté villageoise en Bourgogne du milieu du XVIIIe Siècle à la Révolution* (Paris, 1962); Hilton Root, *Peasants and King in Burgundy* (Berkeley, Calif.: 1982).

48. Antoine Richard, "La vie rurale en Chalosse au XVIIIe siècle," *Bulletin de la Société de Borda* (1946), 3–11; Harriet Rosenberg, *A Negotiated World* (Toronto, 1988), 55–58.

49. Woloch, "The State and the Villages in Revolutionary France," 237–42.

50. Olivier Audevart, "Les Elections en Haute-Vienne pendant la Révolution (1789–1799)" (unpublished master's thesis, U.F.R. des Lettres et Sciences Humaines de Limoges, 1988), 272–73, 278–79.

51. Fossier et al., *Pouvoir municipal et communauté rurale*, 19; A.D. Côte-d'Or L 268; A.D. Rhône 1L 340; Marx, *Recherches sur la vie politique de l'Alsace*, 62; Malcolm Crook, "The People at the Polls: Electoral Behavior in Revolutionary Toulon, 1789–1799," *French Revolutionary Studies*, 5, no. 2 (1991), 169.

52. A.D. Côte-d'Or L 228–230; Audevart, "Les Elections en Haute-Vienne," 276–77.

53. Fournier, "Démocratie et vie municipale en Languedoc," 2: 531.

54. Gueniffey, "La Révolution française et les elections," chap. 7; Edelstein, "La Place de la Révolution française," 141.

55. Crook, *"Aux urnes, citoyens!,"* 156–57.

56. Fournier, "Démocratie et vie municipale en Languedoc," 2: 564–65.

57. Audevart, "Les Elections en Haute-Vienne," 122–23.

58. Ormières, "Politique et Religion dans l'Ouest," 1041–66; Charles Tilly, *The Vendée* (Cambridge, Mass., 1964), 227–62; Fournier, "La Participation électorale en Haute-Garonne," 56–57; Hervé Pommeret, *L'Esprit public dans le département des Côtes-du-Nord pendant la Révolution, 1789–1799* (Saint-Brieuc, 1921), 143; Timothy Tackett, *Religion, Revolution and Regional Culture in Eighteenth-Century France* (Princeton, N.J., 1986), 52–56.

59. Michael Kennedy, "The Foundation of the Jacobin Clubs and the Development of the Jacobin Club Network, 1789–1791," *Journal of Modern History*, 51 (1979), 733; Jean Boutier and Philippe Boutry, "La Diffusion des sociétés politiques en France (1789–An III): une enquête nationale," *Annales Historiques de la Révolution Française*, 1986, no. 266, 365–398.

60. A. D. Marne 1L 303.

61. A. D. Côte-d'Or L 232–233.

62. Fournier, "Démocratie et vie municipale en Languedoc," 2: 593.

63. Charles Tilly, Louise Tilly, and Richard Tilly, *The Rebellious Century, 1830–1930* (Cambridge, Mass., 1975), 26–29.

64. Charles Tilly, "Some Problems in the History of the Vendée," *American Historical Review*, 67 (1961), 29; Crook, *"Aux urnes, citoyens!,"* 163; Audevert, "Les Elections en Haute-Vienne," 127; Edelstein, "Vers une 'sociologie électorale,' " 522–23.

65. Edelstein, *"La Feuille Villageoise,* the Revolutionary Press, and the Question of Rural Political Participation," *French Historical Studies*, 7 (1971), 175–203; Donald Sutherland, *The Chouans* (Oxford, 1982).

66. Lefebvre, "La Révolution française et les paysans," 246–61; Albert Soboul, "The French Rural Community in the Eighteenth and Nineteenth Centuries," *Past and Present*, 1956, no. 10, 78–95.

67. Claude Langlois, "Napoléon Bonaparte Plébiscité?," in *L'Election du Chef de l'Etat en France de Hughes Capet à Nos Jours* (Paris, 1988), 91.

68. Edelstein, "Integrating the French Peasants into the Nation-State," 324–25.

69. Crook, *"Aux urnes, citoyens!,"* 161–64.

70. Peter Jones, *Politics and Rural Society* (Cambridge, U.K., 1985), 305–27.

71. Edelstein, "La nationalisation de la participation électorale des Français (1789–1870)," *Revue d'Histoire Moderne et Contemporaine* (forthcoming).

9

CITIZENSHIP AND THE PRESS IN THE FRENCH REVOLUTION

Jeremy D. Popkin

The revolutionary notion of political citizenship, as Pierre Rétat and other contributors to this book have stressed, harked back to the classical world of Greece and Rome. The printing press and its products, however, were pure artifacts of modernity and, indeed, their impact was one of the principal reasons why the eighteenth-century world differed from the periods that had preceded it. By making the invention of printing the distinguishing characteristic of the eighth epoch in his *Esquisse d'un tableau historique des progrès de l'esprit humain*, the philosophe Condorcet underlined the importance of the rupture with the past that Gutenberg's invention represented. The fact that access to the printing press was designated a fundamental citizen right in 1789, and that the spokesmen of the revolutionary movement insisted from the outset that the press was indispensable in order to constitute the nation as a body of citizens under the conditions of modern life, thus indicated a determination to define citizenship in a new way, one appropriate for the modern world. At the same time, however, the citizen armed with the printing press proved to be a profoundly ambiguous figure, both a model of the "new man" the revolutionaries sought to create and a new elite threatening to monopolize a power to which all citizens supposedly had equal access. The effort to create a notion of citizenship appropriate to an age of modern communications thus posed difficult problems. In practice, the right to publish began to be restricted by 1792, and it became one of the last of the basic attributes of citizenship defined in 1789 to be given effective legal protection in the course of the nineteenth century.

FREEDOM OF THE PRESS AS A RIGHT OF CITIZENSHIP

The press as such was mentioned only briefly in the Revolution's basic charter of citizenship, the Declaration of the Rights of Man and of the Citizen of 1789.

Article 11 specified that "the free communication of opinions being one of the most important of man's possessions, every citizen has the right to speak, write, and publish (*imprimer*) freely, subject to the penalties determined by the law for abuse of this freedom." In the declaration, as in most of the drafts of a list of rights that had preceded it, this right of self-expression in print appeared to be a simple consequence of the revolutionaries' general notion of individual rights, often associated, as it was in the declaration, with religious freedom. Whereas freedom of conscience or of thought were rights the individual exercised in private, freedom of the press had an inherently public dimension: it implied the right to communicate with others. The abbé Sieyès underlined this by proposing to guarantee not only freedom of publication but also freedom of distribution.[1]

Press freedom was the only right mentioned in the declaration whose exercise depended on the existence of modern technology. As Hans-Jürgen Lusebrink's study of the numerous *éloges de Gutenberg* from the revolutionary era shows, the people of 1789 were acutely conscious of the historical rupture introduced by the invention of printing, which they saw as the start of the process of enlightenment that culminated in the French Revolution itself and in the issuing of the Declaration of Rights.[2] Modern historians have followed a different route to the same conclusion. According to Roger Chartier, the generalization of reading, made possible through printing, was crucial to the development of the modern autonomous individual: "Personal communion with a read or written text liberated the individual from the old mediators, freed him or her from the control of the group, and made it possible to cultivate an inner life."[3]

In recognizing freedom of the press as a citizenship right, the constitution makers of 1789 were thus consciously recognizing one of the preconditions of their entire political structure and situating their efforts in a modern world, distinct from the ancient polities from which the notion of citizenship originally derived. The enunciation of a citizenship right that could only be exercised thanks to Gutenberg's invention also implied a certain elasticity in the notion of rights: they could change as technology progressed. Perhaps the legislators of 1789 unwittingly cleared the way for the drafters of the Republican party's platform of 1980, with its assertion that driving an automobile constitutes a right of American citizenship.

The right to freedom of expression in print was, however, a right that not every citizen could exercise personally. In fact, citizenship did not require that one even be capable of expressing oneself in print: literacy was not required for citizenship. Nor did anyone imagine that all citizens would rush to express their opinions in print; the right of expression in print would be exercised by some on behalf of the community as a whole. The formulation in the Declaration of Rights did ensure, however, that access to the printing press would not become the privilege of a closed group: its inclusion as a right of all citizens, regardless of their actual ability to exercise it, acted as a guarantee against the development of a privileged class. Unlike the political rights of voting and holding office, however, the right to print was not made dependent on any specific qualification, such as possession of a certain amount of wealth. Indeed, there was no bar to its being exercised by individuals who were formally excluded from the definition of active citizens, such as women,[4] children, domestic servants, foreigners, or even the insane. (Throughout the Revolution, there were observers who claimed that this last group had a virtual monopoly on the printing press.)

The traditional Marxist critique of the liberal association of press freedom and citizenship has been, to paraphrase the American press critic A. J. Liebling (himself not a Marxist), that it limits freedom of the press to those who own one. The men of the revolutionary era clearly understood that economic considerations would affect the circulation of ideas in print, but, with the exception of a few radicals in 1794 and 1795, they regarded the subjection of the political press to the laws of the market as inevitable and even desirable. Jacques-Pierre Brissot, whose June 1789 pamphlet on press freedom is one of the most interesting discussions of the subject from the revolutionary period, argued that the market mechanism would reconcile press freedom with the need for a unified and patriotic public opinion: patriotic readers would buy newspapers that supported their cause, and thus condemn their rivals to bankruptcy. Since newspapers were relatively cheap, Brissot dismissed the notion that their cost would bar any substantial sector of the citizenry from access to the market and therefore from the chance to exercise an influence on publishers and editors.[5]

Whereas Brissot optimistically assumed that all citizens would also be capable of functioning as consumers, more socially conservative writers argued that the press market would in fact favor the wealthy and that this was desirable, since only those with a certain degree of fortune could be trusted to fulfill all the functions of citizenship. The publisher Charles-Joseph Panckoucke, creator of the Revolution's newspaper of record, the *Moniteur*, explicitly favored large and expensive newspapers, published by large enterprises that would have to be "circumspect in order to avoid being disturbed, and running the risk of losing their capital and the money invested in them."[6] Such a press corresponded to the political structure imagined by those who favored property qualifications for the rights to vote and hold office.

Unlike later Marxist critics, the revolutionaries of 1789 thus saw no contradiction between the citizen's right of freedom of expression and the existence of an economic regime founded on private property. They assumed that the citizen would be economically independent, and differed only on the issue of whether these economically independent citizens would include the entire adult population—the implication of Brissot's democratic formulation—or only substantial property owners, as in Panckoucke's version. But what political information did these citizens have the right to find in the press? The declaration of 1789 and its successors spoke of a right to self-expression; they did not specify a right to information. It is by no means self-evident that the people of 1789 assumed that freedom of the press automatically implied freedom to read the words spoken in the National Assembly. This issue was very much a matter of debate in eighteenth-century Europe. The British Parliament had only conceded the right of journalists to publish its debates in 1772, and it retained the formidable power to imprison journalists for breach of privilege if their commentaries became too outspoken; in 1789, Brissot explicitly reserved the same right to what was then still the Estates-General, as a protection against counterrevolutionary agitation.[7] In the Netherlands, the Patriot movement of the 1780s had divided over the question of whether the governing councils of its urban republics should be required to make their proceedings public: opponents of publicity, including the country's leading newspaper editor, Jean Luzac, argued that such openness would make the councillors subject to mob pressure and prevent them from acting like independent citizens.[8] Similar arguments were used to justify the secrecy surrounding the proceedings of the American Constitutional Convention in 1787, and the United States Senate barred reporters and press coverage until 1795.

The issue was very much up in the air in the months preceding the meeting of the Estates-General in France in 1789. The officials of the censorship bureau refused to authorize the publication of that body's proceedings in advance, arguing that only the assembled deputies had the right to decide whether their speeches should be made public.[9] Had it not been for the necessity of rallying public support against the crown and the privileged orders, one can wonder whether even the members of the Third Estate would have come down firmly on the side of full publicity. In the event, the radical minority among the deputies forced the issue. Mirabeau, balked in his first effort to publish a newspaper, retaliated by titling his publication *Lettres à mes commettants*. In this way, he converted the issue from one of his electors' right to information to one of his own individual freedom of expression, and thereby assured the triumph of the principle of publicity. But the revolutionaries quickly made freedom of information a basic tenet of the new order. "Publicity is the people's safeguard," Jean-Sylvain Bailly, the newly installed mayor of Paris, asserted in August 1789; secrecy had come to be regarded as inherently counterrevolutionary.[10] This right to information was, however, essentially a right of the citizenry as a whole, not a right that could be claimed by any specific individual on his or her own behalf. As such, it was closely connected to the revolutionaries' conception of the press's essential role in the new democratic polity created in 1789.

Press freedom thus soon came to include the right to publicize the words and actions of the people's representatives, but those same representatives continued to claim the right to impose limits on printing. Scholars such as Gerd van den Heuvel and Marcel Gauchet have used this fact to emphasize the contrast between French practice, which continues down to the present day in the form of laws against incitement of racial hatred and anti-Semitism in print, and the more libertarian Anglo-American tradition.[11] While Leonard Levy has rightly pointed out that the libertarianism of the Anglo-American tradition in the eighteenth century should not be exaggerated—the threat of prosecution for seditious libel was a considerable deterrent to political commentary[12]—it is nevertheless true that the revolutionaries never meant to grant unlimited freedom of expression.

To fault them for not doing so is anachronistic: even the clearly stated prohibition against national legislation limiting freedom of expression in the American Bill of Rights was not understood until generations later to bar bans on obscenity and on political radicalism that could be asserted to pose a "clear and present danger" to social order. One can wonder whether either the French or the American judicial system would uphold even today Jean-Paul Marat's right to incite the public to take the king and queen hostage and to massacre the commander of the National Guard, the mayor of Paris, the royal ministers, and five or six thousand other unnamed "enemies" of the people.[13] There were certainly ambiguities in the formulation contained in the Declaration of Rights, and there was certainly harassment of extremist journalists even during the Revolution's liberal phase, from 1789 to 1792. Nevertheless, the clearly stated assertion that freedom constituted the norm, and limitation the exception requiring an explicit legal basis, was a sharp break with the practice of France and all the other continental states of the era. This principle remained embedded in revolutionary constitutional law, though not in practice, throughout the 1790s. The Constitution of 1793 included an unqualified statement that "to express one's thoughts and one's opinions, either in print or in any other manner . . . cannot be abrogated," and deputies continued to appeal to the principle of press freedom in Convention debates.

THE PRESS AND THE POSSIBILITY OF DEMOCRACY

That the revolutionaries remained so loyal to the principle of press freedom, despite their inability to tolerate its practice, was due to the tremendous importance they assigned to the press as the means by which the entire population could exercise its rights as citizens. The press was important because the revolutionary generation saw it as the only means of reconciling the demand, derived from classical Greek and Roman models, that all citizens be able to participate directly in public political debate with the reality of life in a country the size of eighteenth-century France, in which it was impossible literally to re-create the classical public forum. It was this impossibility that led the abbé Sieyès and other revolutionary legislators to assert that the National Assembly could, through the magic of the representative system, substitute itself for the citizenry and exercise the powers that classical democracies had reserved for the assembled people.

The difficulties that this claim engendered are well-known; so too is the Revolution's consistent hostility to intermediary institutions, such as political parties, that might have served to bridge the gap between the people and its representatives. Critics of the revolutionaries' "heretical Rousseauism with representatives"[14] have, however, neglected the way in which they used the existence of the press to give plausibility to their claim to have re-created a situation in which the entire body of citizens could participate in law making. The revolutionaries may have been misguided on this point, but they were sincerely convinced that the press supplied the missing link between citizens and representatives that would reconcile democracy and practicality.

The notion that the printing press could permit the reestablishment of true citizenship in the modern world had begun to develop even before 1789. In the wake of the Maupeou crisis of the early 1770s, Lamoignon de Malesherbes had observed that "the art of printing has thus given writing the same public function that speech had in the earliest times, in the nation's assemblies."[15] By 1789, this argument had become a commonplace that one finds in numerous pamphlets and newspaper prospectuses. Le Hodey de Saultchevreuil, the editor of the *Journal des Etats-Généraux* and its successor, the *Journal logographique*, newspapers that promised a full transcript of the parliamentary debates, justified his enterprises on the grounds that, through his work, "the inhabitants of regions furthest from this capital . . . will virtually be present at the sessions of this august Senate, as if they were attending in person."[16]

Brissot, in his 1789 pamphlet demanding the abolition of censorship and restrictive privileges, argued that only printed newspapers allowed a rational form of representative government: through them, "one can teach the same truth at the same moment to millions of men; through the press, they can discuss it without tumult, decide calmly, and give their opinion." The press would overcome the barriers of space and numbers that threatened to make participatory government impossible in the modern world; it would permit the constitution of a public forum without literally requiring the citizens to abandon their homes and their private occupations to take part in politics. Indeed, the use of print marked an improvement on the democracies of antiquity: Brissot maintained that it would favor calm and rational discussion, rather than the demagoguery that had been the downfall of the Athenians. The epidemic of rural violence that swept France in the summer of 1789 seemed to him to confirm the point. "See how much despots are to blame for having obstructed the freedom of the press, and the speed with which it can enlighten, in an instant, the inhabitants of a great country," he wrote in one of the first issues of his *Patriote français*. "With newspapers, one can also destroy the baseless fears that can sometimes cause the greatest evils."[17]

The revolutionaries were convinced that the press would not only provide the basis for a participatory politics suited to the scale of the modern world and more rational than its classical model, but that it would also be the mechanism by which a true civic spirit would be generated. Newspapers "propagate instruction and reflect its influence, they unite all good spirits and all dedicated citizens; they establish communications that cannot fail to produce a harmony of sentiments, of opinions, of plans and of actions that constitutes the real public force, the safeguard of the constitution," Mirabeau wrote in 1789.[18] The press, in this view, was the essential medium through which the multitude of isolated "dedicated citizens" were converted into a real community, capable of playing a constructive political role. Condorcet, too, saw the press as having a vital unifying function. He claimed that the press alone could assure that "debates among a numerous people be truly one; that one be able to say that, since everyone has followed the same presentation, they are truly deciding on the same matter.''[19]

This idea of the press as the technological extension of the classical open forum was the most fundamental argument for the importance of the printed word in the exercise of citizenship. The open-forum argument put particular emphasis on the two-way nature of communication through the press: the citizens would be able to follow their representatives, but they in turn would be able to hear from their constituents. The press was also essential as a medium for the education of the citizenry. A century later, the Third Republic would put its faith in schooling to teach the principles of citizenship. The revolutionaries of 1789, though they, too, counted on education to help the new regime put down roots, were in a hurry to create the ''new man'' that the new democratic polity required as citizens, and the press loomed large in their notion of how such a transformation could be accomplished in a short time. Formulations to this effect were common in the provincial newspapers, which could less easily imagine themselves as active participants in the two-way process of national political debate articulated by Mirabeau, Brissot, or Condorcet. The prospectus for a Breton newspaper launched in 1790 justified the enterprise because it would enable the residents of the region ''to acquire every day just notions that a great people should have concerning its liberty, its power, its laws.''[20] Citizens needed to know not only the content of the new laws, but how to manage the mechanics of exercising their newly defined political rights. The *Annales orléanoises* gave voters precise instructions on the unfamiliar new procedures for participating in elections.[21] The relationship between citizenship and the press could thus be seen both as a dialectical one, in which printing made the exercise of political rights possible, and as a didactic one, in which printed texts conveyed to the citizens what their rights were. In either case, however, the press was essential in constituting the community of citizens. And because it was essential, those who employed it obviously occupied a most important position.

NEWSPAPERS AND JOURNALISTS AS MODEL CITIZENS

Since citizenship could not exist in the modern world without newspapers and journalists, the conduct of those highly visible citizens became a critical issue. As Camille Desmoulins wrote, ''[t]oday, journalists exercise a public function.''[22] The newspaper and its author—the two, as we will see, often tended to become indistinguishable—offered highly visible models of patriotic citizenship for the population at large. The persona of the patriotic citizen-journalist, first articulated, as Pierre Rétat has shown,[23] in 1789, underwent a process of idealization that culminated with the apotheosis of the assassinated Marat in 1793. It is true that few newspapers actually titled themselves *Citoyen*, in contrast to the number that used formulas such as *Ami*, *Tribun*, *Orateur*, or *Patriote*, but, in most cases, the claim to be a good citizen addressing fellow citizens was clearly articulated.

A typical example of the constitution of a citizen persona can be observed in the early numbers of Brissot's *Patriote françois*. The paper's title implied a personification of the journalistic enterprise, in contrast to the old regime newspapers whose titles—*gazette, courrier, nouvelles*—normally insisted on identification as an institution. Whether the qualification of "French patriot" referred to the newspaper or its chief editor was ambiguous. Although the paper's epigraph, "A free newspaper is a sentinel always on watch for the people," borrowed from a spokesman of the English "Commonwealthman" tradition, did not make direct reference to the concept of citizenship, it certainly implied that the publication would fulfill a vital citizenship role. Brissot's declaration of intentions in the paper's inaugural number reflected similar tendencies. "The point is to spread the enlightenment which prepares a nation to receive a free constitution," he announced. "It will devote itself above all both to defending the rights of the people . . . and to keeping it from allowing itself to be led into continual fermentation, which would perpetuate disorder and postpone the constitution."[24]

In the pages of his paper, Brissot sometimes reported his own performances as a patriotic citizen, as in the number of August 6, 1789, where he reprinted part of the speech that he had delivered in his district assembly, asserting the right of "all assemblies of men in civic communities . . . to give themselves a municipal constitution"; the *Patriote françois*'s readers could thus watch the paper's editor contributing to the very definition of citizen rights. They could even more frequently read editorials that defined the proper behavior of a citizen: "If a simple style is the hallmark of a free man, simplicity of manners, and above all of dress, is even more so" (August 7, 1789); "one cannot recommend too strongly to the soldiers and citizens responsible for dispersing popular crowds to carry out their functions without brutality" (August 9, 1789). Brissot praised individuals whose conduct was that "of an excellent citizen," such as de Kéralio, author of a patriotic brochure, who "since the 13th of July, has devoted himself courageously to the defense of his district, and who contributed greatly to the inculcation of order among a youthful population not accustomed to discipline."[25] Having warned that an excessive faith in great men was one of the besetting weaknesses of free polities (August 7, 1789), Brissot gave a clear example of the conduct an alert citizen ought to follow in this regard by criticizing Mirabeau and warning against an excessive reliance on the good intentions of those in office (August 18, 1789). And the *Patriote françois* provided a commentary on its own behavior, underlining the importance of the press's critical function: "One begins to hear complaints about the degree of liberty that gazetteers and journalists are taking in discussing the operations of the National Assembly. The Assembly would be mistaken to listen to these complaints" (August 18, 1789).

The fusion of newspaper and journalist into a model of the perfect citizen was carried to its extreme in the radical revolutionary press, especially in Jean-Paul Marat's *Ami du Peuple* and in the various versions of the *Père Duchêne*. Marat, as has often been pointed out, merged his identity completely with that of the pamphlet-journal he published from 1789 to 1792: he literally made himself "the friend of the people." His self-proclaimed role was to spur them to rise up and create a true democracy, with "a constitution whose base would be the declaration of rights, and in which the sovereignty of the people would be consecrated together with the authority of the electors over those they choose, the standing convocation of the civic assemblies, the right of the citizens to resist any arbitrary decree by force of arms"[26]—in other words, a true community of citizens. To this end, Marat proposed and acted out a set of behaviors that constituted a model for citizenship: constant vigilance against potential enemies of freedom, defense of those whose rights were violated, a willingness to sacrifice private interests to the public good. The citizen-journalist's martyrdom at the hands of Charlotte Corday dramatically confirmed his frequent promises to lay down his life for the people and enabled the Jacobins to cast him as the ultimate model of the good citizen.

The persona that Marat constructed for himself was, of course, a hard act to follow. The popular pamphlet-journals attributed to the Père Duchêne proposed a less ascetic model, closer to the real life of at least some of the urban sans-culotte population. The fictitious Père Duchêne, the supposed author of these pieces, was portrayed as a flesh-and-blood figure who carried out the full range of his civic obligations without giving up his private existence, as Marat had. Particularly in Jacques-René Hébert's version, there was regular stress on the fact that the Père Duchêne was married, that he worked for a living, and that he liked to relax with his pipe and his bottle. But he also attended his section assembly, stood ready to defend his country, and regularly discussed public affairs with his fellows. The vivid dramatic episodes recounted in serio-comic form in many of these pamphlets regularly put the Père Duchêne in the presence of the high and the mighty—the king, the queen, the leading political figures of the Revolution—and invariably enabled him to demonstrate that the good sense and patriotic instincts of an ordinary citizen were more powerful than the wiles of the people's enemies. The Père Duchêne was, of course, a fantasy figure, but he was close enough to reality to serve as an effective guide for civic behavior.[27]

REALISM, UTOPIANISM, CITIZENSHIP, AND THE PRESS

The association of press freedom, journalism, and republican citizenship born in 1789 proved enduring; it reappeared, for instance, in 1848, when one of the first acts of the Provisional Government was to stage a public ceremony honoring the newspaperman Armand Carrel, killed in a duel in 1836. At the same time, however, it quickly became clear that the journalist was no ordinary citizen, and that those who wielded the power of the press most effectively could do so in ways that disrupted the functioning of the constitutional system within which citizen rights were to be exercised. Journalists like Marat who articulated an activist persona in their writings did not do so for the purpose of modelling a strict obedience to authority. On the other side of the political spectrum, the self-proclaimed *honnêtes hommes* who edited the Directory-era right-wing press contributed mightily to the revenge of the qualification "Monsieur" over the revolutionary form of address, "Citoyen."

From the outset of the revolution, the abuse of press freedom preoccupied its leaders as much as its protection. Brissot, as we have seen, anticipated this problem as early as June 1789 and affirmed the Estates-General's right to silence press critics. Marat saw no contradiction between his admiration for the English laws guaranteeing freedom of the press, which he claimed allowed "a writer, speaking for the country, to drag any public figure, no matter how high his rank, through the mud," and his own calls for "good citizens" to "assemble and demolish any printing show that produces our enemies' libels."[28] But it was not just the radical revolutionaries who called for bans on anti-civic publications: in January 1790, the abbé Sieyès introduced a bill that would have made French press laws at least as restrictive as the Sedition Act passed in the United States in 1798. The measure was never enacted, but it showed that distrust of the press spanned the political spectrum. The prominent citizen-journalist could easily turn into a dangerous demagogue. "How does it happen that this petty individual does so much harm to the public welfare?" one of Brissot's political enemies demanded in 1792. "It's because he has a newspaper."[29] And measures against the press and the journalists could easily be justified in terms of maintaining equality within the civic community. The celebrity-journalist could not really be an ordinary citizen, equal to everyone else.

The Montagnard regime of 1793–1794 had a profound distrust of journalists who overdid the emphasis on their personal virtues as citizens. In the debates of the Jacobin Club, Robespierre consistently opposed the creation of an official club newspaper, for fear that its editor would be in a position to dominate his fellow members by slanting coverage. And yet the press remained essential to the Montagnard conception of republican citizenship: the patriot-citizen needed to know about the most recent government decrees and feats of patriotic heroism on the battlefield. The government of Year II (1793–1794), although it stopped short of creating a state press monopoly, not only imposed censorship but subsidized the circulation of pro-Montagnard newspapers; until Hébert was proscribed, army officers were ordered to read the *Père Duchêne* aloud to the troops. The visible existence of the press was essential if the conviction that the Republic was a representative government was to be maintained: even at the height of the Terror, the revolutionaries remained under the spell of the argument that the press was essential to the functioning of democracy in a large state.

As the Montagnards came to conceive of citizenship as adherence to a unanimous community, however, they were naturally driven to eliminate any signs of dissidence in the newspapers. Even before his group came to power, Robespierre had warned that "the interest of the Revolution may demand certain measures to repress a conspiracy founded on the freedom of the press."[30] Like the other individual rights of citizens, the right to publish fell victim to the dialectic of revolutionary government: the press's collective function as the link between governors and governed was preserved at the expense of its individualistic function as the expression of citizens' opinions.

The Montagnards inaugurated a tradition of restrictions that persisted under all subsequent regimes until the Third Republic. The Constitution of 1795, although it repeated that "no one can be prevented from speaking, writing, printing and publishing his thoughts," also provided explicitly for the temporary suspension of this and other citizen rights "when circumstances make it necessary." The Thermidorians may have restored individual rights in the economic sphere and in some other areas; they did not do so in the domain of the press. The general confidence in the association between press freedom and progress that characterized the last decades of the Old Regime and the early years of the Revolution had broken down: the newspaper press in particular had come to be regarded as the medium by which either the uneducated mob or the retrograde forces of religious fanaticism threatened to destroy the republican constitutional structure and the system of citizenship rights on which it rested.[31] Under Napoléon, many of the censorship restrictions of the Old Regime were temporarily revived, but the tradition that prevailed for most of the nineteenth century more closely resembled that inaugurated under the Directory: the enunciation of a basic right of press freedom, accompanied by a wide range of significant restrictions. Of the various individual liberties mentioned in the Declaration of Rights of 1789, freedom of the press was one of the last to be given meaningful legal protection. Only with the enactment of the republican press laws of 1881 can one speak of a real consolidation of the individual citizen's right to publish freely.

The generation of the French Revolution, the first to define a notion of citizenship appropriate to an era of mass communication, thus discovered that the press was intimately linked to both aspects of the definition of modern citizenship: that which stresses individual freedom and that which stresses collective membership in the polity. For that reason, the press has proved indispensable to the functioning of both Western liberal and democratic regimes, in which civil society is distinguished from the state, and of totalitarian ones, which, far from eliminating the press, have put heavy stress on its importance. (One can argue that it has proved easier to implement the totalitarian version of the press as cement of the univocal body of citizens than to create a working version of the press as expression of the citizens' competing interests.) The various dilemmas that showed themselves as early as the summer of 1789—the tendency of the successful newspaper writer to become separated from and more powerful than, hence distrusted by, other citizens; the influence of economic considerations over the press—have never been fully resolved. In the realm of the press, as in many other respects, the libertarian and democratic ideals articulated in 1789 remain goals to be striven for, rather than prescriptions capable of easy fulfillment.

NOTES

1. Cited in Christine Fauré, ed., *Les Déclarations des droits de l'homme de 1789* (Paris: Payot, 1988), 103.

2. Hans-Jürgen Lüsebrink, " 'Hommage à l'écriture' et 'Eloge de l'imprimerie.' Traces de la perception sociale du livre, de l'écriture et de l'imprimerie à l'époque révolutionnaire," in Frédéric Barbier et al., eds., *Mélanges de la Bibliothèque de la Sorbonne*, no. 9: *Livre et Révolution* (Paris: Aux Amateurs de Livres, 1989), 133–44.

3. Roger Chartier, ed., *History of Private Life: Passions of the Renaissance*, trans. A. Goldhammer (Cambridge, Mass.: Harvard University Press, 1989), 116.

4. There was some discussion in 1789 about whether women were permitted to direct printing shops. Carla Hesse, *Publishing and Cultural Politics in Revolutionary Paris* (Berkeley: University of California Press, 1991), 31.

5. Jacques-Pierre Brissot, *Mémoire aux Etats-généraux. Sur la nécessité de rendre dès ce moment la presse libre, et surtout pour les journaux politiques* (Paris, 1789), 10, 52–53.

6. Charles-Joseph Panckoucke, "Sur les journaux anglois," *Mercure de France*, 30 January 1790.

7. Brissot, *Mémoire*, 52–53.

8. Jeremy D. Popkin, *News and Politics in the Age of Revolution* (Ithaca, N.Y.: Cornell University Press, 1989), 181.

9. Archives nationales (Paris), V(1) 549.

10. Bailly, proclamation of 13 August 1789, cited in Pierre Rétat, *Les Journaux de 1789: Bibliographie critique* (Paris: CNRS, 1989), 195.

11. Gerd van den Heuvel, *Der Freiheitsbegriff der Französische Revolution* (Göttingen: Vandenhoeck and Ruprecht, 1988), 100–103, 108; Marcel Gauchet, *La Révolution des droits de l'homme* (Paris: Gallimard, 1989), 176–78.

12. Leonard Levy, *Emergence of a Free Press* (New York: Oxford University Press, 1985).

13. *Ami du peuple*, 18 December 1790.

14. Gauchet, *La Révolution des droits*, xiv.

15. Cited in E. Badinter, ed., *Les 'Remontrances' de Malesherbes 1771–1775* (Paris: Flammarion, 1985), 273.

16. Prospectus, *Journal logographique*, 1790.

17. Brissot, *Mémoire*, 10; *Patriote françois*, 27 August 1789.

18. Mirabeau, prospectus for *Etats-Généraux*, 1789.

19. Marquis de Condorcet, "Sur les conventions nationales," cited in Lucien Jaume, *Le Discours jacobin et la démocratie* (Paris: Fayard, 1989), 232.

20. Prospectus, *Journal des municipalités, districts et départements de l'Ille et Vilaine, des Côtes du Nord, du Finistère, de la Loire Inférieure et du Morbihan* (Rennes), 1790.

21. *Annales orléanoises*, 23 January 1790, 16 February 1790.

22. Cited in Claude Bellanger et al., *Histoire générale de la presse française* (Paris: Presses Universitaries de France, 1969–1974), 1: 453–54.

23. Pierre Rétat, "Le Journaliste révolutionnaire comme 'écrivain patriote,' " *Il Confronto letterario*, no. 15 (supplement), 111–20.

24. *Patriote françois*, 28 July 1789.

25. Ibid., 9 August 1789.

26. *Ami du Peuple*, 30 November 1791.

27. For a more extensive discussion of the *Père Duchêne* texts and their political significance, see Jeremy D. Popkin, *Revolutionary News: The Press in France, 1789–1799* (Durham, N.C.: Duke University Press, 1990), 151–68.

28. *Ami du Peuple*, 19 January 1790, 21 December 1790.

29. Debate of 30 November 1792, cited in A. Aulard, ed., *La Société des Jacobins* (Paris: Cerf, 1891–1898), 4: 528.

30. Speech to the Convention, 19 April 1793, in *Oeuvres de Maximilien Robespierre*, ed. Marc Bouloiseau and Albert Soboul (Paris: Société des Etudes Robespierristes, 1938–1958), 9: 452.

31. See Jeremy D. Popkin, ''The Newspaper Press in French Political Thought, 1789–1799,'' *Studies in Eighteenth-Century Culture* 10 (1980), 113–33.

10

THE RIGHT TO PRIMARY EDUCATION IN THE FRENCH REVOLUTION: FROM THEORY TO PRACTICE

Isser Woloch

In their magisterial study *Lire et Ecrire*, François Furet and Jacques Ozouf demonstrate statistically that schooling and literacy were products of social development on whose rhythms the Revolution and subsequent regimes seemed to have scant impact. The first Republic, they found, neither advanced popular education nor ruined it. As Furet and Ozouf trace the broad outlines of literacy and schooling in France across three centuries, their originality lies in their emphasis on the role of social demand. "The school is a product of local societies before being an element of their transformation," they conclude. The nature of a community, its level of social development, its individual and collective sources of wealth usually determined whether or not that community offered primary schooling to its young, regardless of the regime or its policy.[1]

The Revolution's apparent lack of impact on literacy does not mean, however, that its shelf of abortive plans and extravagant visions remains the only legacy worth studying. As reflections of the evolving revolutionary mentality, such projects as Talleyrand's, Condorcet's, or Le Peletier's—those "great mobilizing visions of the Revolution," in Branislaw Baczko's phrase—have indeed been dissected time and again.[2] In this chapter I will steer between that corpus of texts and the long-durational trends demonstrated by Furet and Ozouf. I wish to consider instead how the Revolution actually attempted to make a difference, for the National Convention not only imagined but created a "right to education" and a vehicle for implementing that right: *instruction publique*. That this policy did not in the end accelerate the spread of literacy reflected not simply the insuperable social obstacles, but the dilemmas and hesitations in the commitment itself, and finally the fact that it was never really put to the test by being adequately funded for a sustained period of time. Nonetheless, armed with the concept of *instruction publique*, the revolutionary state undertook to promote and improve primary education. It began a campaign of state penetration that left its mark on the new civic order despite its equivocations and ultimate failures.

The state's potential role in education was of course much discussed during the Enlightenment, and in the domain of secondary education the French monarchy occasionally intervened aggressively. But on the question of popular education—in marked contrast to Prussia and Austria—eighteenth-century discourse in France did not advance much beyond a stirring of concern. Before 1789 the French monarchy had not been galvanized into action, nor did the prerevolutionary *cahiers* attach much urgency to the issue. As best we know, only 1 to 3 percent of the parish *cahiers* spoke of it at all, while the general *cahiers* had little to say about primary education either. There was every reason in 1789 to suppose that elementary schooling would remain a purely local matter as always, supported by parental tuition, communal subventions, or both; subject to informal clerical supervision; and geared to socializing the young into the beliefs and decorum of a Catholic way of life.[3]

The Revolution overturned such assumptions. By 1791 influential deputies inscribed primary education on the Revolution's long-term agenda, and by 1793 others catapulted it to a central position in republican ideology. This was not to say that primary schooling would necessarily become secularized, that Catholicism would be driven from the classroom. Rather, in this domain, as in the area of poor relief, the state was poised to become the arbiter of policy as against the Church or local society. Initially, deputies such as Talleyrand and Condorcet presented plans for refashioning the entire structure of French education—elementary schools, secondary schools, universities, and research institutes. Such comprehensive proposals rarely came to a vote, however, and in the end, successive revolutionary assemblies failed to approve any. Meanwhile, popular education assumed an unparalleled ideological and instrumental importance. Republicans came to regard universal primary schooling as the hallmark of a progressive nation and as a key to the prospects of the French Republic. Schools would impart literacy and numeracy but would also inculcate republican values. In tandem with new symbols, images, and public festivals for all citizens, republican primary schools for the young would constitute a revolutionary pedagogy intended to wean the French people from its ignorance and prejudices. The revolutionary passion for national integration, for spreading norms and institutions uniformly across France, also shaped policy on education—as well it might, considering the sharp disparities in schooling among regions and social groups, between town and country, between male and female.[4]

In June 1793 the Jacobin Convention enshrined the idea of universal education in its new Declaration of the Rights of Man: "Education is the need of everyone," it proclaimed, thus resolving a question that had vexed such philosophes as Voltaire. "Society must do everything in its power to favor the progress of public reason and to put education within the reach of all citizens." In this sense elementary schooling, necessary for everyone, stood apart from the hierarchy of more advanced educational institutions. The Convention could in fact act on it independently rather than as part of a master plan, and the egalitarian atmosphere in Paris now placed a premium on doing so. The Convention resounded with promises to establish schools everywhere and with reports on ad hoc local efforts.[5] None of this added up to a real policy, however. How could universal, free primary education actually be brought into being?

Several false starts delayed an effective response to that question. First, the Convention took up a proposal introduced in behalf of the recently assassinated Jacobin deputy Michel Le Peletier. The Le Peletier plan took off from the Jacobin premise that citizens ought to experience a common education (*éducation commune*), for only by such contact could equality and fraternity develop among children of diverse social backgrounds. The more problematic assumption of this blueprint held that access to schooling was not merely a right to which citizens were entitled or an obligation of the state to provide, but that parents were obliged to accept republican schooling for their children. As Danton melodramatically declared, "I too am a father, but my son does not belong to me, he belongs to the Republic." Primary schooling was too vital for the commonweal to be left to circumstances or the discretion of families. Le Peletier therefore proposed to create state boarding schools where children between the ages of five and twelve would be taken to experience veritable equality in food, clothing, lodging, work, play, and learning. Robespierre and the Jacobin Club publicly endorsed the plan, as homage to the Montagnard martyr. Despite pointed criticisms of its "chimerical" qualities, the Convention echoed that homage by adopting a modified version of the proposal on August 13, 1793, when it decreed that such state boarding schools should be offered as an option without being obligatory. The willingness to endorse this Spartan fantasy even symbolically may have been an ominous portent of the Jacobin mentality, but in fact it had no practical impact on the fate of primary schooling. While historians have been mesmerized by Le Peletier's *maisons d'égalité*, the Convention on the very next day "suspended" application of its decree, never (as far as I know) to consider it again.[6]

Finally passing from rhetoric to action in December, the Convention adopted the Bouquier Law. A deceptively simple but oddly ambivalent approach, Bouquier's plan seemed to incorporate a liberal anti-statist viewpoint alongside the spirit of Jacobin egalitarianism. At first glance it accommodated familiar local patterns of primary schooling. Indeed, the Bouquier Law did not create a veritable system of public schooling at all; rather, it committed the republic to paying the tuition (*retribution scolaire*) of each student at a standard rate. Schooling would also be "free" to parents in the latitude they would have to find teachers who suited them. All teachers were required to come under the umbrella of this plan, but their hiring did not depend on any official body. They simply had to secure a *certificat de civisme* and announce their intention to open a school. What they did in the classroom was a matter between them and the parents, since they would not be subject to special surveillance. In theory the plan accommodated ex-priests or nuns as much as ardent sans-culottes chafing to spread the revolutionary gospel in the classroom.

In reality this aura of maximal freedom was disingenuous. While teachers would not be officially screened for their skill, they could teach only after securing a *certificat de civisme* from their municipality or revolutionary committee. True, every public or quasi-public functionary required this bill of civic reliability in the Year II (1793–1794), but traditional Catholic teachers might shrink from seeking it, either on principle or from fear of the consequences should they be turned down. The freedom of parents was limited in another respect as well, for again the Convention visualized primary schooling not simply as a right of citizens (which the state would facilitate by paying all tuition charges) but as an obligation. Though manifestly lacking any ability to enforce this, the Bouquier Law required parents to send their offspring to school. As Danton again put it, "In the Republic no one is free to be ignorant."[7]

The Convention implemented this "democratic law" immediately, and four months later queried the districts about its progress. The response was dismaying. In the 400-odd districts providing specific information, officials estimated that where there should have been about 23,000 schools, only 6,831 were operating, the majority concentrated in about fifty districts. Elsewhere "the absolute famine of teachers" effectively nullified the Convention's hopes. Numerous Old-Regime teachers reportedly balked at working for the Republic or could not acquire a *certificat de civisme* even if they wished to do so. At the same time cooperative teachers were demoralized by "the meagerness and instability of their pay," which depended on enrollment.[8] After Thermidor, however, the fate of the Bouquier Law became moot in any case when deputies, whether in good faith or demagogically, assailed it as an emanation of Robespierrist terrorism. And, because it established no standards of qualification for teachers, some also attacked the law as a sanction for revolutionary "vandalism" and ignorance. Now the advocates of a more structured and ambitious program seized the initiative. Reviving parts of an earlier stillborn plan that he had proposed in collaboration with Sieyès and Daunou, Joseph Lakanal offered a different approach to creating public primary schools.

Lakanal's plan would place primary education more firmly under government supervision, raise the status of teachers, liberate them from a dependence on the vagaries of enrollment, and expand the program of study beyond reading, writing, and arithmetic as Condorcet had once proposed. At the same time it would restore the freedom of parents to choose private schools or no schooling at all. In sum, the Lakanal Law aimed very high while accepting a number of practical limitations. And instead of acting with its usual impulsiveness, the Convention gave extended consideration to a detailed proposal on education, with ample debate, modification by amendment, final approval, and follow-up.[9] Thermidorian in provenance but surprisingly Jacobin in spirit, the Lakanal Law of November 1794 became the hallmark of republican policy on education, a freely debated and artful compromise of conflicting imperatives, extremely ambitious without being impossibly utopian.

Every commune with one thousand or more inhabitants would have an *école primaire* employing both an *instituteur* and an *institutrice* salaried annually by the state at twelve hundred and one thousand livres respectively (with supplements for those teaching in the largest towns). Bourgs and towns would have a proportionate number of additional teachers, while smaller villages were to be amalgamated into *arrondissements* at roughly the same threshold by their district administration. The teachers would be recruited, examined, and certified in a *concours*, or competition, by a three-man *juri d'instruction* appointed by each district administration. These administrations were then to maintain surveillance over the schools and sign pay vouchers. The *instituteurs publics* were enjoined to teach a curriculum of reading, writing, arithmetic, the Declaration of the Rights of Man, the Constitution, republican morality, the principles of the French language, elements of geography, the history of free peoples, and notions about natural phenomena. Religion did not figure in this program.[10]

Apart from their state salaries, *instituteurs publics* could not accept supplementary payments from parents for tutoring or boarding their children; whether they could lawfully engage in a secondary occupation was unclear. By virtue of their state salary, however, teachers would be liberated from a dependence on parental tuition, communal subvention, or actual enrollments. To pay a four-figure annual salary to a humble elementary school teacher in the countryside was extremely controversial, and some deputies believed that this might subsidize negligent or underemployed teachers with public revenues. But Lakanal was adamant, for only in this way could competent teachers be attracted to rural schools, where the salary would indeed seem appreciable: "Only in this way can I foresee equality in education." Like Jacobin policies on public assistance, the Lakanal Law sought to redress the dearth of public services in rural communities. By eliminating tuition and putting teachers on public salary, it not only hoped to provide primary education for the indigent but also offered an incentive for schooling to tight-fisted parents who were not poor.

Lakanal made his ostensibly secular public schools more palatable to conservatives by permitting the establishment of private schools outside the system. Despite impassioned arguments by several ex-Montagnards that this would destroy any hope of *éducation commune* for the nation's children, the Convention sanctioned private schools or *enseignement libre*, as it was called, alongside *instruction publique*. Gilbert Romme then insisted that private schools must at least be subject to strict surveillance and standards set by public authorities. Lakanal himself agreed, seeing this as a compromise between the collective interests of the Republic and the prerogatives of parents. But the Thermidorian majority, adamant about shielding traditional religious teachers from interference, refused to place any constraints on private schools. In the same libertarian spirit, the Convention abandoned the pretense of the Bouquier Law that parents must send their children to school. Nor did the new law require that French be the exclusive language of instruction in areas where the populace spoke German, Breton, Flemish, or local patois. While insisting that *instruction publique* should promote the use of French everywhere, the new law conceded that local languages could be used as an "auxiliary medium" of instruction, in effect abandoning the battle to impose French in non-francophone regions.[11]

The Lakanal Law affirmed the right of all citizens to schooling and the Republic's obligation to provide and fund it. Of course no revolutionary law could conjure away the existing social and cultural obstacles to universal public education, but Lakanal's plan seems a reasoned attempt to confront them. Implemented energetically through the districts (still coordinated from the center as institutions of revolutionary government), the Lakanal Law guided the most significant attempt to create and finance a national system of primary schooling in France until the far more modest initiatives of Guizot in the 1830s. In practical terms, the Revolution's most important action in the field of primary education began with the Lakanal Law of November 1794 and ended with its demise one year later.

THE DEMAND FOR SCHOOLING

Assuming the responsibility for paying *instituteurs publics*, the Republic naturally did not wish to squander public funds on an excessive number of schools, but it also had to consider the practical needs of varied communities. Lakanal had acknowledged that the smallest communes would generally not have their own schools under his plan, which in that sense was more rigid than the Bouquier Law, but he defended amalgamated rural school districts lest "the schools become communal rather than national, which is less favorable to national unity." Nonetheless the law provided for exceptions to the population threshold "in localities where the population is too dispersed . . . upon the documented request of the district administration and a decree of the national legislature."[12]

The Executive Commission on Public Instruction (a division of the former Interior Ministry) warned the districts "neither to make the schools too scarce nor to multiply them excessively." Since it was promoting a substantial curriculum, the government reasonably wanted schools large enough "so that the number of students can contribute to forming and maintaining a useful emulation." By the same token the state did not wish to pay substantial annual salaries in communes so small that *instituteurs* would not be effectively occupied. The Convention had additional reason to require substantial *arrondissements* for its primary schools, since it faced a likely shortage of teachers. On 25 nivôse III (January 14, 1795), it therefore raised the recommended population threshold to one school per fifteen hundred inhabitants.[13] Some districts accordingly readjusted the *arrondissements* they had drawn for rural schools and reduced the number of schools in their towns. The district of Château-Thierry (Aisne) cut the number of prescribed schools from fifty-three to thirty-two; Cerilly (Allier) from thirty-two to eighteen; Sens (Yonne) from forty-seven to thirty-six; Dijon

(Côte d'Or) from seventy to fifty-six.[14] This of course made it even harder for small communes to demand their own schools instead of being amalgamated into an *arrondissement* of two to four villages.

Nonetheless such demands came forth frequently. Small rural communes petitioned the districts to be treated as exceptions to the threshold of 1,000 or 1,500. On their own authority certain districts granted such requests: Soissons authorized a school for a village with 595 inhabitants, L'Ure granted a public school to a commune of 490, and Chaumont approved schools for communes of 498 and 527.[15] With its widely dispersed patterns of settlement, the district of Provins (Seine-et-Marne) proved exceptionally accommodating. It admitted that out of forty-five rural *arrondissements*, twenty-four did not conform strictly to the law's guideline, "so as to make these establishments truly useful by placing the students in greater proximity to the teachers." In Saint Girons (Ariège) the district authorized fifteen schools in villages with populations below 1,000, "considering that the inhabitants of places that cannot in any way be amalgamated with others should not be deprived of education."[16] Of course certain district directorates preferred the virtues of amalgamated schools and rejected such exceptions, while others simply threw up their hands over the "particularism" and narrow "self-interest" of communes that insisted on being the seat of the amalgamated *arrondissement* or on having their own school.[17]

If the rural communes were putting self-interest first, however, it was an enlightened self-interest of a most compelling kind. The dispersal of the rural population and the small size of numerous communes dragged against national uniformity and administrative efficiency in many ways, but they were especially poignant in the matter of schooling. "The amalgamation of communes that are too far from the *arrondissement*'s school provokes a general dissatisfaction in the rural communes," explained the district of St. Quentin (Aisne). "What father would consent to expose his children to perishing of the cold on impassable roads?" The petitions by small communes for their own *écoles primaires* evoke a rural topography of isolated communities separated from each other by rugged terrain, mountains, ravines, marshes, unfordable rivers, torrential streams, or forbidding forests. Even when primitive *chemins vicinaux* connected rural communities, those roads usually became altogether impassable in the rain. A trip that may have been feasible for children in mild weather might become unacceptable during winter—the optimum season for schooling in communities where children worked in the fields during the summer.[18]

In petitions to the Convention, like the "Protest by the inhabitants of the commune of Oriemont (Seine-et-Oise)," rural citizens complained that the new law would benefit only larger communes with concentrated populations unless exceptions were granted. They estimated that in two thirds of France, three of four communes would have to be amalgamated, meaning in effect "that of every three communes there will only be one that can benefit from the nation's beneficence." Boutigny (Seine-et-Marne), for one, with a population of only 741 but with 130 children said to be of school age, was to be amalgamated with St.

Fiacre, a considerable distance away. Its inhabitants therefore protested that the commune's children "will be deprived of the education that the nation has promised to everyone, except insofar as the parents are forced to pay for a private teacher." Citizens in small villages like Corcelle (Ain) or Etaulle (Charente Inférieure) now felt entitled to "a teacher salaried by the Republic." As the national agent in Montmédy (Meuse) observed, the inhabitants of excluded communes "already know full well that they all contribute to the salaries of these teachers by paying their taxes."[19]

Trading the flexibility of the Bouquier Law (payment by the state per student) for a fixed salary designed to make the teachers more independent and secure, Lakanal hoped precisely to favor rural communities by assuring attractive remuneration for their teachers. The resultant formula was clearly too rigid and underestimated the legitimate resistance to amalgamated rural schools. Judging from the lobbying by communes and the sympathetic reaction of many district officials, however, some of the demand for free schooling in small rural communes could be met by multiple exemptions or fine-tuning of the law. Meanwhile, villagers proposed ad hoc arrangements to draw on the "national beneficence" in ways that suited their needs. In St. Pol (Pas de Calais), for example, officials proposed that a district be permitted to collect the full sum due it under the law on the basis of total population, with freedom to distribute it to as many teachers as it wished to employ—in proportion to the population of each commune and the number of pupils in its school, on a sliding pay scale of 600 to 1200 livres.[20]

The most common proposal for circumventing the population threshold of the Lakanal Law turned on the schoolmistresses. The Convention had accepted the conventional wisdom about separating the sexes in classrooms: each primary school was to have two sections; alongside the *instituteur* for boys, each school was to have an *institutrice* for girls. In its way this entailed a remarkable vision for separate but essentially equal schooling, which would diverge only toward the end when girls were to be taught domestic skills such as knitting and sewing. It would also have opened a substantial employment opportunity for women. Unfortunately, the paucity of candidates for these positions and the deficient qualifications of those who did present themselves quickly became evident. Even ignoring the nominal requirements and accepting female candidates with the most rudimentary skills and illegible handwriting, the vast majority of *juris* evaluating them still expressed utter frustration. Of the eleven *institutrices* who applied, reported the *juri* in Dijon, only one was really qualified, while "the other ten need instruction themselves." With only rare exceptions, districts had little choice but to certify three, four, or five times as many men as women.[21] In the long term, perhaps, the commitment to republican *institutrices* might have borne fruit as a new generation of young women acquired basic skills, had their own children, and then sought jobs. For the present, however, the Lakanal Law was headed for failure in providing separate but equal schooling for girls.

This setback, however, could be turned to advantage. The money already pledged by the state for the salary of so many nonexistent *institutrices* could be diverted to hire additional *instituteurs* for smaller rural communes—provided that the Convention reconsidered its stand on single-sex education. The administrators of the district of Chartres (Eure-et-Loire) thus hoped to establish the seventy public schools they wanted instead of the prescribed forty "by using the funds earmarked for the positions of *institutrices* that remain vacant, since very few candidates have presented themselves."[22] Five deputies sent on a mission by the Convention to monitor implementation of the Lakanal Law encountered similar views. Jard-Panvillier reported that *juris* and district directorates had urged him "to replace the [nonexistent] *institutrices* by the same number of *instituteurs* who, in such cases, would teach children of both sexes . . . thereby multiplying the number of teachers without increasing the cost to the public treasury." His colleague Bailleul sympathized with requests to divide rural schools by age rather than sex. Women could teach all the younger children, making it easier to find apt *institutrices* who need only know how to read, and incidentally assuring that girls received a better education later on in company with the boys. These deputies could not authorize such practices in direct contravention of the law, but the Convention might still have revised the law as such demands for flexibility mounted.[23]

THE SUPPLY OF TEACHERS

With or without such changes, however, the demand for schools under the Lakanal Law far exceeded the supply of qualified *instituteurs*. While more plentiful than female applicants, male candidates were still in short supply in most districts, and their qualifications were woefully inadequate. In theory, *instituteurs* would be teaching penmanship, spelling, grammar, and arithmetic as well as a smattering of history, geography, science, and republican morality—evidently a very tall order for the schoolmasters of the Old Regime who formed the bulk of the present pool. Among the forty candidates examined in Adour (Hautes Pyrénées) the *juri* could not find "a single one who mustered even half the knowledge required by this law." *Juris* in Montflanquin (Meuse) and l'Aigle (Orne) expressed the same chagrin at certifying teachers "who can scarcely read correctly and know neither spelling nor grammar. Naming them as *instituteurs*, it seems to us, will not fulfill the aim of the law and will burden the government with paying unmerited salaries." The meticulous *juri* of Dijon's district concluded that not a single candidate in the *concours* for rural schools had the requisite general qualifications, while only eleven out of forty-five could read and write reasonably well.[24] The *juris* got around their dilemma by certifying deficient candidates "provisionally," though usually in the belief that most were "too elderly to hope for any improvement." Younger teachers, whose zeal exceeded their knowledge, might be redeemable if they received some training. But even if the earnest members of these *juris*—*pères de famille* themselves—could not enforce the law's standards of ability, they could at least uphold moral standards by weeding out notorious drunkards and miscreants.[25]

A few officials referred to the new Normal School in Paris as a resource holding out some hope for the future, but that experiment was about to collapse. In November 1794 the Convention had established the *Ecole Normale* in the capital to provide a crash course in "the art of teaching various fields of human knowledge" for candidates nominated by each district in the Republic. After their course the men were supposed to return home and establish training institutes of their own to produce a new generation of local *instituteurs*. The Executive Commission on Public Instruction staffed the *Ecole Normale* with eminent scholars such as the mathematician Lagrange, the chemist Berthollet, the historian Volney, and the literary critic La Harpe. Unfortunately their lectures were far above the heads of their students and had nothing to do with the art of primary education. After a few months the Convention took note of the ensuing disarray and in May 1795 abruptly shut down the school and sent its twelve hundred student-teachers back home.[26] No training schools were subsequently established in the provinces, though some of these men did become *instituteurs* themselves. Months later they were still waiting in vain for the follow-up materials they had been promised.[27] Meanwhile military mobilization had claimed an entire cohort of young men for the army, depriving civil society of potential new recruits for teaching. *Juris* and local officials therefore petitioned for special dispensations to appoint soldiers from their localities. The *juri* of Rodez (Aveyron), which faced a drought of apt candidates, thus requested indulgence for three of its volunteers who had more learning than stamina, and who would therefore "serve the Republic more effectively in the career of public school teaching than in the armies." P. L. Ginguené, head of the Executive Commission on Public Instruction, estimated that *juris d'instruction* were seeking discharges for about six hundred soldiers with "very weak physical conditions"—a minuscule number from the perspective of the war effort. But military administrators apparently could summon neither the will nor the means to facilitate this modest assistance.[28]

Altogether, local officials implementing the Lakanal Law faced a host of problems: pressure for the establishment of additional schools in small rural communes; practical obstacles to separating boys and girls in the classroom because of the dearth of *institutrices*; a shortage of male teachers and the poor qualifications of most candidates; competition with the army for the services of younger men; and bitter local controversies over the disposition of nationalized rectories that were supposed to be made available to the Republic's teachers. To some degree these problems were offset by the dedication and zeal of many local officials; by the occasional success of a district in establishing a substantial complement of schools; and by the eagerness of communes to link themselves to an incipient system of *instruction publique*. There were grounds for disappointment and frustration, for lower expectations, but not for despair.

The Lakanal Law ultimately foundered because of the unanticipated economic disaster that befell France in 1795, after the Thermidorians abandoned price controls and unleashed a wave of hyperinflation. The collapse of the *assignat*'s value hit hardest at rentiers, urban workers, and public employees dependent entirely on paper money. Poor harvests and harsh weather that year compounded the agony. In such circumstances, the great strong point of the Lakanal Law, the fixed salary of twelve hundred livres for *instituteurs publics*, became derisory. Indeed, it turned into a liability, since it was to be the teachers' sole form of remuneration.

The precipitous devaluation of this salary soon dominated the reports reaching the Convention and the Executive Commission. The *juri* of Bergues (Nord) bewailed "the excessive price of foodstuffs which makes a salary that in ordinary times would call forth a favorable response now seem mediocre." Worse yet, teachers already appointed were resigning. In Ambert (Puy-de-Dôme) the *juri* warned the Convention that "the teachers—not finding in the salary accorded to them by the law an income sufficient to procure even half the grain necessary for their consumption—are abandoning their schools to give themselves over to any other occupation. Every day we receive new resignations." Even in districts like Brive (Corrèze) that had certified a large roster of teachers, the once-attractive salary now yielded less than half a year's subsistence by the spring of 1795, and many *instituteurs* handed in their resignations. The situation deteriorated with each passing week. By the beginning of September 1795 the Executive Commission reported to the Convention that "a general cry has gone up over the frightful distress of the teachers. Lacking even the absolute necessities, most are languishing in the horrors of deprivation."[29] The *instituteurs* most likely to endure were those who had already taken possession of former rectories not previously sold off as *biens nationaux*, which the Lakanal Law had pledged to them, an especially useful perquisite if the rectory had a vegetable garden. *Instituteurs* might also persevere in the hope that arrears in their salaries would eventually be paid in hard money.[30] Those who faced starvation while they waited, however, had no choice but to abandon their positions, either to carry on as private teachers paid in kind by parents or to find other work.

In the end even the presumptive allies of *instruction publique* turned against the Lakanal Law. Ginguené, head of the Executive Commission on Public Instruction, concluded that the plan was simply too ambitious. *Instituteurs* capable of teaching the prescribed curriculum were in extremely short supply, and those who did come forward found that the hyperinflation "rendered their salary virtually nil." The time had come to beat a strategic retreat in primary education, he argued, while concentrating the state's resources on the Republic's new secondary schools, the *écoles centrales*. The Commission recommended that the Republic abandon the idea of paying salaries to teachers, "leaving them the right to draw a salary from the parents who have the means of paying for their children's education—a tuition which will always be very low in the countryside."[31]

In its last days, purged by now of most outspoken Montagnards and in a sour mood of austerity and social conservatism, the Convention adopted this prescription for neglect: Under the Daunou Law of October 1795, only the cantonal seats were obliged to maintain an *école primaire*, and *instituteurs publics* would receive only a small indemnity for lodging but no public salary. In this limited number of public schools the prescribed curriculum would be minimal as well— reading, writing, arithmetic, and "the elements of republican morality." Beyond that the new Constitution of the Year III (1795) guaranteed the right of citizens to form private educational establishments.[32]

The Daunou Law, which effectively lasted through the Napoleonic era, abandoned the principle of universal, free primary education. It also left the *instituteurs publics* on their own (save for free lodging or a small indemnity), with no salary from the state and an essentially empty title. As some *instituteurs* in Moissac (Lot) would later complain, not only were they reduced to indigence, but "they enjoy no prerogative whatsoever in society, no dignity, no distinctions. They live amid contempt."[33] Yet if the logic of Daunou and Ginguené was simply to return primary education to the traditional local marketplace, neither the Thermidorian Convention nor the Directory was actually prepared to go quite that far. Though emptying it of real content, the Daunou Law left standing a kind of shell—a thin network of ostensibly state-sponsored schools. For the moment, these schools required tuition payments, and their teachers did not draw public salaries. For the time being, too, the libertarian spirit of the Daunou Law left private schools entirely free from any kind of surveillance or regulation— free to rival and overwhelm these public schools on the issue of religious instruction.[34] But in the hearts of many republicans, free public schools remained an integral feature of a proper civic order. The inordinate expectations invested in that ideal had receded, but the issue was far from settled and would surface again in 1798. The concept of *instruction publique* remained as a legacy of revolutionary thought and in particular of the Lakanal Law—a commitment by the state to make schooling normative and a kind of public service; to spread schooling as widely as possible; to certify teachers in some fashion; and, with a new generation of teachers, to raise the quality of schooling.

Nor was *instruction publique* necessarily secular. While the prescribed content of Lakanal's public schools was indeed meant to be secular, secularism was not crucial to the plan. Under intense community pressure, many *instituteurs publics* willingly or reluctantly capitulated to the parents' "imperious demands for instruction in religious doctrines and practices," even as they taught their pupils "elements of republican morality" and collected their salaries from the Republic in 1795. As Bailleul, a deputy on mission to implement the Lakanal Law, conceded, private teachers were thriving because they "give children the traditional education and inculcate religious principles. . . . Public school teachers fear seeing their classrooms deserted if they are deprived of the same option." His colleague Dupuis similarly authorized *instituteurs publics* to use traditional Catholic materials in their classrooms, for if he barred them, "the parents will take fright and be furnished with a specious pretext for decrying republican education."[35]

Under future regimes public schools might exclude or enthrone religious instruction; they might promote republicanism, loyalty to the emperor, or fealty to the restored Bourbons. Either way, primary schooling became normative for the nation in 1794, and the French state never renounced for very long the mission of prodding local communities into accepting that norm. At the least, the Revolution had produced a permanent change of perspective among the governing elites of most political persuasions. Officials in every successive regime denounced the deficiencies of community-driven, tuition-supported traditional popular education. This view was obviously no by-product of republican anti-clericalism. The opinions of Napoleonic prefects and Catholic University rectors under the Restoration rivaled the scathing comments of the Directory's Voltairian departmental commissioners. Officials continued to deplore the quality and haphazardness of traditional primary schooling across the whole period after 1789, until the criticism reached a crescendo in Guizot's inquest of 1832.

Naturally there were exceptions. *Idéologues* such as Ginguené, Daunou, and Destutt de Tracy seemed content to let the local demand for schooling find its own level. And certain legislative advocates of religious liberty during the Convention and Directory (whether from liberal principles or conservative politics) insisted on the right of parents to seek traditional schooling for their children, whatever its character. The most significant and puzzling exception was, of course, Napoléon Bonaparte, for whom popular education held no priority at all. For the most part, however, responsible officials of each successive regime deplored the state of popular education and clung to some notion of *instruction publique* as a potential antidote.[36]

Their critique of traditional schooling focused on the apparent complacency of local communities toward barely literate, part-time schoolmasters. Incompetent teachers and indifferent or undemanding parents—whether motivated by penury, "avarice," or the imperatives of the family economy—formed an intolerable circle of mediocrity. Responsible contemporaries deplored the very vagaries of the social demand factor that Furet and Ozouf portray as the crucial variable. Since the state could not directly influence the demand side, so to speak, its effort focused on the supply side—exactly as it did in Prussia in the same period, without the complications of revolutionary ideology or anti-clericalism.[37] The state concerned itself with promoting schools; housing schoolmasters; and bolstering the pay, status, and qualifications of teachers—all of which might accelerate the spread of education and ultimately improve its quality. After the failure of the Lakanal Law, the governing elites showed a healthy respect for the inertia and traditionalism of social demand. But armed with the elastic notion of *instruction publique*, they did not permanently surrender before them.

NOTES

1. François Furet and Jacques Ozouf, *Lire et Ecrire: l'alphabétisation des français de Calvin à Jules Ferry* (Paris, 1977), especially 1: 39–42, 54–58, 80–81, 97, 109–15.
2. Most recently by Dominique Julia, *Les Trois couleurs du tableau noir: La Rév-*

olution (Paris, 1981), and Branislaw Baczko, *Une Education pour la démocratie: textes et projets de l'époque révolutionnaire* (Paris, 1982).

3. On the *cahiers*, see Maurice Gontard, *L'Enseignement primaire en France de la Révolution à la loi Guizot 1789–1833* (Paris, 1959), 66–77. Gontard's volume is extremely useful but suffers from a lack of modulation and interpretive insight. On the *petites écoles* of the Old Regime, see R. Chartier, M.-M. Compère, and D. Julia, *L'Education en France du XVIe au XVIIIe siècle* (Paris, 1976).

4. On these disparities, see Furet and Ozouf, *Lire et Ecrire*, and Dominique Julia et al., *Atlas de la Révolution française*, vol. 2: *L'Enseignement 1760–1815* (Paris, 1987), chap. 1.

5. For the succession of projects and laws as well as excerpts from the debates, see the monumental work by James Guillaume, *Procès-verbaux du Comité d'Instruction Publique de la Convention Nationale* (Paris, 1891–1907). For an excellent overview of all aspects of education, see Robert R. Palmer, *The Improvement of Humanity: Education and the French Revolution* (Princeton, N.J.: 1985).

6. See, for example, Baczko, *Une Education pour la démocratie*, 33–37, 345–87; Julia, *Les Trois couleurs*, 92–111; Palmer, *Improvement of Humanity*, 138–46; and J. R. Vignery, *The French Revolution and the Schools: The Educational Policies of the Mountain, 1792–94* (Madison, Wis.: 1965).

7. See Gontard, *L'Enseignement primaire*, 100–06, 113–22; Baczko, *Une Education pour la démocratie*, 46–49, 415–20; and Palmer, *Improvement of Humanity*, 179–83.

8. A.N. BB^{30} [Bureau de la surveillance de l'exécution des lois]: "Lois démocratiques" and A.N. F^{17} 1331B: "Instruction rédigée au nom du Comité d'Instruction Publique" [hereafter C.I.P.] 26 pluviôse an II.

9. Guillaume, *Procès-verbaux*, 5: 142–51, 177–85, 223–38.

10. Cf. Julia, *Les Trois couleurs*, chap. 6.

11. Guillaume, *Procès-verbaux*, 5: 232–33; Baczko, *Une Education pour la démocratie*, 427–37.

12. Guillaume, *Procès-verbaux*, 5: 177–85, 223–38, 244–46.

13. A.N. F17 1347 [Exécution de la loi du 27 brumaire III]: dossiers 1 & 2. A.N. F17 1344/35 [Papiers de Lakanal]: District de Castelsarrasin, 6 ventôse III.

14. A.N. F17 1344/35: District de Montmarsan to Lakanal, 19 prairial III; A.N. F17 1347, d.1 & 2; A.N. F17 10138: Juri d'instruction [hereafter j.i.] de Dijon, 10 ventôse III.

15. See A.N. F17 1347: Demandes d'écoles primaires dans les communes dont la population ne s'élève pas à 1000 habitans. Also F17 1344/35: Districts de Montmarsan and Cusset, prairial III; F17 1347, d.2: District de Narbonne, 21 pluviôse III; District de Chartres, 4 nivôse III.

16. A.N. F17 1344/35: District de Provins to Lakanal, 13 floréal III; District d'Albi to Lakanal, 19 prairial III; P. V. District de Saint-Girons, 6 nivôse III; P. V. District de Quillan (Aude), 4 pluviôse III; G. Clause, "L'Enseignement à Reims pendant la Révolution (1789–1800)," *Actes du 95ème Congrès national des sociétés savantes*, vol. 1: *Histoire de l'enseignement de 1610 à nos jours* (Paris, 1974), 682.

17. A.N. F17 1347, d.3: Districts de Sens, la Neste, Verneuil, Poitiers; d.2: District de Sarlat [ventôse III]; F17 1344/35: District de Montargis, circular, 27 ventôse III.

18. A.N. F17 1347, d.4: District de St. Quentin, Tableau, 3 prairial III; Agent national de Ramberviller, pluviôse III, j.i. de Tarbes, 18 prairial III.

19. A.N. F17 1347, d.4: Réclamation faite par les habitans d'Oriemont, 30 frimaire

III; La Société populaire d'Etaulle (Charente Inférieure), 30 frimaire III; La Municipalité de Corcelle, ventôse III; La Commune de Gargilesse (Indre), nivose III; Les habitans de Boutigny, n.d.; Les Citoyens de huit communes de campagne situées dans les Landes, floréal III; L'Agent national de Montmédy, 26 nivôse III.

20. A.N. F17 1347, d.1: approx. twenty petitions from the Eastern departments; also Albert, Envoyé par la Convention dans l'Aube et la Marne to C.I.P., 3 prairial III, and Georges Sangier, *Le District de Saint-Pol de Thermidor à Brumaire* (Lille, 1946), 783–85.

21. A.N. F17 10138: j.i. de Dijon to C.I.P. [ventôse III]. This complaint was virtually universal. Exceptional districts with substantial complements of *institutrices* included Brive and Marseille.

22. A.N. F17 1353: District de Sens to C.I.P., 1 floréal III; A.N. F17 1347: District de Chartres, 1 ventôse III; District de St. Pol, 5 floréal III; District d'Epinal, 23 nivôse III.

23. A.N. F17 1350: Bailleul from Valognes, 25 floréal III; Jard-Painvillier from Beauvais, 23 floréal III. Cf. j.i. d'Angoulême to Lakanal, 15 prairial III (F17 1344/35).

24. A.N. F17 10138: j.i. Bordeaux, Dijon, l'Aigle, Blois; A.N. F17 1344/35: j.i. Ardour, Cerilly; district of Montflanquin.

25. See Jean Vassort, "L'Enseignement primaire en Vendômois à l'époque révolutionnaire," *Revue d'histoire moderne et contemporaine* 25 (October 1978), 639–40.

26. See Baczko, *Une Education pour la démocratie*, 471–83; Julia, *Les Trois couleurs*, 153–71; Palmer, *Improvement of Humanity*, 209–20.

27. Letters from several former students of the Ecole Normale in A.N. F17 1331A, vendémiaire IV and F17 1353.

28. A.N. F17 1353: Rapport par le Commission Exécutif d'Instruction Publique [hereafter Comm. Exec.I.P.], germinal III; F17 1347, d.1: j.i. de Rodez to C.I.P., 25 ventôse III.

29. A.N. F17 10138: j.i. de Bergues to C.I.P., 16 ventôse III; j.i. d'Ambert to C.I.P., 11 prairial III; F17 1344/35: P.V. District de Brive, 10 floréal III. See also a mass of petitions from *instituteurs* in A.N. F17 1353 including at least two "élèves de l'Ecole normale." A.N. F17 1149: Comm. Exec.I.P. Rapport, 3 vendémiaire IV.

30. Correspondence about the rectories and gardens in A.N. F17 1352. *Instituteurs* were still claiming arrearages under the Lakanal Law as late as September 1797, usually in vain.

31. A.N. F17 1149: Comm. Exec.I.P. "Observations sur les Ecoles primaires," 4 vendémiaire IV.

32. Guillaume, *Procès-verbaux*, 6: 336–37, 580, 793–94, 869–70; Gontard, *L'Enseignement primaire*, 151–55; Baczko, *Une Education pour la démocratie*, 499–523.

33. A.N. F17 10138: Les instituteurs de Moissac (Lot) to Conseil des 500, 11 floréal V.

34. The important article by E. Kennedy & M.-L. Netter, "Les Ecoles primaires sous le Directoire," *Annales historiques de la Révolution française*, no. 243 (January 1981), suggests how this competition looked in 1797–1798.

35. A.N. F17 1350: Bailleul from Valognes, 25 floréal III; Jard-Painvillier from Beauvais, 23 floréal III; Dupuis from Troyes, 6 floréal and from Besançon, 23 floréal III. See also A.N. F17 1344/35: District de Sancerre to Lakanal, floréal III; District de Montargis to Lakanal, 7 prairial III.

36. See the chapter "Primary Education: Retreat and Consolidation," in my *The New Regime: Transformations of the French Civic Order 1789–1820s* (New York, 1994).

37. See Anthony LaVopa, *Prussian School Teachers: Profession and Office, 1763–1848* (Chapel Hill, N.C., 1980), chaps. 1–3.

11

CITIZENSHIP AND MILITARY SERVICE

Alan Forrest

Throughout the revolutionary decade the concept of citizenship was continually being discussed and its implications extended. This is most clearly demonstrated in the texts of the various constitutions of the 1790s that sought to add flesh to the Declaration of the Rights of Man and define the duties that were implicit in the enjoyment of liberties. In returning to the Rights of Man, the politicians were doing more than just staking their claim to moral legitimacy. They were also, as Marcel Gauchet has observed, admitting that they found it well nigh impossible to agree on any simple and comprehensible definition of the proper relationship between the individual and the collectivity. With the passage of time they would move further and further from the spirit of Sieyès' wording. Whereas the declaration was an integral part of the Revolution's first constitution, that of 1791, it was supplanted by a different formula in the republican Constitution of 1793, and in the more conservative document of the Year III (1794–1795), rights were explicitly balanced by duties: the rights of man were extended to become "*les droits et les devoirs de l'homme et du citoyen.*"[1] In part these changes reflect phases in the politics of the Revolution, but more importantly, they are evidence of a regime coming to terms with the reality of government. It had to extract tax revenues, police crime, control inflation, feed the towns, put down outbreaks of counterrevolution. More generally, it had to persuade its population to undertake civic tasks, among them tasks that many found distasteful. There is little doubt that for many Frenchman the performance of any form of personal military service figured high among the duties that they least relished. If that was the meaning of citizenship, there were many among them who had to be persuaded of its benefits.

Of course, the Declaration of the Rights of Man was not intended to form a blueprint for government. In the late 1780s Sieyès had been principally concerned with freeing Frenchmen from the various impositions placed on their liberty by the monarchy. The declaration was, in this sense, a joyous and resounding declaration of new freedoms, an insistence that the supposed tyranny of the Ancien Régime must be ended. It granted rights but imposed no obligations on the individual; rather it was the collectivity that was obliged to provide a framework in which the individual could enjoy his inalienable rights. The fact that in practice some might have to fight and die to defend these freedoms was passed over in silence. The only mention of obligation concerned money payments. *"Pour l'entretien de la force publique et pour les dépenses d'administration,"* stated clause 13, *"une contribution commune est indispensable."* But again nothing was said to indicate that some might have to contribute more than others. *"Elle doit être également répartie entre tous les citoyens, en raison de leurs facultés."*[2]

Very soon general expressions of liberal intent had to give way to something more concrete. The Declaration of the Rights of Man might be placed symbolically at the head of the 1791 constitution, but it could do no more than guide the constitution-makers. The state must also know what it can expect of its citizens, especially in such matters as its own defense. Yet the constitution said little about the extent of this obligation. It was more concerned with controlling the military, especially the officer class. Thus the fourth section of the constitution, subtitled "De la force publique," deals essentially with matters of organization rather than obligation. The force was to be organized for internal security as well as for defense against an external enemy. It was to be composed of an army and a navy; of a special force for the maintenance of order inside France; and, in a subsidiary capacity, *"des citoyens actifs, et de leurs enfants en état de porter les armes, inscrits sur le rôle de la garde nationale."*[3] The rest of the section is devoted not to the recruitment of this force but to questions of authority and internal discipline. The deputies were concerned with ensuring that the army remained loyal to the government, acting only in accordance with explicit orders. Indeed, they went to some pains to limit the freedoms that soldiers enjoyed as citizens, lest these freedoms become a threat to the civilian population. The army and navy were to be subject to their own laws and to military discipline. Above all, as clause 12 made clear, *"la force publique et essentiellement obéissante; nul corps armé ne peut délibérer."*[4]

But what should be the civil status of soldiers? Officers, of course, were already a privileged group in society, a noble elite cut off by breeding and education from the men they led. But what of the men? What rights of citizenship should they enjoy? The problem was complicated in the early stages of the Revolution by the division of France's citizens into *actifs* and *passifs*: only those who paid the equivalent of three days' wages in tax were to enjoy full political rights. This was a deliberate calculation. In Sieyès' words, *"ceux-là seuls qui contribuent à l'etablissement public, sont comme les vrais actionnaires de la grande entreprise sociale. Eux seuls sont les véritables citoyens actifs, les véritables membres de l'association."*[5] Yet in the case of the military this was an uneasy distinction. It was difficult to deny that men who might be called upon to die for the freedoms of others were *"actionnaires"* in the *"entreprise"* of the nation. Should not their patriotism or their sacrifice be rewarded by the people they were defending? Not everyone agreed. The image of the army during the last years of the Ancien Régime was generally unflattering: soldiering had too often been a career of last resort, the only available outlet for the younger sons of poor peasant families or the destination of troublesome boys at odds with their parents or with the law. Voltaire's image of *"un million d'assassins en-régimentés courant d'un bout à l'autre de l'Europe,"* marauding, pillaging, raping, and murdering, may have been an insensitive caricature of an eighteenth-century army, but it commanded wide credence among the propertied in society.[6] Could such people seriously aspire to the privileges of *actifs*?

It was a problem of which the revolutionaries were well aware. They were conscious of the illogicality of defending a free people with an Ancien Régime army, an army denied any voice in the affairs of the nation. The credibility of their revolution seemed tainted by an institution that was built on the same assumptions as the armies of tyrants. They sensed the need for an army composed of free men, an army of citizens. But they were also afraid of the military, afraid of royalism and treason by the officers, of disorder and mutiny by the men. It was the loyalty of the officers that exercised them most. Though the great exodus of army officers would not take place until the king's flight to Varennes, there was a steady trickle of nobles into emigration during 1789 and 1790. By the end of 1791 the situation would become desperate: as many as 60 percent of the officers would either resign or emigrate, appalled by the treatment reserved for Louis and angered by the oath of loyalty the Assembly tried to impose upon them. Some units, as Sam Scott has shown, lost nearly all their officers in the rather undignified rush toward the frontiers.[7]

But the perceived threat to stability did not come wholly from the officers. Despite the libertarian rhetoric that flooded France in 1789, conditions in the regiments changed little from those during the Ancien Régime. Discipline remained harsh and demeaning. Besides, the army was being increasingly deployed inside France to enforce measures of the police, and soldiers came face to face with the aspirations of civilians and a language of citizenship that had not penetrated their barracks. At the Bastille many of them showed their sympathies with the crowd, and the ambivalence of their position became even more marked during the months that followed. Mutinies were savagely put down by officers fearful for their own authority, and they did so with the full approval of the Assembly. Yet the deputies could not pretend that the problem would go away. During 1790 about one-third of the royal army experienced some form of insubordination, with over 40 percent of the units involved receiving overt support from the general public. At Nancy in August, the most serious mutiny of the period involved foreign mercenaries as well as French troops.[8] Increasingly it was the government's own authority that was at issue.

Fear of the military led ministers to make concessions, to grant the troops more rights in law. But as yet these concessions fell short of full political rights; they did not conceive of soldiers expressing their own views on the matters of the day. What they did accept, from 1791, was that the nature of the individual soldier's engagement was changed: he no longer took an oath of fealty to an individual, the king; instead, his contract was with the collectivity, the state. Soldiers fought as Frenchmen in the name of France. Increasingly, too, the Assembly brought their civil status into line with that of their civilian counterparts. By the terms of the law of February 18, 1790, soldiers were allowed, if they qualified through their tax payments, to exercise the rights of active citizens for, the assembly argued, despite the long absences their job entailed, their homes were on French soil. They should therefore enjoy the same voting rights as other active citizens, provided that, at the time of the election, they were not serving on garrison duty in their own canton. There was even a respect in which soldiers were given a degree of privilege over their fellows, since the law prescribed that long and honorable service in the army could act as a substitute for taxes. *"Tout militaire qui aura servi l'espace de seize ans sans interruption et sans reproche jouira de la plénitude des droits du citoyen actif et sera dispensé des conditions relatives à la propriété et à la contribution,"* it declared, on condition, once again, that the soldier was not on garrison duty in his own canton at the time of the election.[9]

The Jacobin Constitution of 1793 went still further in guaranteeing the status and honor of the individual soldier. It stressed equality, declaring that there should be no commander-in-chief of the French forces and that any rank or position of subordination a man might occupy during his service had no relevance once he returned to civilian life. Service in the cause of the Revolution, in other words, was seen to be compatible with full citizenship, with equality before the law. Again, the document laid emphasis on the rights of the individual citizen and sought to reassure him that these rights would be respected even during his period in uniform. But what had seemed adequate in 1791, when the country was still at peace, no longer sufficed in times of war. So the 1793 constitution also turned to the obligations that fell upon citizens when their country was in danger. These were treated in the broadest of brushstrokes, in two clauses that explained that the people had rights, too, rights that might take precedence over those of the individual. *"La force générale de la République,"* it stated rather vaguely, *"est composée du peuple entier"* (clause 107). Less opaque, and rather more menacing, was clause 109: *"Tous les Français sont soldats,"* it declared; *"ils sont tous exercés au maniement des armes."*[10]

This clause was never interpreted literally, of course. The armies would never have been able to cope with the influx of raw recruits, and the country would have starved. But the idea that citizenship involved duties, and specifically the duty to defend the community in war, was unambiguous. What is more, it was an idea that was now firmly engrained in constitutional law. In the last great revolutionary constitution, that of Year III (1794–1795), military service was placed among the principal duties incumbent on French citizens, and the extent of their obligation was spelled out. Once again all Frenchmen had military duties to absolve; and to clarify what this might mean, it drew a clear distinction between *"la garde nationale en activité"* and *la garde nationale sédentaire."* It was in the latter, effectively a reserve from which men might be called up in an emergency, that service was to be universal. *"La garde nationale sédentaire,"* declared the constitution, *"est composée de tous les citoyens et fils de citoyens en état de porter les armes."* And, in case that still concealed ambiguities, it went on to argue that service was a sine qua non of citizenship. *"Aucun Français ne peut exercer les droits de citoyen s' il n' est inscrit au rôle de la garde nationale sédentaire."* Those who would become active soldiers would, of course, be selected from this pool, though on the method of that selection the constitution was less informative. *"L'armée se forme par enrôlements volontaires et, en cas de besoin, par le mode que la loi détermine."*[11] As in 1793 there were numerous clauses defending the rights of the men who were incorporated, insisting, for instance, that the overall command could not be entrusted to any single man. But the balance of rights and obligations had changed. The emphasis was now on the duties of the citizen, on the military obligations of the individual toward the revolutionary state.

The explanation lies partly with the army itself. By 1795 many of the abuses that had damaged the image of soldiering and the self-esteem of the troops in the early months of the Revolution had been removed. Officers were no longer distant figures from another social world, men who were encountered only when discipline was to be imposed and punishments inflicted. Increasingly they were men like themselves, corporals and sergeants who had been promoted to officer rank as a result of their military experience and tactical skills. They were men to be admired and emulated, men who spoke the same language as their troops. Soldiers had rights by law, and if there was a special military code, there were also military tribunals where their cases could be heard. Under the Jacobin Republic they had other sorts of rights, too: the right to join clubs and popular societies, to read the political press, to attend the theater. In some Jacobin clubs near the northern and eastern frontiers, their contribution was so great that civilians were edged out and military caucuses risked taking over; at Wissembourg, indeed, the local club was rebaptised the *"société patriotique et militaire."*[12] In the many revolutionary festivals staged to celebrate victories or to sing the praises of republican virtue, the soldiers always had an honored part.[13] There were promises of pensions for their dependants and of land for returning servicemen. In many different ways their role in French society was being recognized, their value to the Revolution publicly acknowledged. Above all, the declaration of war and the dependence on the army for the continued survival of the state gave the troops a sense of their own importance and of the dignity their service bestowed.

Of course not all the problems of the Ancien Régime army were dispelled overnight. The deep-seated suspicion of officers so widespread among the revolutionaries took a long time to overcome; under Bouchotte's ministry, for instance, officers were systematically spied upon and could be held responsible for military reverses. Three commanders of the Armée du Nord, Luckner, Custine, and Houchard, were consigned to the guillotine.[14] The change to a mass army involved new tactics, and these took time to work. Problems of supply remained serious throughout the 1790s. Rampant inflation and recurrent economic crises meant that pay often came through late or was devalued to virtual worthlessness. And the inherent tension between an army of political militants and an army of military professionals was never completely resolved, though by the time of the Directory it was clear that revolutionary enthusiasm was no longer enough to win promotion or "gain military favor.[15] These were, in short, difficult years of adjustment, which saw a revolution in military discipline, in strategy, and in mentalities, but the prestige of the army was not itself at issue. Soldiers were continually reminded of their importance and told of the Republic's gratitude. They were encouraged to believe that they were fighting a political as well as a military campaign. All the armies, from the beginning of the Convention to its end, were accompanied by deputies on mission whose job it was to ensure that government policy was loyally carried out (it is instructive that military missions were continued even after *floréal* Year II (April–May 1794), when the others were officially abandoned).[16] And they were subjected, particularly in the Jacobin period, to an unremitting campaign of political education which helped to secure their loyalty and increase their self-esteem.[17] Winning helped, too. The fact that for much of the period they were part of a victorious army, surging across Europe, did much to boost their morale, even if, for many among them, their dearest wish was for a rapid peace settlement and for the opportunity to return home.

France's legislators could claim that by a series of root-and-branch reforms they had shaped their armies to the ideals of the Revolution and had made them compatible with the dictates of citizenship. They believed that this democratization had practical benefits, that an army of citizens would constitute a better fighting force. To the new officer class, Dubois-Crancé held out the prospect of political as well as military gains. "*Demeurez dignes de la cause sacrée que vous défendez,*" he urged them, "*et des nouveaux bienfaits que la Nation va répandre sur vous en effaçant jusqu'aux dernières traces les distinctions aristocratiques qui survivent encore à la Révolution dans l'armée de la Liberté et de l'Egalité.*"[18] As for the men, they were fighting for a cause in which they believed, and that alone would suffice to turn ordinary soldiers into republican heroes. Commenting on Dubois-Crancé's plans for the restructuring of the armies, Robespierre was clear that victory would be built upon liberty and self-belief. "*La destinée des hommes libres est de vaincre les esclaves, et leur devoir est de croire qu'ils ne peuvent être vaincus par leurs ennemis; ils sont invincibles en effet, dès qu'ils croient l'être.*" The proposed reorganization of the armies, the *amalgame* that sought to remove any lingering distinction between the line army and the new volunteer battalions, was a key measure in creating that mentality. "*Elever les âmes des soldats,*" declaimed Robespierre, "*leur offrir tous les avantages qui peuvent flatter des hommes armés pour une si grande cause; faire disparaître les vices d'une organisation qui est l'ouvrage du despotisme et de l'aristocratie militaire; . . . voilà, sans contredit, l'opération la plus analogue à la fois aux besoins actuels de l'Etat et aux maximes sur lesquelles reposent notre liberté.''*[19]

Ironically, creating an army fit for citizens proved to be a less intractable problem than finding citizens fit for the army. Many were reluctant to accept that their new status implied military obligations to the state, and the problem was compounded by the military tactics the Revolution was compelled to adopt. France fought with mass armies, far bigger than those that had served Louis XV, far bigger, too, than the armies of other European powers; and since the Revolution never succeeded in creating an outstanding cavalry, it had to depend all the more on the infantry.[20] Continued success depended on a steady flow of fresh recruits, yet successive levies showed how reluctant many communities were to give up their young men to the military—and with good reason. Every village in France had its quota of old men, poor and physically broken, who were an eloquent testimony to the realities of eighteenth-century soldiering. There were other problems, too, problems that were regional before they were national. France was still a very localized society, where people traveled little and saw defence in terms of their own community, their own village, their family *mas*. In many areas, like the Auvergne and the Pyrenees, mountainous terrain and fast-flowing rivers impeded the best efforts of the recruiting sergeant. Peasant farming was labor-intensive, and for young peasant boys an absence of some years in the regiments could effectively end their hopes of land, and hence of security. Rural policing had never been effective, and communities enjoyed a surprising degree of autarchy. Villagers further resented the intrusion of a state they still imperfectly understood, especially when its agents came to seize their sons and drag them off to the frontiers.[21]

These were longstanding problems, and they help explain the somewhat anxious emphasis placed on military obligation in constitutional law. It might be argued, indeed, that civic consciousness was something the Revolution never really succeeded in creating, despite all its rhetoric, continual nagging, and final resort to terror. Nor was the lack of *civisme* restricted to the young men of the community, to the recruits and their immediate peers; there is a weight of evidence to show that parents, farmers, employers, neighbors, mayors, priests, entire communities connived at acts of disobedience and made themselves accomplices to *insoumission*. They shared the doubts and fears of the young, offering them shelter and employment and protecting them when the village was visited by gendarmes or swept through by a *colonne mobile*. When the need arose they would even join the young men in armed attacks on the gendarmes or help to free those who had been taken prisoner.[22] As policing became more intrusive, so resistance could grow in violence, leaving policemen dead by the roadside and mocking the pretensions of the state. Such incidents demonstrate the extent to which the problem of military service was not really a problem of the army at all; it lay in civilian society, for it would always be easier to imbue young men with a sense of patriotism once they were in the regiments than to persuade village France of its obligations to the state. Throughout the decade from 1789 to Brumaire the government would receive many reminders of this unpalatable truth. The Revolution's new civic order, in Isser Woloch's felicitous phrase, would be a long time in the making.[23]

If citizenship implied obligation and an element of sacrifice, then military service might realistically be regarded as the litmus test. No aspect of revolutionary policy demanded such a fundamental uprooting of people from their homes or such a brutal break with community tradition. Young men were being torn from their families and from the cultures they knew and understood, often to fight for a cause that was not theirs. Village communities were being required to accede to the demand that they give up their sons, the young men who in so many cultural and traditional ways provided leadership for the whole community. Religious and linguistic ties were roughly overridden. Mayors were ordered to support the state against the instincts of their own communities. Son was being turned against father, neighbor against neighbor, as the gendarmerie attempted to enforce the law. Citizenship could become more than a little uncomfortable.

The response of local people was predictably patchy. In some areas, notably the great plains of the north and east where people were accustomed to defending their homes against invasion from across the Rhine, tradition ensured that men would always be found to serve the Republic, just as previously they had served the monarchy. But in much of rural France the appeals of the state evoked at best a lukewarm response. Neither the demand nor the language in which it was couched struck a chord in communities where soldiering had never been seen as an honorable or natural occupation for the young. It was not that they were cowardly, nor that they were expressing any political protest; rather it was a simple fact of local tradition. For many their rightful place was in the community, where they would be ready to defend the other villagers in the event of attack. In vain did the revolutionary authorities insist that the young place the common weal above individual interest, contrasting the virtuous service of "*la chose publique*" with the political crime that was "*égoïsme.*" The words were meaningless. The same Pyrennean hamlets that refused military service to the state proved perfectly willing to arm and equip *miquelets* or *chasseurs basques* to defend their people and their livestock against incursions from Spain, a duty whose utility they could understand.[24] In many of the more peripheral regions of France it was the insistence on the nation and on national defense that was contested. Military service was accepted when it was placed in a more localized context.

But the revolutionaries seldom made that concession. Ideologically they thought in national terms, and the aim of their military reforms was the creation of a truly national army to replace the line army they inherited. They rapidly abolished the provincially based regiments that had played such a prominent role during the eighteenth century, and they had no place for foreign mercenaries, for the regiments of Swiss and Irish, Germans and Swedes who had served the kings of France. The massacre of a Parisian crowd by Swiss guards on August 10, 1792, only confirmed what they already believed: that mercenaries were the troops of tyrants. But the corollary of that was not without its perils. If they could not rely on foreign manpower, they had to insist that the French people bear the human cost of war unaided. Inevitably that meant an increased burden, both emotionally and economically; and it was a burden that had to be imposed. Even so, the manner of its imposition is instructive. Personal service was not imposed on all alike, and the government's refusal to resort to a simple system of conscription caused much resentment. This leads us to ask: What was the extent of the military obligation the Revolution sought to extract from the individual citizen?[25]

In 1791 the call was for genuine volunteers. There was no question of obligation, since it was assumed that the young of France would rush to inscribe. And the initial response was encouraging: the armies found all the recruits they required, and in some areas men had to be turned away. The revolutionary authorities could with conviction claim that in the new volunteer regiments they were molding an army committed to the cause of liberty. But even at this stage caveats should perhaps have entered. If France produced a hundred thousand men for the new volunteer regiments, recruitment for the line fell by fifty thousand, and among the new volunteers were old-line soldiers who chose to abandon their former regiments. Again, there was no war to fight in 1791: those who offered themselves did not necessarily envisage active service; some saw the army as a more adventurous form of national guard duty; others were convinced that their commitment ended after a single campaigning season. And—perhaps the most damaging factor of all—the call for volunteers in 1791 would be only the first of many. Yet that call was made to all single men without family obligations and aged sixteen to forty-five. Could the pool be trawled in successive years? The question was soon answered by the relatively slow response to the levy of 1792, when it became apparent that a large percentage of those who were prepared to volunteer had already done so the previous year. On that first occasion voluntarism worked well, and its publicity value for the Revolution was enormous, but it could not provide a long-term solution to the problem of manpower, especially once war was declared and the armies started to suffer severe losses.

Increasingly, therefore, revolutionary recruitment law followed the constitution in making military service one of the obligations of citizenship. In the *levée des 300,000* of February 1793 the first step was taken when local quotas were allotted for recruitment. Where insufficient volunteers could be found, other mechanisms had to be adopted, mechanisms that were left to the discretion of local people. The law merely stated that the recruitment process should be carried out "by whatever means they found most suitable, by a majority vote." Some communities opted for a ballot; others used the highly tendentious *scrutin révolutionnaire*, whereby the entire population was assembled to nominate the most patriotic among them to serve. A few tried to evade the duty altogether by raising enough money to buy the services of outsiders. None of this seemed very satisfactory, and complaints of cheating and unfairness were legion. Nor were sufficient men found, even by imposing supplementary levies; by the end of July only about half the required 300,000 had been incorporated in the battalions. More men were desperately needed, and balloting, however unpopular it had proved in the more recalcitrant areas of the country, seemed the least offensive expedient to adopt. For the *levée en masse* in August, therefore, the government insisted that ballots be held throughout France. This time the government expressly stated that all citizens had military duties to the state. Everyone was to be involved, not just the most vigorous or most republican. "Young men will go off to fight," declared the Convention's decree of 23 August; "married men will forge weapons and transport food supplies; women will make tents and clothing and will provide the service in hospitals; children will shred old linen; old men will be taken to the public squares to offer encouragement to the warriors and to preach the hatred of kings and the unity of the Republic."[26]

The *levée en masse* was intended to produce an army 750,000 strong, and it did produce around half a million, providing the basis of the armies that would continue to fight for the Directory in Italy, Germany, and across much of Europe. This was the "citizen army" of revolutionary legend, the "nation in arms." But how close did the Jacobins really come to equating military service with citizenship? The obligation that fell on all young men was simply to be available for service, to be in a pool of reservists out of which the armies would be created. But the reserve imposed no duties; a *billet blanc* in the ballot was still the passport to peace of mind. The entire sacrifice was in practice borne by the serving troops, and even at the height of revolutionary expansionism the generals had no need—and certainly no desire—to receive into the ranks everyone who was theoretically liable to serve. Indeed, with the passage of time and the greater professionalization of the army, it became clear that huge numbers of raw, untrained recruits were the last thing that the military required. They wanted to hang on to the well-trained, professional soldiers already in their ranks, which in turn made it more difficult for seasoned veterans to get permission to return to their families. Military service was not only arduous and dangerous; it was also increasingly open-ended, a fact that was not lost upon civilian society.

Inequalities took other forms, too. The needs of the military were unpredictable from one year to the next. Thus there were years of heavy recruitment (1793 and 1798–1799) when men in their upper teens and lower twenties stood a high chance of being taken; but between these dates levies were few and undemanding. Again, not all regions of the country were treated alike. The army, eager for loyal and dependable troops, sought soldiers in areas of France with a proven record for soldiering accepting that patriotic cities like Paris or traditional recruiting grounds like the Marne should provide more, even if the principle of equality emerged somewhat dented. Those seeking exemption on medical grounds could often feign injury, and for much of the period, at least until the *levée en masse*, the principle that a man could buy himself out by paying for another to serve in his stead was officially tolerated. The army connived at this, since many of the officers were doubtful of the value of troops whose motivation was so clearly suspect, and the earlier governments of the 1790s had no desire to interfere in commercial dealings between private citizens.[27] But the implications of this policy were only too clear to others. Those who preferred to evade their responsibilities might realistically hope to succeed, and the suspicion remained that those who were being asked to serve were the poor, those without the money or the connections necessary to find a replacement. In civilian society the belief that the rich were able to escape their obligations made recruitment more difficult, while among serving soldiers these inequalities were even more bitterly resented. Some soldiers admitted in their letters home that they envied those of their friends who had survived the lottery of the ballot; others confessed to admiration for men who had deserted and made it back to their villages. Many expressed their concern that, if money could be found, every effort should be made to spare their younger brothers from their fate.[28]

Some, of course, came to like the army, to cherish the camaraderie of the barracks, to take pride in conquest and promotion. Or else, having lost the best years of their lives, they saw little reason to return to a village that would have no place for them. Among those who scattered, as tradition maintained that they should, when the defeated French armies crossed back onto French soil in 1814, were men who had served since the Revolution, who had been conscripted in the Year VII (1798–1799), been requisitioned during the *levée en masse*, and even, in a few cases, who had volunteered in 1791 or 1792. They had spent their entire careers in the military, serving the king and the Republic, the Directory and Napoléon. From the District of Rambouillet in the Seine-et-Oise we have a register of all the soldiers and NCOs who abandoned their units during that confused spring of 1814.[29] There are 680 names in all, mostly conscripts of the final years of Napoléon's campaigns, but including some who had completed more than a quarter of a century in uniform. Nicolas Becquet, from Villiers-Saint-Frédéric, had been requisitioned in 1793; he had never been promoted during his long career, eight years of which had been spent in captivity in England. Eustache Godefroy, from Mittainville, had served without a break from August 1793 until his desertion in May 1814; he frankly admitted to being worn out, *"usé,"* and was granted his *réforme*. A few could boast even longer service. Pierre David, from Limours, had joined the army as a *palefrenier* in the king's bodyguard in 1792; transferred to the artillery he continued to serve as a common soldier throughout the revolutionary and Napoleonic wars. Another who joined in 1792 was Jean Tupin, from Forges; again he had given long service, first in the line, then in the *voltigeurs*, until he finally deserted during the campaign of 1812. But the record for long and devoted service, at least in Rambouillet, must go to Jean-Baptiste Lamay, from Clairefontaine, who had volunteered in 1791 to defend the Revolution and had subsequently grown old in the service of the emperor.

The revolutionaries sought to link military service to the rights of citizenship. In a society where the people were held to be sovereign this was a natural case to argue, and it did not go unheeded. Over a million men were incorporated in the armies over a ten-year period, but the levels of response, both from the young men themselves and from their families and friends, tell us that the lesson was not yet fully understood, that the language of *nation*, *patrie*, and *citoyenneté* was still unfamiliar to many Frenchmen. For these ideas to enter popular culture would take much longer, certainly until well into the nineteenth century. By that time the state would have acquired some of the administrative and coercive apparatus necessary to effect such a transformation, and the inexorable demands of Napoléon's conscriptions in the years up to 1814 would have ensured that the young came increasingly to regard service as a *rite de passage*, a necessary if unwelcome duty that fell on them as they approached adulthood. By 1814 a second generation was going to war; among the conscripts in Napoléon's Grande Armée were sons of the men who had volunteered in 1791 or been balloted in 1793. Habits had been formed, an essential part of the process of civic education, but in the 1790s the context was very different, and military service was a demanding benchmark by which to judge qualities of citizenship. There were, after all, so many variables. Some men enjoyed military life or came from regions with a tradition of soldiering. Others still thought of the army as a form of servitude, of a *billet noir* in the ballot as a civil death sentence. Some genuinely believed that the army presented them with the opportunity to defend a revolution in which they firmly believed. Others, and they were the majority, saw service as just another of the many demands made upon them by the state. Personal circumstances, too, were different. For many artisans, military service could be slotted relatively easily into their years of apprenticeship and training. But peasant boys from the *pays de petite culture* might conclude that years in the army meant giving up all their lifetime's dreams: marriage, land, the independence that would bring status and respect in their village community. The state might think that it was making an equal demand on all, but in the eyes of many of its new citizens it was not. It was that perception that did the most to undermine the ideal of a citizen army, the notion that military service was a true attribute of citizenship.

NOTES

1. Marcel Gauchet, "Droits de l'homme," in François Furet and Mona Ozouf, eds., *Dictionnaire critique de la Révolution française* (Paris, 1988), 685.

2. John M. Roberts and Richard R. Cobb, eds., *French Revolution Documents*, 1:171–73.

3. Jacques Godechot, ed., *Les Constitutions de la France depuis 1789* (Paris, 1970), 63.

4. Ibid., 64.

5. Abbé Sieyès, *Préliminaire de la Constitution: reconnaissance et exposition raisonnée des Droits de l'Homme et du Citoyen* (Versailles, 1789), quoted by William H.

Sewell, Jr., ''Activity, Passivity, and the Revolutionary Concept of Citizenship,'' in *The Political Culture of the French Revolution*, ed. Colin Lucas (Oxford, 1988), 110.

6. Emile-G. Léonard, *L'armée et ses problèmes au dix-huitième siècle* (Paris, 1958), 229–30.

7. Samuel F. Scott, *The Response of the Royal Army to the French Revolution* (Oxford, 1978), 106.

8. Ibid., 95–96.

9. Jean-Paul Bertaud, *La Révolution armée: Les Soldats citoyens et la Révolution Française* (Paris, 1979), 63.

10. Jacques Godechot, ed., *Constitutions*, 90–91.

11. Ibid., 131–33.

12. Arthur Chuquet, *Wissembourg* (Paris, 1893), 44.

13. See, for example, Robert Legrand, ''Les fêtes civiques à Abbéville,'' *Bulletin de la Société d'émulation historique et littéraire d'Abbéville*, 1978, 373–426.

14. John A. Lynn, *The Bayonets of the Republic* (Urbana, Ill., 1984), 13–14.

15. Albert Meynier, ''L'armée en France sous la Révolution et le Premier Empire,'' *Revue d'études militaires*, 1932, 17–23.

16. A. Picq. *La Législation militaire de l'époque révolutionnaire* (Paris, 1932), 33.

17. During Bouchotte's ministry this was sufficiently marked for Jean-Paul Bertaud to talk of the army as an ''*école du jacobinisme*.'' Bertaud, *La révolution armée*, 194.

18. Ibid., 93.

19. Robespierre, ''Observations sur le plan d'organisation de l'armée proposé par Dubois-Crancé au nom du Comité Militaire,'' in *Oeuvres* (New York, 1970), 3:258–59.

20. Lynn, *Bayonets*, 279.

21. Alan Forrest, *Conscripts and Deserters: The Army and French Society during the Revolution and Empire* (New York, 1989), 74–97.

22. Ibid., 232–35.

23. Isser Woloch, ''Napoleonic Conscription—State Power and Civil Society,'' *Past and Present* 111 (1986).

24. J. Ansoborlo, *Les Soldats de l'an II en Pays Basque* (Bayonne: 1988), 65–68.

25. A fuller account of the successive recruitment laws and their effects can be found in my *Soldiers of the French Revolution* (Durham, N.C., 1990), chap. 3.

26. Albert Soboul, *Les soldats de l'an II* (Paris, 1959), 119.

27. Bernard Schnapper, *Le Remplacement militaire en France* (Paris, 1968), 16–18.

28. Forrest, *Soldiers*, 168–69.

29. A. D. Seine-et-Oise, series R (non-classée), *régistres de contrôle* for the districts of the Seine-et-Oise following the dispersal of 1814, register for the District of Rambouillet.

PART III

Responses to Limitations of Citizenship

12

WOMEN'S REVOLUTIONARY CITIZENSHIP IN ACTION, 1791: SETTING THE BOUNDARIES

Darline Gay Levy

The first seven months of 1791 marked a dramatic escalation of revolutionary democratization in Paris. At this critical juncture, deputies in the National Assembly were working to complete a constitution for a limited monarchy in which the electoral base of the sovereign citizenry would be narrowed and the powers of sovereignty delegated and divided between the legislature and the royal executive. At the same time, liberal and radical political communicators and organizers intensified their efforts to mobilize public opinion, encourage the multiplication of grass-roots political organizations, and initiate and direct mass-based activities of surveillance and control.

A principal issue around which these campaigns crystallized was trust: the trustworthiness of military and political leaders at all levels and, more basically, their commitment to supporting the revolutionary principle that all authority derived its legitimacy from a sovereign citizenry and was responsible to its supreme will. Resistance to the civil constitution of the clergy, the departure or rumored departure of members of the royal family, the passage of legislation to regulate the press or control collective demonstrations of political opposition—all were reworked and exploited by radical leaders determined to mobilize opinion and organize democratic participation around politics of censuring, surveillance, and control of public officials and elected leaders.

The meanings assigned to citizenship by participants in this political drama were staggeringly diverse, often competing and conflicting. Almost invariably, they were gendered in such a way as to foreclose or narrowly restrict women's access to equality of rights and powers inherent in principles of revolutionary democracy. However, it also is true that these gendered meanings of revolutionary citizenship were plural and unstable. Individuals and groups, women and men of all ranks, continually tested these meanings and contested them in political acts, applying a rich variety of strategies to the work of transforming, circumventing, or subverting them.

Throughout the fall and winter of 1790–1791, journalists writing for Prudhomme's *Révolutions de Paris*, one of the most radical political journals of the period, issued urgent directives to the public, especially *le peuple*: they must acquire a political education; step up their vigilance against foreign enemies; increase their surveillance of public authorities at all levels and exercise the right to sanction their acts; and organize their activities—in short, claim the rights, responsibilities, and powers of a sovereign citizenry.[1]

Abruptly, in the eighty-third number of the *Révolutions de Paris* (February 5–12, 1791),[2] in the midst of urgent communications with the public about its political rights and obligations in a period of mounting threats to the nation's safety, one of Prudhomme's writers introduced an article on another subject: "On the influence of the revolution on women," the first of a number of pieces on this theme.[3] The journalist explained that "[s]everal women have complained to us about the revolution"; they had written letters; they were pressing him to reply. He summarized the substance of this correspondence: "[F]or the past two years, it seems that there has been only one sex in France." The correspondents called attention to women's nullity in the nation's primary assemblies, sections, and clubs: "[W]omen are no more in question than if they did not exist." They referred to the shabby treatment of women at the National Assembly: they were allotted a few benches to attend sessions as if a favor were being granted. The two or three women who managed to make an appearance before the bar were dismissed after a perfunctory hearing while the Assembly passed to the order of the day. The correspondents recalled that at earlier periods in the nation's history, women enjoyed the vote and a deliberative voice in representative bodies. Their letters added up to an indictment of the new revolutionary order for denying political rights to women and a legal status as active citizens.

To these communications—*cahiers de doléances* of a sort—the writer for the *Révolutions de Paris* responded with an article intended to set the record straight, to quash once and for all, with reasoned arguments, demands for the empowerment of women that were the other face of his correspondents' indictments of a gendered revolutionary politics of domination and exclusion. In a piece in a later number of the *Révolutions des Paris*, this journalist would refer to the "principles we professed [in the article in no. 83] with regard to [women], following the immortal author of the *Social Contract* and the *Nouvelle Héloise*."[4]

The journalist intended his article to be a straightforward Rousseauian account of the necessary influence of the revolution on women: the revolution that eventually established principles and practices of democratic politics for men also would, and should, clarify differences between men's and women's natures, sharpen the divisions between their roles in the public and private spheres, and overall, drastically narrow the parameters of women's citizenship. Woman was constitutionally frail, dependent by nature; her natural virtues were private virtues, her natural place was in the home; whatever she knew of the outside world passed first through the censoring review of men. However, the journalist also insisted on illustrating this Rousseauian philosophy of women's nature using the news. As it turned out, revolutionary news—coverage of oaths taken by *citoyennes* in the Société fraternelle; a review of exploits of *les femmes du peuple* on July 14, 1789; summaries of sharply worded letters to the editor from *citoyennes* who were devouring the political news, reading it independently and responding critically—all tended to dissolve Rousseauian metahistorical definitions of women's nature and fate into open-ended accounts of the irrepressible, uncontainable, political-military involvement of women of all ranks in revolutionary political life.[5]

In addition, the publisher of the *Révolutions de Paris* and his writers shared a political commitment to mass mobilization that clearly took priority over their commitments to Rousseauian views of sex, gender, and politics. Crisis journalism, the use of the press to create and sustain a climate of permanent emergency, was a powerful instrument for promoting democratic mobilization. In times of crisis, it would have made no sense to eliminate by definition half the population of the capital and the nation out of deference to Jean-Jacques Rousseau. In addressing the question of women's roles during national emergencies, the journalist baldly occluded Rousseauian woman and brought into relief 13 million embodiments of feminine energy unbound and in action—although somehow still under the direction of the press: "*Citoyennes* of all ages, all ranks! Leave your homes, all of you at once; rally from door to door and march toward the city hall (*maison commune*) . . . station yourself at the head of each battalion. . . . Armed with incendiary torches, stand before the gates of the palace of your tyrants." And yet, once the state of emergency was over, "*Citoyennes!* we would want to see you return to your homes and once again take up the accustomed yoke of domestic duties . . . reign sweetly inside your households, teach the rights of man to the stuttering child . . . but do not compete with us."[6]

Analyses of contradictions and tensions that mark "On the influence of the revolution on women" tell us little about how the unstable combination of meanings in this text was in fact received, read, and acted upon by the readers— the public—especially the women toward whom the article was directed. Much of our difficulty in addressing such issues has to do with locating the evidence.

On February 22, 1791, a little over a week after the eighty-third number of the *Révolutions de Paris* was distributed, nineteen women identifying themselves as "*citoyennes* from the rue du Regard in the faubourg Saint-Germain" sent a signed address to the members of the Cordeliers Club about a state of national crisis, how it concerned them, and what they were planning to do about it.[7] This address, we suggest, also can be read as their response and challenge to the author of the article "On the influence of the revolution on women."

These *citoyennes* wrote at a moment of generalized unrest that had reached near-insurrectionary proportions in the capital, as reports of departures and planned departures of members of the royal family circulated in the press and provoked debates in political clubs and popular societies, along with calls for preventive action.[8]

Writing at this critical juncture, the authors of the address to the Cordeliers Club situated themselves in the private and public spheres simultaneously:

Listen to us, brothers of the Cordeliers Club. We emerged from the depths of our retreats to which the duties of motherhood relegated us; we suspended our household labors momentarily; we met; we spoke about the misfortunes that assail the still fragile edifice of liberty on all sides; and here is what your sisters, *citoyennes* from the rue du Regard say to you. (Citoyennes, Adresse, 2)

The *citoyennes* did not proclaim duties, rights, and powers of citizenship in abstract declarations; rather, they projected themselves into complex, intertwining roles as historical subjects who enacted all three—as they raised and educated their children; acquired political information; decided how to act on the basis of it; organized, creating a space in which to meet and discuss the import of the news and its impact on the welfare and safety of the nation; forged new political ties, reaching out from their homes on a single street in their neighborhood to communicate the results of their deliberations in their address to one of the most democratic, active, and best connected political clubs in the capital—a club that encouraged women to attend and participate in meetings.[9]

" . . . and here is what your sisters . . . say to you." They incorporated into their address the outcome of their deliberations—a combined plea and warning: their brothers must remain alert and armed, keep up their watch over governing authorities, or face the consequences of their laxity—loss of everything from their sisters' esteem and their spouses' respect to their own liberty. Their exhortation included a declaration of political-military intentions and commitments: until now they had "consoled" themselves for "having been able to do nothing for the public good" by devoting themselves to "raising the spirit of our children to the height of free men." However, should their brothers default or betray them, then "driven by indignation, pain and despair," they would rush into "public places," defend the liberty that had made their brothers into men, save *la patrie*, or die (Citoyennes, Adresse, 3–4).

In their conclusion, the *citoyennes* issued a disclaimer; in the same sentence, they disavowed it: "Brothers, our alarms are imaginary, they never will materialize; we would like to believe that, for your sake as well as for our own. . . . Your *watchfulness* is ever the same . . . we would praise you for it if free souls knew how to praise, or needed to be praised."

"Greetings and perseverance to our brave brothers in the Cordeliers Club. We commend *la patrie* to you; we leave off discussing it with you only to talk about it with our children." In these last lines, the *citoyennes* signaled that although their political exchange with the Cordeliers Club had been interrupted momentarily, they would continue to perform in the multiple interlocking political roles they had authored for themselves and scripted into their address, roles that linked their civic activities in the private sphere (principally their practice of patriotic motherhood) to a broad spectrum of empowering behaviors in the public arena.

The assembled members of the Cordeliers Club, after listening to a reading of this text, could barely contain their enthusiasm for an address "that radiates principles of liberty, the purest civic mindedness, and the most beautiful courage, expressed with all the energy and virtue of patriotism." They voted unanimously to print the address complete with signatures and to express the club's gratitude and admiration to "these worthy *Citoyennes*."[10]

Within a week, the address printed by the Cordeliers Club found its way into the offices of the *Révolutions de Paris*, where it was picked up by the journalist who had written "On the influence of the revolution on women." In the eighty-sixth number of the journal, this writer published extensive excerpts from the address, along with a running commentary in notes, an account of its warm reception of the address at the Cordeliers Club and his own reply to the *citoyennes*.[11] He introduced the text as "an address that demonstrates, at last, the salutary *influence of the revolution of women*." He noted that the authors "appeared to be penetrated with their duties." Furthermore, they "rendered homage . . . to the principles we professed with respect to them [in the article in no. 83] following the immortal author of the *Social Contract* and the *Nouvelle Héloise*" . . . or did they? In a note, the author confessed his puzzlement, more likely his misgivings. "Could this address from the women of the rue du Regard have been drawn up with the intention of replying indirectly to our article 'On the influence of the revolution on women'?"

The annotations allow us to follow the journalist's thinking as he read and selectively transcribed the text. By the time he reached the second paragraph, he began interpreting this indirect reply not as an homage to Rousseau or to himself but as a challenge, a threat. He first pinned down this threat to a verb: to relegate, which he underscored. He cited: "we came out of the depths of our retreats to which the duties of motherhood *relegated* us.' " In a note, he attempted to shore up the divisions between public and private spheres and men's and women's roles by supplying the right word for the text, one that carried the connotation of correct, gender-appropriate attitudes and behaviors as he understood them.

"To attach" should be substituted for "to relegate"; to relegate evokes an association with "penalty, constraint, punishment," as when you "relegate an unfaithful wife to a forced retreat" [a telling example]; whereas the duties of motherhood "must attach a woman to her home, must make her love the interior of her household; a good mother must not think of herself as *relegated* to the cradle of her children."

Following the annotated citations from the address and a puzzling comment that he would have liked to see eleven more signatures, the writer referred to the extract from the minutes of the Cordeliers Club for February 22: "the reading of this address was covered with applause. . . . It received homage of gratitude and a just admiration.''

Here, the journalist could not restrain himself. ''As for us, here is what we would have made it our duty to say in reply to these worthy *citoyennes*.'' In effect, he challenged the decision of the Cordeliers Club to recognize and confirm the complex multiple parts in the public and private spheres that the *citoyennes* from the rue du Regard had written out and appropriated as their political identities. In a response overloaded with sharply worded commands, interrogations, rebukes, and put-downs, the writer proceeded to evacuate political crises from the news in order to justify a major rescripting of political roles for *citoyennes*. In the opening lines of their address, the *citoyennes* described themselves as immersed in precisely the Rousseauian behaviors the journalist had lauded in his ''On the influence of the revolution on women.'' They situated themselves appropriately—and he cited from their address—''in the bosom of [their] households''; they said they were entirely occupied with teaching their children to recite the constitution by heart. What had gone wrong? The *citoyennes* had informed themselves about a grave crisis. He cited: ''we learn with pain, with fright, about the attacks of enemies of the public good . . . we spoke about the misfortunes which assail our liberty.

Their reaction to these news reports of a crisis at hand provoked everything that followed: their decision to meet, their discussion of the state of affairs, their work on a signed address into which they scripted multiple, transgressive, and intentionally permanent political roles for themselves, and their communication of this text to the Cordeliers Club. Their scenario for the practice of citizenship in times of crisis differed markedly from the one the journalist had drawn up in his article ''On the influence of the revolution on women.'' Nonetheless, he had given *citoyennes* their cue when he insisted that states of emergency not only precipitated women's entry into the political arena, they also justified their political-military performances—although never without outside direction.

After the events, a practitioner of crisis journalism took the authors of the address to task—first, for having misread the news. At worst, what was at hand was an impending crisis, not a full-fledged crisis. ''The enemy is not yet at our front doors. Stop sounding the alarm, and peacefully await the moment of peril[!]'' ''It is not yet necessary for you to rush headlong into public places. This beautiful patriotic zeal is not yet in season.''

Conveniently ignoring his opening speculation that the *citoyennes* might have been reading the *Révolutions de Paris* and responding to his article, he questioned whether they could have any access to the news. ''Centered on your duties, with which you appear [sic] to be penetrated, how are you informed about what is happening outside your homes?'' He questioned their ability to process the news intelligently, to understand how or when to translate critical discussion into political action: ''Eh! How can you know that we don't always speak with the intention of acting?''

For the interim, while crisis was only in the offing, while it still was possible to bracket this issue of gender roles in times of grave emergency, the journalist considered himself entirely at liberty to question the political initiatives and acts of the *citoyennes* in the public sphere. They incited their brothers to greater vigilance; the journalist, who a week earlier had commended such efforts, now dismissed and trivialized them: "Why do you seem to be doubting our perseverance? . . . We know what we have to do." The *citoyennes* said they had met to draft their address to the Cordeliers Club; the journalist chastised them for their transgressions into the public sphere: "We do not take it into our heads to give you lessons about how to love your children; save yourself the trouble of *coming into* our clubs [sic] in order to lay down the citizen's responsibilities for us" [emphasis added].

In the absence of dire emergencies, the *citoyennes* must ignore the political conjuncture; current political affairs should not be their concern—unless or until their men instructed them otherwise. The opening lines of his reply to the *citoyennes* had been a piece of fraternal advice: "Sisters, go back into the bosom of your household, take up your domestic labors once more, and do not leave the crib of your children again." He last word was an imperious order: "Women [*femmes*], from now on, come out only with us, or when we summon you" (385).

The substitution of "*femmes*" for "*citoyennes*" and "*soeurs*"—forms of address that carried connotations of complex bonds between the individual and the nation, and between fraternal equals—was not innocent. In another article in the same issue of the *Révolutions de Paris*,[12] the journalist clarified his meaning. As part of an argument for excluding women from the regency, he insisted that *femmes* were not *citoyennes*: "In our Constitution, women are not recognized as *citoyennes*; that is to say, they do not possess any political quality at all, not even the right to be represented personally, even if they are property owners." If the opposite were true, "our mothers, daughters, wives and sisters must be allowed to vote in our primary assemblies and run for municipal office, etc."

These arguments from revolutionary constitutional law were undergirded by principles derived from the immortal author of the *Social Contract* and the *Nouvelle Héloise*.

So, by virtue of what principles are our women deprived of a political character? By virtue of the vow of nature, which did not create women for [high] office in the body politic. These functions call for hard work, acquired experience, powers of mind and reasoning that do not belong at all to a sex with a weak and delicate constitution. . . . In a word, women were born for domestic virtues and cares. Their duty does not extend beyond that. (382)

In the spring of 1791, the likelihood that this kind of discourse would significantly alter the incidence or patterns of women's political participation was not great. The writer for the *Révolutions de Paris* who rescripted the roles of the *citoyennes* from the rue du Regard and invoked the French constitution and the immortal Rousseau to rationalize a radical narrowing of the parameters of women's citizenship and a thorough mining of the ground for their claims to a legal status as citizens wrote after the fact—after the fact of their having replaced his prescribed roles for women in revolution with roles they constructed for themselves, assumed, played out, publicized, and bound up inextricably with their political identities.

Had the *citoyennes* read the journalist's "On the influence of the revolution on women"? Were they "replying indirectly" to it? Very possibly. The timing of this writer's article and the address of the *citoyennes*; common elements in the repertory of gender roles from which the journalist and the *citoyennes* worked (patriot mothers and wives, vigilant sentinels, female combatants); similarities in themes treated in the two texts (like national emergency as the occasion for multiplying women's political roles and expanding the sphere of their activity)— all strongly suggest that the *citoyennes* had the journalist's article in mind. If they read it, they did not do so passively. Instead of taking his directions, they directed themselves, they produced their own text. The Cordeliers Club's confirming response reinforced—it did not replace—their prior act of self-authorization.

In his article, the journalist had created parts for female players that keep them alternating between near-demonic and domestic behaviors, in public and private spheres, in wartime and peacetime—always under his imperious direction, "*Citoyennes* of all ages, all ranks! come out of your homes, all of you at once." The *citoyennes* on their side, cast themselves in multiple inextricably enmeshed roles that required that they continually cross the boundary lines between public and private spheres—or dissolve them—as they took on a remarkable number and variety of activities: patriotic mothering, political organizing and networking, the drafting of political communications, surveillance. They also projected themselves into parts as combatants ready to put their lives on the line in an ultimate test of the integrity of these invented political identities. Their vacillation at the end of their address—was the crisis real or had they imagined it?—may well have been strategic. Their expressed interest in a continuing political dialogue with the Cordeliers Club—"we leave off discussing [*la patrie*] with you only to talk about it with our children"—testifies to their determination to persist in performing in parts that cemented their ties to the nation—for the present, into the future, and notwithstanding the political *conjuncture*. They further affirmed and strengthened their commitment to these particular political identities and ties by signing their address and by representing themselves from the outset as *citoyennes*.

Announcements in the radical press that "[i]n our Constitution, women are not recognized as *citoyennes* . . . they do not possess any political quality at all"; that "women were born for domestic virtues and cares[,] [t]heir task does not extend beyond that" did not suffice to dissolve these kinds of political bonds, not in the spring of 1791. In the late fall of 1793 strikingly similar discourse placed in the service of the Jacobin regime not only rationalized, but also contributed to provoking, a far-reaching legal exclusion of women from the public sphere.[13] The year 1791 was not 1793. During the first half of 1791, authority at the political center was divided, splintered; it did not coalesce around a single ideology and efficient repressive bureaucratic machinery. In this partial power vacuum, the radical press, political clubs like the Cordeliers, and popular societies all reached down and out to promote democratization, to encourage and direct the mobilization of groups excluded from the political status and rights of active citizenship. These communicators and organizers were caught up in rivalries and power struggles, including struggles to control the meaning of fundamental political concepts like citizenship—precisely because such terms defined the base and boundaries of the revolutionary nation. Their ideologies were riddled with internal inconsistencies and contradictions; their strategies for mass mobilization frequently backfired or went in directions they could not have anticipated and could not control. The meaning of women's revolutionary citizenship was one among many fiercely contested issues around which their differences and conflicts and the internal tensions and fissures in their professed beliefs continued to coalesce, deepen, and multiply, while the issue itself remained unresolved. Institutional pluralization and ideological fissuring favored performances like the one played out on the rue du Regard, in the Cordeliers Club, in the pages of the *Révolutions de Paris*, and in the public spaces of revolutionary Paris. Throughout this period, women of all ranks, collectively and individually, persisted in exploiting a relatively open, fluid, indeterminate political climate. They seized available opportunities; they recast or invented political roles for themselves; they brought a rich repertory of strategies to a struggle in which they, along with the rest of the nation, were caught up, a struggle to shape and legitimize their political identities as citizens.

At approximately the time the *Révolutions de Paris* published its censorious dossier on the address by nineteen *citoyennes* to the Cordeliers Club, along with related discourses supporting the exclusion of women from the public sphere, the *Orateur du peuple*, another radical journal, was reacting with indignation and outrage to reports that coercive military authority had been enlisted to track down the *citoyennes* from the rue du Regard.[14] The *Orateur* condemned the truculent, abusive, accusatory behavior of fifteen or sixteen National Guardsmen, Lafayette's toadies, who had descended on the shop of "the patriot Roullier," a wholesale wine merchant in the rue du Regard. In Roullier's absence, the *Orateur* reported, they guzzled his wine, sang bawdy songs in front of his children, and drank to the health of the king, the queen, and Lafayette, but not the nation. They also interrogated Roullier's wife about the location of "the club of the women from the rue du Regard, who signed an address to the Cordeliers Club." Dame Roullier told them she did not know whether such a club existed. She was not telling the truth, however. Dame Roullier was one of the nineteen *citoyennes* from the rue du Regard who had signed the address. The *Orateur*, without calling attention to this fact, advised both Roullier and his wife to file a complaint and noted that two patriot lawyers had been charged with defending Dame Roullier.

In this same piece, the *Orateur* mentioned that in their drunken state, the National Guardsmen had "spewed out a thousand gross insults" against a group of "courageous women" who had thrown a bust of Lafayette, "their idol," out of a window.

Who were these "courageous women"? That is another story, one that includes the defenestration of Lafayette's bust, reported in the *Orateur*, but also carries us beyond that incident to their other exploits that are linked to an exploration of the parameters of women's citizenship in action during the first seven months of 1791. Here, I briefly review several episodes.

About two weeks before he published "On the influence of the revolution on women," Prudhomme printed the article "What is the People?" in the eighty-first number of the *Révolutions de Paris*.[15] In a footnote, the publisher returned to a piece he had published seven weeks previously containing detailed proposals for the formation of an ultrapatriotic legion of tyrannicides.[16] "Tyrannicides" had provoked several letters to the editor from "good republicans" volunteering to enter the "sacred battalion." One volunteer came in person, unannounced.

A fact, and not the least extraordinary fact of the revolution, [Prudhomme observed] is the visit we received from a young girl, gifted with all the graces of her sex and all the energy of our own. "My name is Constance Evrard," she told us; "I live in the rue de Grenelle-St.-Germain. If you were missing a tyrannicide to complete the battalion, count on me. [*sic*]. I quickly would have discarded my women's clothing to don that of a sex all of whose courage I feel I contain in myself. I have shed tears over the death of our patriots; I willingly would give all my blood to spill that of the enemies of *ma patrie*."[17]

In unambiguously laudatory language, Prudhomme described Constance Evrard as a member of a rare hybrid species who had wandered into his offices to serve, if not save, the Revolution. Without using the term, he depicted a *femme-homme extraordinaire*—extraordinary precisely because she combined in her person the purest masculine and feminine characteristics of revolutionary virtue, "all the graces of her sex, and all the energy of our own."[18] Prudhomme contrived to leave his reader with the impression that although she had not been expected, she had been warmly welcomed; did he seriously consider her a worthy candidate for the highly select elite corps of ultrapatriots described in "tyrannicides"? Brutus was a role for a man. Could Constance Evrard play Brutus? In his summary of their conversation, Prudhomme allowed this "young girl" her word on the question. Her words more than confirmed his portrait of her hybrid patriotic virtues. She testified to her impulse to throw herself into gender-appropriate expressions of mourning for dead patriots, but at the same time, she depicted herself as the embodiment of all the classic qualities of male republican virtue: courage to fight, the will to triumph over the enemy, fortitude in the face of death. She said that, if needed, she was ready to change costumes, exchange roles, spill all her blood while playing the part of a man—"all of whose courage I feel in myself."

Notwithstanding a certain indeterminate openness and fluidity in the political culture of revolutionary Paris in 1791, such declarations still came dangerously close to subverting prevailing models of appropriate gender roles. If Prudhomme experienced any discomfort, he disposed of it by relegating the entire issue of *femmes tyrannicides* to the category of hypothetical cases and lost opportunities. At the beginning of his note, he assured his public that the battalion of tyrannicides was more than complete and prepared to move at the first news of an invasion. As if to hold the prospect of the enrollment of this "young girl" further at bay, Prudhomme transcribed her words in the conditional tense, more or less. Whatever his reservations, however, his openness to playing with the idea of a *femme-homme tyrannicide* only added to the confused messages issuing from the office of the *Révolutions de Paris* about the meaning of women's citizenship in action.

In February 1791, not long after her visit to Prudhomme's office, Constance Evrard and several other women, including her close friend Pauline Léon—the "courageous women" mentioned by the *Orateur du peuple*—smashed the bust of Lafayette and threw it out of a window.[19]

On June 21, just after the flight of the king and royal family from Paris became known, Constance Evrard, Pauline Léon, and Léon's mother were stopped at the Palais-Royal by a troop of bodyguards "and almost assassinated" for speaking up against this "infamous treason."[20] The reporter on the beat for *Le Babillard* reported that "the woman living at no. 64, rue de Grenelle" (Evrard's address) had opined that day that the way to deal with proclamations of martial law was to cut off the head of whoever carried the red flag; she herself offered to carry the severed head around town on the tip of a pike, the reporter said.[21]

On Sunday evening, July 17, just after the mass petition signing and massacre on the Champ de Mars, a *chasseur volontaire* in the battalion of the Petits-Augustins arrested a woman in connection with a violent dispute in the courtyard of a house on the rue de Grenelle, opposite the Fontaine de Grenelle. In addition to the woman, the dispute involved a sieur Muller, a National Guardsman and a pharmacist by profession, his wife and other family members, his employees, and his neighbors. Mme Muller accused the woman of making insulting and injurious remarks about M. Muller—calling him an assassin, for one thing.

At 10:30 P.M., accompanied by parties and witnesses to the dispute, the *chasseur* brought this woman before the police *commissaire* in the Section Fontaine de Grenelle.[22] In her interrogation, she identified herself as Constance Evrard, twenty-three years old, a native of Arcy, in the Pays des Vosges, who had been working for the past three years as a cook at the home of a former treasurer of France at no. 64, rue de Grenelle.

Questioned at length, Evrard was unexpectedly forthright for a woman apprehended in the aftermath of a declaration of martial law and a massacre of petitioners protesting the reinstatement of Louis XVI. She stated that she had been present at the Champ de Mars with Pauline Léon and Léon's mother and that her purpose was to "sign a petition like all good patriots." Asked what was in the petition, she answered that she wasn't too certain, that she "didn't have it read to her," but that she believed that the aim of the petition was to "have the executive power organized in another way." When questioned about her political affiliations, she offered the information that she often joined groups that met in public places, like the Palais Royal and the Tulieries Gardens; that she sometimes attended meetings of the Cordeliers Club, although she was not a member.

Her interrogator wanted to know whether it was true that her name had been printed in several journals. She replied that her name had appeared in the *Révolutions de Paris*. She also offered some additional information, noting that some time ago, she had gone to see Prudhomme to renew a subscription. She complimented him on the article on tyrannicides, adding that she had mourned the death of Loustalot (a celebrated writer for the *Révolutions de Paris* who had died the previous summer). She emphasized that she had expressed her enthusiasm about "Tyrannicides" to Prudhomme, telling him that "if she had been a man, she didn't know how far her patriotism could have led her"; she was very surprised to find her name printed in the journal the following week.

With whom did she associate habitually and what journals did she read? She said that *les Léon*, mother and daughter, were her only company. As for her reading, she read "Prudhomme, Marat, Haudouin [Audouin], Camille Desmoulins, and very often the *Orateur du Peuple*."

From Evrard's interrogation and the testimony of others, it is clear that she was outraged by the behavior of the National Guard on the Champ de Mars that afternoon. Dame Muller, in her testimony, said that Evrard and the Léon women had called Sr. Muller, her husband, "an assassin, a hangman, a scoundrel who was killing everyone at the Champ de Mars" and that Evrard had threatened to stab Sr. Muller within three days. On her side, Evrard insisted that she did not threaten to stab Sr. Muller; if she did say that, she didn't remember it. She did acknowledge that on her way home from the Champ de Mars, and full of indignation about the behavior of the National Guard toward unarmed citizens, she met Sr. Muller, who was headed toward the Champ de Mars with his battalion; when she encountered Dame Muller, her neighbor, Evrard reproached her because Sr. Muller had gone there "just like the others." A witness, an embroiderer, testified that he overheard Evrard say to his neighbor, the owner of a dairy shop, that Lafayette "would fall."

After hearing the testimony, the police commissioner ordered that Constance Evrard be taken immediately to the Department of Police; there, the following morning, July 18, the decision was made to release her, on the double condition that she appear before the authorities whenever summoned and that "her master" assume responsibility for guaranteeing her appearance.

Although Constance Evrard worked as a cook for a former treasurer of France, we have no evidence that she considered her employer or anyone else "her master" or that she was in the habit of answering docilely to the summons of the authorities in place. As a reader of Prudhomme's *Révolutions de Paris*, she would not have missed the meaning of the journal's celebrated epigraph: *"Les grands ne nous paraissent grands que parce que nous sommes à genoux. Levons nous."* If Evrard was inclined to answer to anything, it was to an imperious need to make a place for herself in the Revolution, to identify herself as a *bonne patriote* by her acts, to practice citizenship.

How did she know what a *bonne patriote* was? As Prudhomme's writer put it in his reply to the *citoyennes* from the rue du Regard: "How did you become informed about what is happening outside your homes?"

Evrard gave herself an education in radical revolutionary citizenship as she involved herself in a broad range of political activities that political leaders and communicators were urging *le peuple* to take on. She attended meetings of the Cordeliers Club, where specific political measures were formally linked to principles like popular sovereignty. She participated in informal discussions of political news in public places, including the Palais-Royal and the Jardin des Tuileries. She was part of an expedition that carried out the defenestration of a bust of Lafayette, emblem and symbol of a suspect military leadership. At the Palais-Royal, immediately after the flight to Varennes, she publicly denounced the treason of the king. She petitioned on the Champ de Mars on July 17 for a referendum on the future of monarchical executive authority—a direct challenge to the legitimacy of the royal executive as well as to the authority of the legislature under the new constitution, and an affirmation of the general will of the sovereign people.

She also devoured the news. Evrard told the police commissioner in her section that she read five journals, organs of the radical press; she subscribed to one. How could a cook have gotten her hands on as many as four radical journals? Possibly by frequenting the *cabinet littéraire national* of Mme Vaufleury, where they were available for the price of six sous.[23]

As a reader of these papers, Evrard was exposed to multiple and frequently diverging perspectives on the news. Different journals turned in contradictory reports and interpretations of the same event: the writer for the *Révolutions de Paris* berated the *citoyennes* from the rue du Regard for organizing: "We do not . . . give you lessons on how to love your children; save yourselves the trouble of coming into our clubs to lay down the citizen's responsibilities for us." At about the same time, the *Orateur du peuple* exposed efforts by Lafayette's National Guardsmen to locate the club of the *citoyennes* from the rue du Regard. A single writer might be of several minds or embrace incompatible objectives in the same article—the case of the author of "On the influence of the revolution on women." Tensions, fissures, changing emphases in a journalist's or a journal's position might blur or confuse the message: in Prudhomme's *Révolutions de Paris*, an article by a staff writer could emphasize convictions that the publisher, in his annotations, challenged or radically altered. There is no evidence that the journalist who wrote the article on tyrannicides had given a thought to including *femmes-hommes extraordinaires* in the elite battalion he dreamed up; on the other hand, Prudhomme himself decided to treat Constance Evrard—a female subscriber and would-be volunteer for the "sacred battalion"—gingerly, with praise, and in print.

In the end, Evrard made one kind of sense out of a rich, complex mix of political information and commentary—her own. By the middle of July, her convictions had led her from the offices of Prudhomme, where she avowed her radically republican commitments, to the Champ de Mars, where she acted on them, signing her name to a petition that challenged the king's legitimacy and the authority of the legislature to speak for the sovereign nation. By the end of that day, she had taken the risky step of insulting a member of Lafayette's National Guard for his involvement in the bloody repression of the petitioners on the Champ de Mars.

Evrard's straightforward answers to questions during her interrogation can be interpreted as evidence of her political innocence, but they can also be read as a continuing affirmation of the integrity and coherence of a political identity she had constructed, fixed, and played out several times as her role, in the many public arenas of revolutionary Paris. From the rue du Regard to the Champ de Mars the distance was not all that great.

Citizenship is central for understanding the meaning of the French Revolution as a democratic revolution, one which tried to make power legitimate by making it responsible to the will of individual members of the sovereign nation.

In our collaborative work on gender and citizenship in revolutionary Paris, Harriet Applewhite and I have interpreted formulations and practices of revolutionary citizenship as sites or fields of continuous, often bitter power struggles: struggle about who is to be included and who excluded from membership in the political nation; struggles about the nature and limits of individual rights and responsibilities in the political community; struggles about boundaries between legitimate and illegitimate exercises of authority.

Democratic theory posits the principle of a citizenry equal in rights, responsibilities and access to positions conferring power; in practice, however, all modern democracies are riddled with inequalities of rights and powers; gender is one axis along which inequalities and exclusions are structured and experienced.

Exclusive or restrictive gendered meanings of citizenship suffused revolutionary culture; were encoded in constitutional and statutory law; informed contract theories of the foundation of political society; were reflected in revolutionary imagery and symbolism; and were structured into the revolutionary political vocabulary.

However, it also is true that during the first seven months of 1791, a period of rapid radicalization, when definitions of the sovereign nation and the location of its general will were fiercely and continuously contested, all meanings of French revolutionary citizenship, along with the ideologies attached to them, were plural and unstable, marked by complex internal tensions and fissures. Women, along with other marginalized or excluded groups, continually tested and contested these meanings in discourse and act, applying a rich variety of strategies to a struggle to widen, dissolve, newly imagine, and reconstruct the boundaries of prevailing definitions and practices of citizenship. In 1791, the outcomes of that struggle were not certain. In any case, outcomes, even once they have happened, are never certain.

NOTES

1. For discussion of these and related issues in the *Révolutions de Paris*, see no. 68 (23–30 October 1790), 113–20; no. 72 (20–27 November 1790), 361–70; no. 81 (22–29 January 1791), 133–38; no. 83 (5–12 February 1791), 237–39; no. 85 (19–26 February 1791), 316–23.

2. *Révolutions de Paris*, no. 83, 226–35.

3. Based on strong similarity of themes, styles, and positions, and pending further research, I am suggesting the possibility of a single author for the following articles in *Révolutions de Paris*: "On the influence of the revolution on women," no. 83; "On Divorce," no. 85; reply to the *citoyennes* from the rue du Regard, no. 86; "On the regency," no. 86.

4. *Révolutions de Paris*, no. 86 (26 February–5 March 1991), 383.

5. *Ibid.*, no. 83, 229–31, 226.

6. *Ibid.*, no. 83, 233–35.

7. *Club des Cordeliers. Société de amis des droits de l'homme et du citoyen. Extrait des délibérations du 22 février 1791* ([Paris], 1791). This publication includes the address, "Les citoyennes de la rue du Regard, faubourg Saint-Germain, à leurs courageux frères du Club des Cordeliers . . . ", which will henceforth be cited in parentheses as Citoyennes, Adresse.

8. See *Révolutions de Paris*, no. 83, 237–38; no. 84 (12–19 February 1791), 275–85; no. 85, 313–16.

9. Robert Barrie Rose, *The Making of the Sans-Culottes: Democratic Ideas and Institutions in Paris, 1789–92* (Manchester, U.K., 1983), 111.

10. *Club des Cordeliers . . . Extrait des délibérations du 22 février 1791*, 4.

11. *Révolutions de Paris*, no. 86, 382–85.

12. *Ibid.*, no. 86, 380–83.

13. See Darline Gay Levy, Harriet Branson Applewhite, and Mary Durham Johnson, ed., *Women in Revolutionary Paris, 1789–1793* (Urbana, Ill., 1797), 213–17.

14. *Orateur du peuple*, 5, no. 17 [early March 1791], 135–36.

15. *Révolutions de Paris*, no. 81, 133–39.

16. *Ibid.*, no. 74 (4–11 December 1790), 445–53.

17. *Ibid.*, no. 81, 137.

18. I thank Catherine Montforet for communication of her unpublished paper "Charlotte Corday: *'femme-homme'* extraordinaire." In the early months of 1791, a radical publisher could entertain such models of sexual amalgamation. By summer-fall 1793, as Montfort makes clear, the Jacobins were condemning *femmes-hommes* as dangerous, aberrant, and monstrous.

19. Léon was a founding member of the Society of Revolutionary Republican Women; Evrard also joined. This radical club exclusively for women was organized in the spring of 1793. For documentation of the defenestration incident, see Dominique Godineau, *Citoyennes tricoteuses. Les femmes du peuple à Paris pendant la Révolution française*

(Aix-en-Provence, 1988), 372, 375–76. For Léon's version of the incident, see Levy, Applewhite, and Johnson, eds., *Women in Revolutionary Paris*, 158–60.

20. See Levy, Applewhite, and Johnson, eds., *Women in Revolutionary Paris*, 158–60; Godineau, *Citoyennes tricoteuses*, 372, 375–76.

21. *Le Babillard*, no. 17 (21 June 1791), 7.

22. Archives de la Préfecture de Police, Paris, Aa 148, fol. 30.

23. Jeremy Popkin, *Revolutionary News: The Press in France, 1789–1799* (Durham, N.C., 1990), 35–37.

13

WORK AND CITIZENSHIP: CRAFTING IMAGES OF REVOLUTIONARY BUILDERS, 1789–1791

Allan Potofsky

The role of the "organization of labor" in the carving out of an identity of revolutionary citizenship is an elusive problem. Once upon a time, that problem was resolved in the heroic image of the sans-culotte. According to Soboul's and his followers' synthesis on sans-culottism, the artisan earning his living by work with his hands was the supreme citizen-worker of the revolutionary order, who alone could be counted upon to defend the Republic under siege from enemies within and without. In this view, the politicized artisan fully incarnated moral and social categories of revolutionary citizenship.[1]

The recent skepticism that meets "the myth of the artisan" in revolutions from 1789 to 1848 has dimmed and blurred that once-vivid portrait of the revolutionary citizen-worker.[2] Recent scholarship exposes the tenuous connections between "the organization of labor" and concepts of citizenship. Even the imagery of sans culottism is interpreted as essentially invented by revolutionary journalists in search of an authentically collectivist tradition to call their own. The citizen-worker as sans-culotte appears more fully suited to the iconography of the radical Revolution than to its social history. The problem of work in current historical literature has thus been severed from political representations of work—in conventional terms, social structure has come to be treated as a completely separate sphere of inquiry from the political culture of the Revolution.[3]

To return to the problem of work, then, is to revive questions about its many representations in the Revolution. How did workers conceptualize themselves as citizens of the revolutionary order? Were those who worked considered typical of general citizens of the nation, as with the Third Estate writ large? Or, were those who worked depicted as a special subgroup within the nation, as in the example of the sans-culottes of the Year II of the Republic?[4]

This chapter will examine several images of citizenship in documents representing the building industry of the capital during the Revolution's constituent phase. The period here covered, 1789–1791, corresponds to the earliest articulation of a public works policy, and thus represents the initial attempt to project the Revolution onto the building site. This process unfolded as a matter of course in the earliest period of the Revolution and was later exemplified in the Panthéon français. As builders recast the church of the patron saint of Paris, Ste. Geneviève, into a monument to the nation's heroes, the Panthéon, they would also sculpt the civic identity of all those who toiled on the nation's work sites.

From the beginning, the builders constituted themselves as an articulate and active constituency because they understood themselves as profoundly affected by revolutionary policies. The health of the construction industry was utterly dependent on the building of public edifices, on public works projects, and on the availability of networks of credit, all of which were threatened in the transition from the Old Regime to the new civic order. For these valuable material reasons alone, revolutionary builders, from the large scale entrepreneur to the former journeymen, petitioned often and with great passion on many of the social and economic policies of the Revolution. Besides these utterances, their presence would be felt through other means of communication. Their sheer numbers assured that they would surface often in police reports on crowds of the Revolution. At the time of the Revolution there were about 18,500 employers and workers in the entire industry, comprising 6.3 percent of the working population of Paris.[5]

While the original impetus to appeal to the nation or municipality might have been material, the forms of address chosen by builders embraced newly forged concepts of citizenship. In literature bearing their names, builders were presented as citizens with a distinct bond to the nation: a clear-cut relationship formulated in social contractualist language. Sets of social and economic rights that citizen-builders demanded for themselves were matched by sets of obligations toward the nation. Ultimately, the architects, masons, carpenters, and others who performed "work for the nation" portrayed themselves as having a privileged role in physically constructing the cultural symbols of the new order.[6] The construction trades of Paris derived an identity in erecting public buildings that promoted the image of the Revolution, which in turn represented the Revolution in its capital city to the rest of the world.

INVENTING THE CITIZEN-BUILDER

From the perspective of the building sites of Paris, the Revolution appeared first as a moment of lost employment opportunities. Projects both private and public were halted in the immediate aftermath of revolutionary upheavals. By August 1789, even the last recourse preventing the able-bodied poor from sliding into absolute indigence would be denied them. The ending of the crown's experiment in *ateliers de charité* closed more than a thousand public projects throughout France that had once engaged tens of thousands of men in outdoor road construction and women and children in indoor *filatures* (spinning establishments).[7]

Particularly hard hit by unemployment were the building workers engaged on public work sites, where the crown constructed monuments to its imperial grandeur. Work was suspended at the gatehouses as well as on the walls ringing Paris, on the site of the churches of the Madeleine and Ste. Geneviève, and on parts of the Louvre, then—as it seems always—in the process of being restored. The crisis of unemployment in the early Revolution was aggravated as well by the shutting down of private building sites. As the National Assembly haggled in 1790 over the legal structure of a liberal economy—debating such issues as the price of *patentes* for entrepreneurs and the abolition of commercial courts—private construction in Paris was largely halted. Work sites were immobilized as building entrepreneurs and owners awaited clarification on the true value of their investments in a new economy.

Paradoxically, then, as the Assembly proclaimed the freedom of commerce in five separate decrees between October 1789 and September 1790, the work sites of Paris remained paralyzed. In the absence of a fully achieved commercial code, the exact risks of a liberal economy remained to be determined. Besides, relatively fresh memories of disastrous experiments in economic liberalism, in 1763–1764, 1775–1776, and 1787, caused apprehension among Parisian entrepreneurs and owners involved with construction ventures. Liberty was as perilous to its supposed beneficiaries as it was exhilarating to the deputies in the Assembly who repeatedly decreed its arrival.[8]

The response to the crisis of unemployment in 1789–1790 inspired the creation of an image of the citizen-builder. A tenuous *esprit de corps* was articulated by pleas for help drafted by assorted spokespersons for the building trades. The demand for work in the early revolution forged a fragile alliance that glided over differences of *états* and provoked the creation of a political interest group that spoke in the name of a coalition of construction entrepreneurs and workers. Previously fragmented by corporate jealousy, the builders of Paris now came together as a unified body, ostensibly speaking with one voice on the need to encourage private building projects in the capital.

Audaciously, with one fell swoop, the newly found solidarity of the construction industry sought to efface centuries of contention. The building trades of Paris had always been among the most litigious sector of the Old Regime guild economy. Turf wars over privileges and control over parts of the building process erupted often and were settled before a separate police jurisdiction, the *chambre des bâtiments*, established within the master masons' corporation. The massive documentation of this Old Regime housing authority chronicles in elaborate detail the intracorporate strife that divided builders. Their struggles were epitomized above all by the bitter, enduring rivalry between master masons and architects on defining final authority over the building process.[9]

With the breakdown of the corporate economy, elaborate networks of credit collapsed as well. In the midst of this chaos, an alliance of citizen-builders signed petitions to the National Assembly to suggest means to alleviate destitution and unemployment among the construction trades. One solution was offered in a typical pamphlet written by large-scale entrepreneurs in the late summer of 1790. In stark contrast to Old Regime corporate taxonomy, construction entrepreneurs spoke of the building trades as a unity, as a group of citizens undifferentiated by status or skill and opposed only by their creditors.[10]

The builders, in their own words, "awaited life or death, under the knife of our creditors, crushed by financial obligations and without bread." They portrayed themselves as collectively victimized by an economic policy whose ambiguities intensified wretched social conditions in Paris. In seeking direction from the Assembly, the builders cited the nation's obligations toward its "destitute" citizens. They blamed lack of work on the scant efforts of the Assembly to formulate a coherent commercial code and condemned political immobility as the cause of misery.[11]

What was the notion of citizenship embedded in these appeals for public action? At first glance, this literature summoned forth the charitable obligations of the nation to its people. The "plea" for policies encouraging construction in Paris summoned forth prevailing arguments for "*le droit à la subsistance*" that circulated widely in 1790. All builders were to be provided the means to feed themselves and their families. Here, however, subsistence was not to be provided by charity, which now signified a corrupting force on the poor.[12] Subsistence would henceforth be guaranteed by a healthy, liberated, urban economy, and employment provided by projects launched by thriving private entrepreneurs.

Citizenship meant the enjoyment of full participation in a growing economy to avert the need for public assistance. The entrepreneurs' demand for private ventures was reiterated by former master masons and architects who joined in a petition in the name of the "arts and professions of building" in December 1790. This later petition also conceptualized citizen-builders as a unified block, in seeking "to occupy many tradesmen or enterpreneurs of all *états*" in twenty-two privately run projects in the capital. Like the entrepreneurs in the earlier petition, the master masons and architects depicted the only alternative to indigence as economic liberalism backed by a well-conceived code. In their view, active encouragement of private construction projects was the only feasible solution to the problem of unemployment in the early Revolution.[13]

FROM PRIVATE TO PUBLIC CONSTRUCTION: THE FOUNDING OF *TRAVAUX PUBLICS*

Instead of combatting unemployment by stimulating private initiative, however, the revolutionaries focused their energies on the public sector. As a direct response to the predicament of unemployed builders, the municipality of Paris in early 1790 directed the organization of the *Département des travaux publics*.[14] This administration was to be charged with carrying out *grands projets* launched by the National Assembly. Meanwhile, it was given a more mundane task: the department was the equivalent of the Old Regime jurisdiction, the *voirie*, the police of roads, quais, and edifices. It originally functioned as a regulatory organ to direct the building guilds to fulfill the needs of public safety. Administrators were charged with making sure that "old ordinances did not fall into disuse," and to make sure wily master artisans would not compromise public safety through violations of building codes.[15]

The political self-representation of the building trades was reformulated to suit a new challenge in petitions for administrative posts and jobs in the bureau. The municipality of Paris introduced an aggressively competitive system of petitioning for positions as supervisors, administrators, and architects on public works projects. There, it would no longer be enough to advertise oneself as merely destitute to find work: specific talents and experience were to be considered for gainful employment. The municipality was looking for the industrious and skilled citizen-builder to hire. Ultimately, the formation of a cadre of trained building tradesmen within the Département des travaux publics assured that its mission would be more ambitious than that of surveying cracks in minor structures.[16]

The new self-representation of citizen-builders was eloquently championed by a remarkable proposal published in late 1790 by architects working for the new bureau. Their *mémoire* crystallized the sentiment that new public works projects should serve to alleviate the destitution of only "the most industrious classes." The needs of the nation would be satisfied only by a large-scale revival of craft industry in Paris, which would in turn "occupy in a useful manner the artisans and workers of the Capital."[17]

This pamphlet collapsed a wide range of social prejudices and charitable impulses into a single argument for *grands projets*. While its anonymous authors advocated the embellishment of Paris through a network of boulevards and monuments, their objective was to set forth a stirring justification for the rejuvenation of the nation around the building process. Unlike the earlier petition addressed to the National Assembly, it spoke to a different political context and forged a distinctive political identity for the building trades. It sought to appeal for money to go to public building projects by distinguishing industrious building tradesmen from the masses of indigent poor, who were portrayed as wasting precious funds in recently organized *ateliers de secours* devoted to unskilled work mostly involving road repairs and canal construction.[18]

To strengthen the appeal for funding to employ the able-bodied and skilled, the architects-authors sought to expose the corruption of the indigent and poor who entered the ateliers. Invoking a distinction popularized by the physiocrats, they contrasted the sterile labor performed in the *ateliers* to "the culture of the mechanical arts" represented by the building trades. For while the former were admittedly useful to extend social control over "dangerous classes," they were beginning to fail their own purpose, which was only "a feeble palliative" meant to "employ [people] in the opening moments of the Revolution, and to survey and contain the crowd of individuals that misery would lead astray or reduce to despair.''

The authors of this petition then continue to make a crucial distinction between the useless, stultifying labor in the *ateliers de secours* that were meant only to survey and contain the poor, and the edifying, systematic work of physically building the nation. They resolved that, above all, it is the building process that lends itself to a thorough education of the people in citizenship:

We must therefore breathe new life into such professional and mechanical crafts, to engage in grand public enterprises, whose execution demands the competition of a great number of workers of all types and which are directed to considerations of *utilité générale*. Architecture is, of all the crafts, the one that employs the most extended influence ... [where] artists and artisans of all classes are called to compete to erect public monuments.[19]

At first glance, this document presents a variation on the ageless theme that public assistance corrupts while work edifies. In fact, however, its essential message was far more nuanced, for these architects appealed to the core assumptions of Sieyès: the rights of citizenship ought to be the exclusive property of those who contribute to society. Political entitlement must be based on useful labor. Strictly on the basis of their productivity are the building trades—from the richest entrepreneur to the poorest worker—qualified to enjoy the rights of the nation.

The authors of this *mémoire* concluded that the building trades, in their work, embodied the supreme qualities of the Third Estate. The "competitive" yet cooperative nature of work on large public sites; the unification of professionals and artisans as productive laborers; the "political results" of socially virtuous labor—these distinguished the building process as an education in active citizenship within the French nation.

This rich pamphlet, moreover, resists being reduced to an example of the passive reception of Sieyès's ideas among the Third Estate, for while following Sieyès's reasoning, it also recast his arguments to fresh purpose to suit a shifting context. It sought to distinguish the unskilled poor from productive but unemployed laborers, and to argue in favor of channeling money marked for workshops toward the funding of socially useful public works projects. Thus its authors argue that the "immense sums" of money spent on unemployment could only be justified by "political results" and by promoting "the glory of the Nation." The argument that favored public construction projects over the workshops succeeded to a striking degree: public works projects on the site of the Panthéon were opened in April 1791; the *ateliers de secours* were closed in May 1791.[20]

In the earliest phase of the Revolution, 1789–1791, we thus may detect two forms of citizenship among members of the building trades. First, they appear on the national scene to address themselves to the National Assembly as a unified block that no longer distinguished between status and skill. Here, they are a political constituency unjustly "impoverished" by the lack of a coherent economic policy. They attempt, accordingly, to pressure the National Assembly to formulate policies that would encourage private construction. Second, slightly later, from early 1790 to early 1791, representatives of the building trades speak to the municipality of Paris in more strident terms. They are defined in contrast to the indigent poor; the building tradesmen are the industrious backbone of the nation. Builders demonstrate true fidelity to the Revolution by participating through manual labor in constructing the nation. They deserve public works projects because they have a unique role in crafting physical symbols of the new order.

The building tradesmen henceforth carved out for themselves a special niche in the Third Estate. They were no longer at one with the great majority of the impoverished but virtuous Third Estate; rather, they distinguished themselves by their particularly competitive yet cooperative labor as more dignified and more deserving than the poor. They represent a cut above the rest of the Third Estate by being the most fully industrious of the French.

Are these simple opportunistic self-descriptions to suit different audiences, or do these self-representations of the building trades also have a relationship to the organization of labor during the Revolution? To suggest a few answers, I turn to a third, more sharply focused representation of citizenship, which would emerge directly in response to issues raised on the building site of the Panthéon in Paris. The Panthéon represents a shift from the theory of revolutionary building policy to its practice. On its work site, the transformation of the image of the citizen-builder emerged from work experience, but now expressed by petitions and by actions of members of the construction trades.

ON THE NATION'S WORK SITE: BUILDING CITIZENSHIP AT THE PANTHEON

The construction trades of Paris derived an identity in erecting public buildings promoting the image of the Revolution, and nowhere were the principles of the Revolution more dramatically manifest than in buildings such as the Panthéon. There, the Greco-Roman ideal of fully integrated citizenship was evoked by structures of architectural harmony, and public space was envisioned to exalt public service for the *patrie*. The civic virtue of the Revolutionary patriot, it was believed, could be inspired by constructing eighteenth-century symbolic versions of the agora, the marketplace of ancient Greece which was used as a political assembly for the polis.[21] The Panthéon's rich symbolism, moreover, would extend to its construction policies. Consecrated in April 1791 by the Assembly as a national monument, the Panthéon was intended to fulfill the goals of the Département des travaux publics as articulated earlier by newly hired architects-*fonctionnaires*: to launch a work site that embodied the ideals of a meritocracy of talent.

The construction of the Panthéon was organized as a deliberate departure from the Old Regime system of building the crown's domain. The arrangement of the

Old Regime construction site turned, above all, on privilege. The king's architects, graduates of the Royal Academy of Architecture, were the exclusive supervisors of the king's *grands projets*.[22] The municipality of Paris in 1791, by contrast, set about throwing the construction process wide open, avoiding the corporate body of the crowns' architects for evident political reasons, in favor of hiring a network of expert architects and entrepreneurs to use as verifiers, inspectors, and supervisors of the building site. Much of the elite of the Panthéon represented "new officers" of the new order, types whose artistic sense, training, and craft specialization resembled that of a civil engineer much more than that of an architect. These newly established administrators went about transforming all the activities on the building site. Hiring and firing would no longer be a matter of patronage—of obligations owed to a specific master or entrepreneur—but dictated by the timetable set by supervisors.[23]

The construction of the Panthéon represented a concentrated effort to organize work according to the revolutionary principles of equal access to work and uniformity of contractual conditions. All who qualified, ideally, would find work, and all who worked would receive the same pay for the same labor. Thus, the laborers on the work site of the Panthéon were conceptualized as a group of undifferentiated citizens, freely contracted by the nation and liberated from the constraints of intermediate corporate statutes and regulations.

The revolutionaries intended that a competitive meritocracy would replace patronage. But "merit," following Sieyès's revolutionary formulation of citizenship, meant at the same time political virtue and social utility. Petitions for work on the Panthéon were drafted to advertise a worker as among the most militant of the politically engaged and as among the most deserving of the industrious poor. The process of hiring administrators and workers was thereby deeply politicized. The competitive system of petitioning for jobs meant that former masters and journeymen appealed on the basis of their civic virtue as well as on the basis of talent. Petitions for employment, as administrators or as workers, typically presented the writer as a citizen without resources, the father of a family, a "good patriot," as well as a builder in good standing among colleagues.[24]

Besides competitive employment practices, the innovations on the nation's work site would extend to the organization of labor. The Panthéon was to be a model of a new equitable system of construction. The very division of labor and the establishment of pay scales were fixed by the City of Paris, rather than determined by the ebb and flow of the loosely organized economy of the Old Regime. Work on the Panthéon was to be rigorous and systematic, with every laborer paid daily rates rather than by the task.

The new division of labor was documented by salary rolls before and during the Revolution. Under the Old Regime, workers would be engaged on a given work site as infrequently as not, often for tasks that would only take as little as one-eighth of a day. With the exception of a steady cadre of well-paid assistants, continuity of the work force was erratic, as the individuals changed dramatically from month to month. Pay scales were also tipped in favor of seniority and of what we could call "loyal insiders."

By contrast, the salary rolls for the Panthéon during the Revolution show a cadre of some one thousand workers who were retained for uniform, if high, salaries and for consistent twelve-hour days and six-day work weeks. There was little evident favoritism and no indulgence shown toward those who were sick or injured, who would be rapidly replaced. Rhythms of work and pay were rendered routine and disinterested, tough but fair, on the nation's work site.[25]

The projection of the Revolution onto the Panthéon's building site was thus accomplished in several ways: First, traditional hierarchies between masters and journeymen were jettisoned, and technical experts replaced privileged elites; second, a rugged system of petitioning for work introduced political virtue as a category of employment; finally, the organization of labor was itself made routine and, in the minds of supervisors, "rational." All of these policies represent the recasting of conventional work practices to create a body of citizen-workers. The workers at the Panthéon represented unmediated contractual work that had consented to sell its property, as embodied in its labor, for unflexible and stipulated conditions.

Over the course of 1791, more than a thousand or so masons, carpenters, stonecutters, and other workers were engaged to complete the Panthéon by transforming it from an Old Regime shrine to the alliance of Church and State into a secular temple to the glory of the nation. This politically active, highly skilled, and overworked body of workers would prove a lethal combination, often threatening the social peace of Paris. Ironically, the choice of hiring politically reliable builders would lead to a work force that was highly capable in articulating work-related grievances through the appropriate political channels.

Disturbances on the work site began in the summer of 1791. In June, the Assembly had passed the Le Chapelier law that banned all associations of workers. Shortly thereafter work stoppages that had taken place throughout Paris spread to the Panthéon, accompanied by angry petitions, demanding increases in pay of up to 20 percent and a relaxation of work rhythms set by the municipality. Underlying the conflict throughout the summer were the two distinct yet contradictory objectives of the Panthéon: on the one hand, as a public works site, it held forth the promise of hiring all the unemployed but skilled citizens of Paris; on the other hand, however, as a particular building with limited needs, it followed rhythms of labor that dictated periodically laying off workers. The noted activism of carpenters, for example, was provoked because their primary task—putting up and taking down scaffolding—did not demand the continual engagement of many workers.[26]

The immediate issue of the dismissal of workers on the nation's work site was connected to an even more fundamental concern, outlined in the petitions that called on the municipality to reform the construction practices of the Panthéon. They called into question first and foremost the control of the work process. In July and August 1791, journeymen masons, sculptors, stonecutters, and carpenters on the building site began to contest the right of municipal supervisors to hire and fire workers according to the demands of the Panthéon itself.

During a work stoppage in this period, 380 stonecutters signed a petition claiming that the four municipal supervisors were corrupt; that they skimmed some of the funds meant for paying workers; and that they did not have the right to dictate ''rational'' work practices or salaries. These supervisors were seen as profiteers, whose immediate interest at the Panthéon was strictly personal gain. A work force that had met tough standards of *civisme* had little tolerance for orders from building experts whose political mettle was never questioned.[27]

A consequence of the unrest over the summer of 1791 would be the crafting of this third form of self-representation for the building trades. This was based on civic virtue. The political commitment of a builder was not perceived as a point of distinction from all other poor and industrious workers. A demonstration of the will to see fellow tradesmen as co-citizens was as important as technical expertise in finding and keeping a job at the Panthéon.

The subversive implications of citizen-builders who derived their sense of identity from *civisme* were fully drawn by the architect-theoretician Quatremère de Quincy, the chief inspector of the Panthéon after June 1791. Following the reasoning of other frightened entrepreneurs, he condemned the contentious work force as forming ''factions'' and as fostering ''disorder and anarchy.'' In a ringing denunciation of the workers in August 1791 he focused on the influence of republicanism on their behavior: ''This state of things is the inevitable consequence of the absurd system established between the workers who, by an absurd parody of government, look upon their work as their property, and the building as a republic where they are *concitoyens*.''[28] Apparently, to Quatremère, the building tradesmen had learned the wrong lessons in their education as citizens of the nation on the work site of the Panthéon.

What would be the legacy of the identity of *civisme* and of the conflicts it helped to engender at the Panthéon? Did this self-representation of workers point the way to sans-culottism of the Year II of the Republic? However provocative were the exchanges between the building workers and administrators of the Panthéon, the skirmishes in the summer of 1791 had the clear imprint of traditional corporate politics of the Old Regime.

The principal point of contention was the recasting of traditional hierarchies. The antagonism at the Panthéon centered on the elite agents of revolutionary innovation, not on sans-culotte distinctions between those who worked with their hands and those who did not. The introduction of a new cast of characters on the construction site, the expert-supervisors, with seemingly despotic powers on the building site, sparked the resentment of workers. In August, when these expert-supervisors were replaced at the top of the building hierarchy by the well-known Old Regime building entrepreneur, Poncet, the conflict temporarily died down. Social peace was temporarily restored, despite Poncet's implementation of the municipality's same work regimen and employment schedules, as announced in a poster that proclaimed a massive reduction of stonecutters because "the confusion between such a great number of artisans is prejudicial to the work process."[29] At the heart of the dispute, then, lies the imposition of supposedly rational techniques of organizing work by individuals whose precise capacities and interests were unknown to journeymen. By contrast, Poncet's decisions were accepted probably because it was widely believed that the master's or entrepreneur's practices would be tempered by considerations of tradition or patronage.

As a result of the disturbances that summer, the categories of *civisme* that promised a fragile unity to builders at the opening of the work site of the nation were no longer tenable. The earlier political solidarity of the building trades— united as the poor and as the industrious exemplars of the Third Estate—was fragmented once again into separate crafts. The demands of masons, stonecutters, sculptors, carpenters, and others were formulated in different petitions. While all called for the protection of their jobs, there was no sense of common cause between them.

Apparently, in the absence of alliances over specific political matters, corporate hostilities dating from the old regime came back to the fore. The different métiers portrayed themselves more as competitors than as collaborators on the nation's building site. Despite the measures of the National Assembly to efface corporate distinctions, to mandate into existence the political body of a unified nation, the Old Regime prejudice of distinguishing oneself in terms of task and skill was still alive among the building trades. Ultimately, a coherent political identity of unified citizen-builders would only be forged in the face of Napoleonic repression.

The crisis of a building industry that fragmented the workers at the Panthéon into separate trades raised the problem of self-representation once again. *Civisme* as an identity of builders was not a coherent or consistent image to workers who could not unite on the work site. By the end of 1791, the recasting of builders once again into a politically unified interest group seemed inconceivable. Lingering animosities based on craft or status distinctions seemingly reduced the notion of building as a cooperative education in citizenship into a utopian aspiration.

There remained, however, the interest of building entrepreneurs and contractors in maintaining public confidence in construction: the fear of the building site as a crucible of social unrest was plainly bad for the industry as a whole. This concern is reflected in a pamphlet, published toward the end of 1791, written collaboratively by Girard de Bury, the *procureur du roi* of the just-abolished *chambre du bâtiment*, and two entrepreneur masons. They conceived a detailed proposal for reforming the building site on revolutionary principles. The resulting *Réflexions* were a sophisticated attempt to posit an ideal construction site that incorporated not Sieyès's notions of the exclusivity of the Third Estate, but rather the egalitarian ideals of the Constitution of 1791. These reflections represent a plea for equal access to jobs by all professionals and workers and for a sense of esprit de corps unified under a regime of talent.

The goal of this document was to find the *juste milieu* between civil equality, as enshrined by the constitution, and traditional corporate hierarchy, as dictated by the organization of the building site. These authors proposed a corporate basis for restructuring the trade: a respect for conventional differences was the only basis for encouraging the vigorous professionalization of architects, masons, and carpenters. The lesson learned at the Panthéon, on the tenacity of corporate distinctions, was thus not quickly forgotten.

The achievement of an ideal work site hinged on judging the contending demands of various métiers before the court of public utility. The construction of public buildings was ennobling precisely because, as a process, it served the practical needs of all citizens in the nation. In the words of these masons, "We therefore must not confuse those professions brought forth [*enfantées*] by luxury, and which only have for an objective mere comfort, with those whose labors are of interest to public safety and the life of the Citizen."[30] Here, the building trades are not collapsed into the general class of undifferentiated citizens as in the first form of self-representation; nor, as in the second, are they distinguished from the indigent poor that depended on *atéliers de secours* to survive. This discourse also exhibits little evidence of the third identity of builders, displayed in the *civisme* of workers at the Panthéon. Rather, by late 1791, the spokesmen of the building trades carved out a niche for themselves between poverty on the one hand and the useless luxury trades on the other, which were corrupt for encouraging mere opulence. The building trades here emerged as uniquely occupied with labor in the "interest of public safety and the life of the Citizen." In this, their fourth political incarnation, the image of the building trades as a practical science that served only the public good was the antidote to the fresh memories of unrest at the Panthéon. The builders are thereby portrayed as an inclusive milieu that embraces, in the words of these masons: [A]ll Workers, all Entrepreneurs, all craftsmen who have an equal right to share public works in common; it is thus only fair that they be all called to participate in these works, and that they be employed in harmony with and proportional to their talent."[31]

The meritocracy inherent in "building the nation" is here portrayed as citizenship based on talent alone, stripped of all political virtue. We thus see the builders of Paris move from a portrayal through the image of the destitute citizen-builder to one of industriousness, to *civisme*, and finally to that of talent, in response to shifting contexts of the Revolution.

These four distinct images demonstrate the lack of the hegemony of a single revolutionary notion of citizenship as derived from the organization of labor. They illustrate as well the eclecticism and flexibility of language crafted in response to changing contexts and human experiences. The pamphlets and petitions by builders reveal that the central sans-culotte polemic—the glory of those who work with their hands—was arrived at only after the meandering and sometimes contradictory career of images of the citizen-worker in this early period.

The making and remaking of the identity of the building trades would continue as a process in flux, grounded not in artisanal culture that looked ahead to sans-culottism, nor in social structure alone, but in a constellation of meanings that embraced both. These were images that would eventually transform the builders from a tenuously united milieu to a well-defined hierarchy of conflicting professions, whose ultimate value was in enhancing "the life of the Citizen" of revolutionary France.

NOTES

1. On these moral and social categories of citizenship, see, for example, the response to the enduring question "Qu'est-ce qu'un sans-culotte" in the *Révolutions de Paris*, no. 214 (6–13, November 1793), 177–79.

2. Jacques Rancière, "The Myth of the Artisan," in S. Kaplan and C. Koepp, eds., *Work in France: Representation, Meaning, Organization, and Practice* (Ithaca, N.Y., 1986), 317–34.

3. Steven Laurence Kaplan, "Social Classification and Representation in the Corporate World of Eighteenth-Century France: Turgot's "Carnival," in ibid., 176–228; Richard Mowery Andrews, "Social Structure, Political Elites and Ideology in Revolutionary Paris, 1792–93," *Journal of Social History*, 9 (1985–86), 71–112; Michael Sonenscher, *Work and Wages: Natural Law, Politics, and the Eighteenth-Century French Trades* (Cambridge, U.K., 1989); Lynn Hunt, "The Rhetoric of Revolution," in her *Politics, Culture, and Class in the French Revolution* (Berkeley, Calif., 1984).

4. These two ways of thinking about citizenship are discussed by William Rogers Brubaker in "The French Revolution and the Invention of Citizenship," *French Politics and Society*, 7, no. 3 (1989), 30–49.

5. Figures derived from data in F. Braesch, "Un Essai de statistique de la population ouvrière de Paris ver 1791," *La Révolution Française*, 63 (1912–13), 289–321.

6. "Les travaux pour la Nation" and, after September 1792, "pour la République" are expressions found in petitions for work on the Panthéon by unemployed builders. Archives Nationales (hereafter A.N.), F[13]333[B].

7. A.N.; H[2] 1959 The Bureau de la Ville de Paris authorized 33,333 livres to open *ateliers de charité* during the winter of 1788–1789. On the role of the ateliers of the new Parisian Département des Travaux publics, see the report by one of the department's original administrators, J. B. Edmé Plaisant, *L'Administration des ateliers de charité, 1789–90*, ed. A. Tuetey (Paris, 1906), especially 21–27. See also William Olejniczak, "Working the Body of the Poor: The Ateliers de Charité in Late Eighteenth Century France," in *Journal of Social History*, 24 (1990–91), 87–108.

8. Michel Bruguière, *Gestionnaires et profiteurs de la Révolution: L'administration des finances françaises de Louis XVI à Bonaparte* (Paris, 1986), 44–65; Jacques Godechot, *Les Institutions de la France sous la Révolution et l'Empire* (Paris, 1989), 16–23, 228–32.

9. The papers of the *chambre des bâtiments* are in the A.N., series Z[1J].

10. A.N., AD XIII 13: *Prière à l'Assemblée Nationale pour les Entrepreneurs de Bâtiments, Ouvriers, et Fournisseurs des Bâtiments* (n.d., but 1790 from content). This *prière* denounced creditors who profited from the anarchy of commercial practices, especially 2–3.

11. A vitriolic riposte to the *prière* is in A.N. AD XIII 13: *Observations sur le Mémoire donné à l'Assemblée Nationale par les Entrepreneurs des Bâtiments* (December 1790), written by the *créanciers* who had withdrawn funding from building projects and who were angered at being blamed for the builders' misery.

12. On this *"droit,"* see the comments on a January 1790 report of La Rochefoucauld-Liancourt by Alan Forrest, *The French Revolution and the Poor* (New York, 1981), 27. On charity in the early Revolution and on the later career of the *"droit à l'assistance,"* see Isser Woloch, "From Charity to Welfare in Revolutionary Paris," *Journal of Modern History*, 58 (1986): 779–812.

13. Bibliothèque Nationale (hereafter B.N.), 4o Fm 35337, *Pétition à Monsieur Le Maire, Messieurs les Officiers Municipaux et Notables, Composant le Conseil Général d la Commune de Paris: Par les Arts et Professions du Bâtiments* (December 1790), 5.

14. "Rapport des commissaires du Département des travaux publics" (5 May 1790), in Sigismond Lacroix, ed., *Actes de la Commune de Paris pendant la Révolution* (Paris, 1897), 5:248–51.

15. The concept of a Département des travaux publics was put forth by the *Projet du Plan de Municipalité de la Ville de Paris*, B.N., Lb^{40} 1185 (August 1789), 23. It was only fully put into place by the middle of 1790. See Tuetey's introduction to *L'Administration des ateliers de charité*, v–vii.

16. B.N., Lb^{40} 3267, *Règlement pour les ateliers publics* (11 November 1789). On the implementation of these *règlements*, Archives de Paris: 4AZ 692, "Municipalité de Paris: Lettre écrite par les Administrateurs du Département à MM. les Syndics de la Communauté des Maîtres Maçons" (December 1790).

17. A.N., AD XIII 13: *Mémoire sur la nécessité d'entreprendre de grands travaux publics pour prévenir la ruine totale des Arts en France, et pour occuper, d'une manière utile, les Artistes et Ouvriers de la Capital* (n.d., but late 1790 from context), 1.

18. Plaisant, *L'Administration des ateliers de charité*, 6–14.

19. Ibid., 2–3.

20. On the suppression of the *ateliers de secours*, see Bibliothèque historique de la Ville de Paris (hereafter B.H.V.P.) #743 f.31–2: Letter from the Department des travaux publics to the Section des Arcis; and B.H.V.P. #741, f.103: Letter to the Section Henry IV.

Cf., petitions from *sculpteurs en ornements*, *tailleurs de pierres*, and *charpentiers* written in late April 1791, when both *ateliers de secours* and the Panthéon had been opened. These urged the immediate closing of the ateliers for using the Panthéon's funds; A.N., O^1 1699, F^{13} 1935, F^{13} 1137–1138.

21. Cf. Mark Deming, "Le Panthéon Révolutionnaire," in Barry Bergdoll, et al., eds., *Le Panthéon: Symbole des Révolutions* (Paris, 1989); Mona Ozouf, "Le Panthéon," in Pierre Nora, ed., *Les Lieux de mémoire*, vol. 1, *La République* (Paris, 1987), 138–66; L. Biver, *Le Panthéon à époque révolutionnaire* (Paris, 1982). On the Panthéon in a broader context, cf., Bronislaw Baczko, *Lumières de l'utopie* (Paris, 1979), chap. 6.

22. On the Old Regime construction site, see B.N., V.29997, *Almanach des Bâtiments*, 1790. For lively contemporary critiques of the abuses found there, see Michele de Fremin, *Mémoires critiques d'Architecture* (Paris, 1702), and Marc-Antoine Laugier, *L'Essai sur l'architecture* (Paris, 1755).

23. As described by Quatremère de Quincy. *Rapport Fait au Directoire du Département de Paris sur les Travaux entrepris, continués, ou achevés au Panthéon* (22 October 1793), in A.N. F^{13} 1935.

24. These petitions are collected in A.N. F^{13} 333A-B.

25. The Panthéon's payrolls are scattered through A.N. F^{13} 1137 and O^1 1700. For a contrast with an Old Regime payroll, cf., Archives de Paris: D^{5}B^6 1966, *Brouillon de paie, 1777–85*, Grelet, entrepreneur des bâtiments.

26. For material on disturbances among carpenters, see B.N., F M 35345, *Pétition présentée à la Muncipalité de Paris par les Ci-Devant Maîtres Charpentiers* (30 April 1791); B.N., F M 35346, *Précis presentée à l'Assemblée nationale par les Entrepreneurs de la Charpente* (22 May 1791); B.N., F M 35347, *Précis presenté à l'Assemblée Nationale par les Ouvriers de l'Art de Charpente* (26 May 1791).

27. A.N. F^{13} 1935, 29 July 1791; cf., petition by sculptors, 26 August 1791.

28. B.N. Lb^{40} 165, Quatremère de Quincy, *Rapport sur l'édifice dit de Saint-Geneviève* (1791); also quoted in Sonenscher, *Work and Wages*, 347.

29. A.N., F^{13} 1935, *Département de Paris: Extrait des régistres des délibérations du Directoire*, 24 August 1791.

30. A.N. AD XIII 2B, *Réflexions sur quelques abus qui regnent dans la construction des bâtiments, et sur le moyen de les prévenir ou d'y remédier* (n.d., but 1791 from content), 2–3.

31. Ibid., 3–4.

14

MARRIAGE, RELIGION, AND MORAL ORDER: THE CATHOLIC CRITIQUE OF DIVORCE DURING THE DIRECTORY

Suzanne Desan

"The liberty, existence, union, and prosperity of the Republic rest on the union of marriage, on its unity, stability, purity, respect, and on its indissolubility pronounced by God," wrote Jean-Henri Bancal in his 1797 work, *The New Social Order Founded on Religion*. Confident that a religious republic could exist, this Catholic deputy joined in the attack on divorce in the Council of 500, arguing that the "indissolubility [of marriage] is the true foundation of society, of liberty." This appeal for the stable, patriarchal family was not unusual in 1797. Another opponent of divorce commented, "When a revolution has cut the ancient bonds of society, it is useful to find a new way to build cohesion between the diverse members of society. . . . I propose a king within each family so that we won't need one for all of France."[1]

After the overthrow of Robespierre led to an era of reaction, disillusionment, and questioning, divorce focused particular national attention and anxiety. This issue lay at the crossroads of many hotly contested matters, including religion, morality, gender roles, social stability, and the relationship between the public and private. In September 1792, in its waning hours, the Legislative Assembly had legalized divorce, working on the assumption that marriage was a secular contract and that a nation dedicated to liberty could not demand that individuals alienate their personal liberty permanently in marriage. The law allowed men or women to file under seven broad claims, including "incompatibility" and "mutual consent." Within the next ten years, some thirty thousand divorces occurred, for the most part in urban areas and mainly (about 70 percent of the time) initiated by women.[2]

The relatively easy access to divorce, especially the liberal stipulation allowing divorce based on incompatibility, came under constant critique in the Thermi-

dorian and Directory periods. The winter and spring of 1797 in particular witnessed a prolonged attempt by conservative deputies in the Council of 500 to
outlaw or curtail divorce based on incompatibility. This chapter explores these
crucial debates for insights into the struggle of the late 1790s over what form
of society might best underpin the fledgling, moderate Republic.

Broadly speaking, deputies who leaned toward the right, or toward royalism,
and who were sympathetic to the restoration of Catholicism, argued against easy
access to divorce; some even embraced indissolubility.[3] Anticlerical left-wing
deputies pushed by and large to leave the divorce laws unchanged. But, strikingly,
some of the key players in the divorce debates defied such easy categorization,
with the main pro-divorce advocate of compromise using his pro-Catholic stance
to moderate the influence of Catholic attackers of divorce. After prolonged debate
over whether to suspend divorce based on incompatibility, the legislature ultimately compromised in June 1797 by extending for six months the waiting period
for this form of divorce. Although the law changed little, these debates allow
us to probe the mood of French social thinking en route to the Napoleonic Code,
to investigate the wild-card role of religion in the politics of the Directory, and
to question changing attitudes about domesticity and gender on the part of both
Catholic critics of divorce and their opponents.

THE CONSERVATIVE ATTACK ON DIVORCE

For Catholic deputies, whether they were moderate republicans or unabashed
royalists, divorce raised a central question: Without the moral, emotional, and
ceremonial power of religion, what was the source of moral cohesion within the
family, society, and state? And yet, in the particular political context of 1797,
even after the elections leading to extensive gains by the right in the Council of
500, the restoration of Catholicism and overturning of revolutionary social reforms remained highly charged issues. Catholic opponents of divorce proceeded
with caution, hoping to create an alliance against divorce with conservative
republicans who remained wary of "fanaticism." They launched their main
attack on divorce based on incompatibility and sought to cloak their proposal in
a language of civil contract and to emphasize common concern over moral order,
gender roles, and the relationship of the public and private spheres.

From the very outset, the conservative deputies attacking divorce began in
flamboyant terms to paint the moral disorder and personal suffering that resulted
from the possibility for divorce. They became instant masters of the narrative
of public debauchery and the disastrously broken home. "The lamentations and
cries of a thousand tearful mothers, of a thousand fathers of families, of thousands
of children, about to become widows, [widowers], or orphans, beseech your
justice and should at last touch your *sensibilité*; stop this devastating outpouring
[of divorce] that threatens the republic with ruin," proclaimed Philippe-Delleville
early in the debate. Graphic, heart-wrenching, or blatantly immoral examples
multiplied: a soldier away defending the *patrie* whose wife "burns to leave him

and throw herself into the arms of her seducer''; a young man divorces his newlywed wife to marry her eighty-two-year-old great aunt so that he can inherit her wealth and quickly remarry his true young love.[4]

Even as Catholic deputies gushed forth heartrending images of the devastating impact of divorce, the debaters on both sides of the issue knew that this emotionalism was more than a rhetorical ploy, for the very fragility and changeability of passions lay at the crux of the divorce problematic. Darracq, an anticlerical who fought to leave the laws unchanged, caused a ripple of laughter in the Council of 500 when he observed that one could not "contract a pledge to love eternally, to love all one's life."[5] But marriage as the nexus between contract, passion, and social stability was no laughing matter, especially in the aftermath of the Terror. What exactly would the relationship be between the private realm of sentiment and emotion and the public realm of social and political order? In order to resolve this problem, conservative opponents of divorce promoted both a realignment of the relationship between the public and the private and a reaffirmation of a moral order based on more clearly defined gender roles.

Catholic critics of divorce repeatedly portrayed the institution as invasion into the private sphere of the home. The Year II (1793–1794) in particular had witnessed an intense politicization of private matters, from the naming of children to the choice of how to spend Sunday. As Lynn Hunt has suggested, this intrusion of public politics into the private arena during the radical revolution may have contributed to the urge toward creating a domestic world separate from politics.[6] The opponents of liberal divorce laws implied that this shattering of the public-private line had double meaning: it was the violation of both private conscience and domestic harmony. Earlier in July 1795 Jean-Baptiste Mailhe claimed that the Convention had liberalized divorce laws even further to victimize one imprisoned husband "groaning in the bastilles of the Terror . . . it was a question of isolating the victim, already condemned to death, tearing his wife away from him, [and] throwing her into the arms of another."[7] Linking liberal divorce to the Terror and to the destruction of one man's private life, he could have found no more compelling indictment of the nation's encroachment on the private home. Faulty as his depiction was, it struck a resonant chord. The laws of 4 floréal (April 23, 1794) and 8 nivôse (December 28, 1793) fell with little debate.[8]

Likewise, the Clichien Henry-Larivière also harped on the intrusion into the privacy of conscience as well as home. He rebuked the legislature for creating laws that conflicted with individuals' private religious beliefs. From a different political perspective, Jean-Henri Bancal argued that divorce in effect violated "individual liberty, and property, because the man and woman, . . . united for their entire life, are no longer masters in their homes, when a strange man or woman . . . can trouble the interior of their family, can soon chase them from this sacred asylum, and take their possessions." This slippage equating individual liberty with the defense of home and property against outside encroachments is a striking metaphor, evocative of the changing system of republican values, precursor to the Napoleonic era. It is perhaps especially noteworthy in this context in which the defenders of divorce did not seem to work very hard to reassert their own definitions of individual liberty.[9]

Conservative opponents of divorce for incompatibility explicitly played upon anxiety over gender roles, emphasizing both the weak, susceptible character of the flighty female and the dangerous quality of feminine sexuality.[10] Reversing the 1792 argument that divorce laws prevented the domestic slavery of women, many suggested that the abolition of divorce (at least for incompatibility) would guarantee male fidelity and protect vulnerable women from being seduced or fooled out of their dowries. As the Catholic deputy Duprat pronounced, "Who formulated most of these demands? Women, young wives, some of whom are nursing their babies while others are just about to become mothers. Their weakness and *sensibilité* have been abused: most often [they are] the dupes of some ambitious man or libertine, their greatest error is their charm or their fortune." Susceptible women needed the protection of secure marriages. Conversely, Catholic legislators accused "women above all, [of] forgetting the natural shyness of their sex," and abusing the divorce laws to allow their passions free rein and to escape domestic responsibilities to husband and children. To shock the assembly, Favart read a petition from a wife who resolved that if " 'the day arrives when laws against divorce put this monster [her husband] back in my bed, that day will be his last; I will stab him.' . . . (the council trembles with horror.)" In an interesting assimilation of republican discourse condemning the "empire of frivolous women in the Old Regime," the Catholic deputy Bancal claimed that divorce stemmed from "vice-ridden customs, left over from the monarchy" and had "legally armed frivolous women" against their husbands.[11]

The divorce debates allow an interesting aside on the feminization of religion: some Catholic legislators hinted that perhaps religion, cultivated in the domestic setting, was especially crucial for tempering both the licentious and the gullible sides of female *sensibilité*. Bancal stated the point most directly: "The sweetness, obscurity, retreat, silence, the interior care of the family, prayer, reading of the Holy Scriptures, are the lot and the happiness of the woman who wants to fulfill her duties. . . . Women are sensitive [*"sensible"*] and weak. They need religion to make them strong, to assure their virtue and happiness." This religious domesticity would mitigate against divorce. Bancal's 1797 language bears a notable resemblance to the assertion of the idéologue Jacques-Louis Moreau, who wrote in 1803 that women's "uterine influence [made them] more disposed than men were to believe in spirits and see ghosts; they succumb all the more easily to all superstitious practices and their prejudices are more numerous."[12] While Moreau and Bancal had very different attitudes toward religion, their overlapping vision of the links between feminine *sensibilité*, religion, and domesticity may help to illustrate how religion became increasingly feminized in the nineteenth century. Catholics and non-Catholics alike came to share a cultural expectation that religiosity was tightly linked to the emotional makeup and domestic responsibilities of women.

In addition to emphasizing the invasion of public matters into private life and weaving a dramatic narrative of the immoral impact of divorce law, Catholic deputies pointed out with varying degrees of directness that the desacralization of marriage had weakened and cheapened conjugal bonds. By trying to reduce marriage to a simple contract it had become "a market of human flesh," "[commercial] traffic," a "fraud," or even "prostitution." These legislators repeatedly used images of financial and sexual transactions to contrast the current situation with the true nature of marriage as "a sacred bond," ("*lien sacré*") "the most holy of obligations," "a solemn knot,"[13] In outlining the sacred social significance of this bond, opponents of divorce were quick to appropriate and transform the republican language of civil contract and to expand the social parameters of this "civil bond . . . that has too imposing a character to be destroyed at will," in the words of Favard. (Interestingly enough, the Catholic deputies who attacked divorce for incompatibility were more willing to raise—and reinterpret—the definition of marriage as a civil contract than were those who defended the 1792 law.) For example, Debonnières admitted in June 1797 that marriage was a "civil contract," but asserted that it was "the first, the most invested [*interessé*] of all." It was a "sacred" contract "that can not be broken without danger to society . . . [for] marriage is the fundamental base of society." Likewise, Siméon proclaimed that the conjugal contract was no simple civil contract, for it created a family and involved "interested third parties: the children, the parents of the two spouses, society in general. The law should look out for these third parties and not allow the abrogation of this contract which is *at once public and private* [emphasis added]."[14]

In depicting the social importance and unique character of this civil contract, some legislators argued for indissolubility by evoking the Catholic theological position that marriage made the man and woman into one being, but they cloaked their interpretation in natural rather than religious law. When Siméon described the conjugal bond as a "natural contract by which the two become one," he took pains to distinguish his depiction of marriage from "religious vows," and contended that it was wrong to "believe that everything that they [the religions] have sanctioned was bad and contemptible. . . . The indissolubility of marriage became a religious dogma only because it was already a natural and political dogma." Although he strove to couch his opinions as moderate, Siméon pushed his point on the power of religion, noting that because the conjugal bond was indissoluble by nature, "all Peoples took the divinity as a witness to its lasting quality" and "consecrated and blessed marriage." In the delicate political and religious context of 1797. Catholic deputies strove to give their religious vision some philosophical legitimacy in the revolutionary register, but few present had any doubts as to their source of inspiration. The pro-divorce deputy Darracq was quick to assert that to believe that spouses in marriage were "*duo in carne una* would be to dive back into the sacerdotal errors that we fortunately have escaped."[15]

Another strategy of the pro-Catholic opponents of divorce was to remind the

Council of 500, with increasing frequency and boldness, that religion had a particular ritualistic and emotional power that enabled it to stabilize wayward passions on behalf of social order. They played upon the post-Thermidorian doubt about the regenerative moral power of either revolutionary legislation or the new secular political culture. "Do not think that it's your legislation that makes these [conjugal] bonds respectable; no, it is what remains of morals, of public decency, and of religion that serves as a brake," insisted Philippe-Delleville in the final debates over divorce in June 1797. Jean-Baptiste Mailhe contrasted the irreligiosity and consequent weakness of French marriage with the Athenians and Romans, who had surrounded marriage with "religious ceremonies that made it more respectable" and harder to dissolve.[16]

THE DEFENDERS OF DIVORCE RESPOND

The deputies attacking divorce for incompatibility had annexed the language of civil contract to depict marriage as a peculiarly powerful social contract on the hinge between public and private. Religiosity and ritual throughout the history of civilization had provided moral support and acted as the ideal mediator between private passions and public order, they claimed. Finally, they had depicted in graphic detail the intrusion of divorce into an idealized domestic world and implied that divorce had also thrown gender roles out of whack. Theirs was a powerful assault, touching many flashpoints of anxiety in the Directorial period. In certain ways their attack joined with the shift in the balance of power in the legislature to the right after the elections of April 1797 to frame the debate in largely conservative terms. The issue of moral order became most central.

In some ways the response to the attack on divorce for incompatibility was unexpected. Very few mentions were made about the allusions to religion.[17] Only a few of the defenders of divorce drew upon the 1792 argument that individual liberty in general and, more precisely, the individual right to contract freely stood at stake. In the winter of 1797 Cambacérès, the tireless author of unsuccessful civil codes, commented succinctly in defense of divorce and of his latest civil code that "the needs of morality should not serve as a pretext for attacking individual liberty." And Darracq, a new man in the national legislature, resurrected old references to the "natural rights of man" to argue that marriage without divorce would constitute "the mutual *alienation of their persons*" [original emphasis]. As for Félix Faulcon, the master of the final compromise, although he referred occasionally to individual liberty, he used this argument most extensively in defense of divorce by mutual consent, defined liberty rather vaguely, and made this aspect of his defense by far less pivotal than others.[18]

Rather, as a primary strategy the defenders of divorce engaged in their own battle for control of definitions of morality and the tranquil family life as the underpinning of order in the republic. Divorce laws in fact protected domestic morality and the private family, they asserted. In response to the frenzied depictions of families torn asunder by divorce, the pro-divorce deputies produced their own dramatic tales of families forced to endure wretched lives together or to reveal their gut-wrenching secrets at the moral expense of the whole nation. In a telling example, Lecointe-Puyraveau concluded his 1797 defense of divorce with a vivid portrait of a young woman forced to remain married to the man who had denounced her father during the Terror. If she were not allowed to divorce she would face the executioner of her father daily. "When he approaches her, she envisions in his hand a bloody head suspended by its white hair. She cries out to you: he is the one who has killed my father; he cannot be my husband." "Good enough to figure in a novel," was the phrase chosen by the anti-divorce Dumolard to debunk these scenarios.[19]

The defenders of divorce stressed that divorce based on incompatibility acted as a catchall category. Without this possibility, individuals would have to reveal a multitude of private causes for unhappiness, ranging from "adultery and impotence" to "shameful diseases" to a wife's forced prostitution at the hands of her "wasteful and cowardly" husband, as Oudot suggested. Pro-divorce deputies particularly emphasized the need to avoid scandalous public trials. Félix Faulcon drew on his years as an Old Regime judge to call up repeated images of trials, filled with "scandalous revelations that publicly uncovered the hidden turpitudes of families and familiarized . . . young listeners with contagious descriptions of depravity and vice." Such disclosures would have a corrosive effect on morals and would hardly dignify marriage, thundered the moderate Faulcon.[20]

The attempt of the pro-divorce faction to win back the discourse of sentimentality, domesticity, and moral order suggests how attitudes toward the division between the private and public spheres had changed even among supporters of the Revolution. Certainly the republican cult of motherhood had long promoted an idealized realm of family virtue and happiness, but before Thermidor republican culture had not advocated the segregation of this private sphere. During the radical revolution, virtually no aspect of private life was immune from public scrutiny, and a public citizen must ground his or her political validity in private virtue. Clearly, this politicization of the private took on a particular intensity due to the political climate of the year II (1793–1794); but as Sarah Maza has argued, this ever-expanding public sphere grew in part precisely out of the public disclosure of private scandals in much discussed trials in the final years of the Old Regime.[21] By 1797, however, we have come full circle from this exposure of the private in order to create and then maintain the public sphere. The gulf of the Terror loomed large, and according to the deputies defending divorce, some of them ex-Montagnards, public revelations of private indiscretions were no longer necessary for the public good. They would in fact only be invasive and detrimental to the republican spirit and the moral order. Seeing that Catholic opponents and republican defenders of divorce shared the certainty that domestic privacy, however defined, sustained the political and social order helps us to understand the evolution toward the domestic ideology of the nineteenth century.

As a further political strategy, the defenders of divorce struggled in a variety of ways to occupy the moderate ground. Several deputies espoused the notion that to suspend the law allowing divorce by incompatibility (while waiting for the completed civil code) was an unconstitutional and anarchical political act. Reminiscent of the Terror, such an act played dangerously with the laws and stability of the land. Pons de Verdun warned that such a suspension of law might usher in anarchy, "because what is anarchy, if not an interregnum of the law?" As Félix Faulcon asserted, "*Hélas!* we have only *revolutionized* too much in France; I would like to believe, Citizens, that you do not want to *revolutionize* divorce" [original emphasis].[22]

Most tellingly, this pro-Catholic moderate, who engineered the final compromise in June 1797, deliberately attached his defense of divorce and his position of political moderation to a pro-Catholic stance by circulating a pamphlet entitled *Opinions sur le divorce et sur les ministres du culte*. This joint defense of nonjuring priests and of divorce seemed to appeal deliberately to opposing coalitions within the legislature and sought to defuse the hold of the anti-divorce deputies over any legislators sympathetic to Catholicism. When he presented his commission's minimal proposal to extend the wait for divorce for incompatibility by six months, Faulcon spoke almost more about the need for compromise among factions than about divorce or the proposed change: "It is in suspending one's biases that one becomes truly useful to one's country, and not in attributing (without thought) either dangerous philosophical leanings to those who defend the institution of divorce, or the narrow mindset of an absurd fanaticism to those who want to destroy it."[23] In the end, the six-month delay as a compromise solution to the issue of divorce for incompatibility found backing from a coalition of leftists and moderates who were wary of the growing royalist presence in the legislature. Despite the opposition of Portalis, the Council of Ancients backed this slight change in the divorce law.

In short, for all the discussion of divorce and its ills, the legislative councils did little to change the divorce laws. They left it to the Napoleonic era to make divorce truly difficult to obtain, especially for women. Nonetheless, despite the lack of broad legal changes, the hotly contested debates over marriage, religion, and morality reveal the fault lines of anxiety and the shifting social thinking of the Directory period. Among the supporters of divorce, the erosion of the old defense based on individual liberty bore witness to the uncertainty of the path toward liberal individualism in the late 1790s. In contrast, as the Catholic opponents of divorce attempted to redefine the conjugal civil contract as a unique, socially loaded contract "at once public and private" and to suggest the power of religion to return some moral stability to marriage and society, they began to pave the road toward both the Napoleonic Civil Code and the Concordat. But most striking is the shared concern of both opponents and proponents of divorce with strengthening the lines between the public and private spheres and with creating a strong domestic sphere as the basis of the social and political order— whether republican or royalist, Catholic or secular. The legislative debates over divorce during the Directory may not have changed much in the way of laws, but they helped to lay the foundations for domestic ideology and cast the terms of nineteenth-century negotiations over the relationship among family, religion, state, and society.

NOTES

1. Jean-Henri Bancal, *Du nouvel ordre social fondé sur la religion* (Paris, 1797), 235; Charles Toussaint Guiraudet, *De la famille considérée comme l'élément des sociétés* (Paris, 1797), 26–27, also 4–9.

2. See Dominique Dessertine, *Divorcer à Lyon sous la Révolution et l'Empire* (Lyon, 1981); Marcel Garaud and Romuald Szramkiewicz, *La Révolution française et la famille* (Paris, 1978), 67–89; Roderick Phillips, *Family Breakdown in Late Eighteenth-Century France: Divorces in Rouen, 1792–1803* (Oxford, 1980), and *Putting Asunder: A History of Divorce in Western Society* (Cambridge, Eng., 1988); Francis Ronsin, *Le Contrat sentimental: Débats sur le mariage, l'amour, le divorce de l'Ancien Régime à la Restauration* (Paris, 1990); and James F. Traer, *Marriage and the Family in Eighteenth-Century France* (Ithaca, N.Y., 1980).

3. While the religious beliefs of deputies are difficult to determine, I am calling "Catholic" those who argued strongly in favor of relaxing laws regarding non-jurors and public Catholic worship. Information on the deputies' religious leanings is from reading debates on religious issues during the Directory and from Adolphe Robert, Edgar Bourloton, and Gaston Cougny, *Dictionnaire de parlementaires*, 5 vols. (Paris, 1891). As conservatives suspected of royalism, many anti-divorce deputies faced either deportation or the annulation of their elections after the 18 fructidor coup against the right in September 1797. This list includes Boissy d'Anglas, Debonnières, Dumolard, Duprat, Henri-Larivière, Mailhe, Maillard de la Somme, Portalis, and Siméon.

4. Philippe-Delleville, 11 frimaire an V, *Moniteur* #73, 13 frimaire an V/ 3 décembre 1796; Archives nationales (hereafter AN) AD XVIIIc 365, *Rapport fait par Favard sur le divorce, au nom d'une commission spéciale, 20 nivôse an V* (Paris, an V/ 1797).

5. Darracq, 4 pluviôse an V, *Moniteur* #126, 6 pluviôse an V/ 25 janvier 1797.

6. Lynn Hunt, "Révolution française et vie privée," in *Histoire de la vie privée de la Révolution à la Grande Guerre*, ed. Michelle Perrot (Paris, 1985), 21–51, especially 21–28, 50–51.

7. Mailhe, 15 thermidor an III, *Moniteur* #321, 21 thermidor an III/ 8 August 1795.

8. These laws had shortened the wait for remarriage to ten months for women and eliminated it for men and had allowed divorce based on *de facto* separation of six months or more. Garaud, *Révolution et la famille*, 78–93.

9. Henri-Larivière, 29 prairial an V, *Moniteur* #274, 4 messidor an V/22 juin 1797; AN AD XVIIIc 365, Jean-Henri Bancal, *Opinion sur le divorce, prononcée au Conseili des 500, 12 pluviôse an V* (Paris, an V/1797).

10. On the nature of the feminine, see Suzanne Desan, " 'Constitutional Amazons': Jacobin Women's Clubs in the French Revolution," in Bryant Ragan and Elizabeth Williams, eds., *Re-Creating Authority in Revolutionary France* (New Brunswick, N.J., 1992), 11–35; Elke Harten and Christian Harten, *Femmes, Culture, et Révolution*, trans. B. Chabot, J. Etore, and O. Mannoni (Paris, 1989); Lynn Hunt, *The Family Romance of the French Revolution* (Berkeley, Calif., 1992), especially chaps. 4 and 6; Joan Landes, *Women and the Public Sphere in the Age of the French Revolution* (Ithaca, N.Y., 1988), especially chap. 4; and Dorinda Outram, " 'Le langage mâle de la vertu': Women and

the Discourse of the French Revolution,'' in Peter Burke and Roy Porter, eds., *The Social History of Language* (Cambridge, Eng., 1987), 120–35, especially 124–26.

11. A.N. AD XVIIIc 365, Pierre-Louis Duprat, *Opinion sur la suspension du divorce pour cause d'incompatibilité d'humeur et de caractère, séance du 13 pluviôse an V* (Paris, an V/ 1797); Favart, *Rapport sur le divorce*; Bancal, *Opinion sur le divorce*.

12. Bancal, *Du nouvel ordre social fondé sur la religion*, 245; Jacques-Louis Moreau, *Histoire naturelle de la femme* (1803), quoted in Hunt, ''Révolution française et vie privée,'' 50.

13. For example, see in A.N. AD XVIIIc 365 the speeches of Bancal, Favart, Duprat, cited above, and Siméon, *Opinion sur la suspension du divorce pour incompatibilité, séance du 5 pluviôse an V* (Paris, an V/1797); and the speeches of Philippe-Delleville, 11 frimaire an V, *Moniteur* #73, 13 frimaire an V/ 3 décembre 1796; Golzart, 28 nivôse an V, *Moniteur* #120, 30 nivôse an V/19 janvier 1797; Mailhe, 4 pluviôse an V, *Moniteur* #126, 6 pluviôse an V/ 25 janvier 1797; Dumolard, 12 pluviôse an V, *Moniteur* #135, 15 pluviôse an V/ 3 février 1797.

14. Debonnières, 20 prairial an V, *Moniteur* # 267, 27 prairial an V/ 15 juin 1797; A.N. AD XVIIIc 365; Favart, *Rapport sur le divorce*; and Siméon, *Opinion sur la suspension du divorce*.

15. Siméon, *Opinion sur la suspension du divorce*. See also Bancal, *Du Nouvel ordre social fondé sur la religion*, 230–35, 238–42, 248; Darracq, 4 pluviôse an V, *Moniteur* #126, 6 pluviôse an V/ 25 janvier 1797.

16. Philippe-Delleville, 20 prairial an V, *Moniteur* #267, 27 prairial an V/ 15 juin 1797; Mailhe, 4 pluviôse an V, *Moniteur* #125–26, 5–6 pluviôse an V/ 25–26 janvier 1797.

17. See the comment of Darracq on 4 pluviôse an V/ 24 January 1797 on the ''sacerdotal errors'' of marriage as a sacred union, mentioned above. On 5 pluviôse an V, Lecointe reproached anti-divorce petitioners for timing their attack badly, for they had ''chosen exactly the moment when refractory priests are recovering their most dangerous influence.'' *Moniteur* #128, 8 pluviôse an V/ 27 janvier 1797.

18. Cambacérès, 3 pluviôse an V, *Moniteur* #125, 5 pluviôse an V/ 24 janvier 1797; Darracq, 4 pluviôse an V, *Moniteur* #126, 6 pluviôse an V/ 25 janvier 1797; Félix Faulcon, *Mélanges législatifs, historiques, et politiques, pendant la durée de la Constitution de l'an III* (Paris, 1801/ an XI), 1: 226–37, 236–37, 243.

19. Lecointe-Puyraveau, *Opinion sur le projet de suspension de l'article II de la loi du 20 septembre 1792, séance du 5 pluviôse an V* (Paris, an V/1797), 16; Dumolard, 12 pluviôse an V, *Moniteur* #135, 15 pluviôse an V/ 3 février 1797.

20. Oudot, 20 nivôse an V, *Moniteur* #112, 22 nivôse an V/ 11 janvier 1797, and 28 nivôse an V, *Moniteur* #120, 30 nivôse an V/19 janvier 1797; Faulcon, *Mélanges législatifs*, 1: 208–13, 221–24, 228–29, 244, 249–50.

21. Sarah Maza, ''Domestic Melodrama as Political Ideology: The Case of the Comte de Sanois,'' *American Historical Review* 94 (1989), 1249–64, and ''Le tribunal de la nation: Les mémoires judiciaires et l'opinion publique à la fin de l'ancien régime,'' *Annales: ESC*, 1987, 73–90.

22. Pons de Verdun, 28 nivôse an V, *Moniteur* #120, 30 nivôse an V/19 janvier 1797; Thibaudeau, 20 prairial an V, *Moniteur* #267, 27 prairial an V/ 15 juin 1797; Faulcon, *Mélanges législatifs*, 1: 214.

23. Faulcon, *Mélanges législatifs*, 1: 264.

AFTERWORD

Lynn A. Hunt

Despite our collective title and Pierre Rétat's fine effort to give the concept of citizenship some historical definition, many of the chapters in this book have addressed the apprenticeship of democracy as much as the concept of citizenship. The definition of citizenship was, of course, a prime site of contestation in the apprenticeship of democracy, but that apprenticeship included many other areas of conflict as well. We can think productively about those various areas of conflict and about the differences and similarities in the chapters included here if we imagine them as arrayed in a field between two poles ranging from the theory of democracy, on one end, to its practice, on the other.

The theory pole is most obviously identified with the work of François Furet and most clearly exemplified here in the chapter by Patrice Gueniffey, one of his most promising students. Perhaps to the surprise of the authors, I would also include on the theory end the chapters by Michael Fitzsimmons and Madelyn Gutwirth. Those who emphasized the theoretical aspects of French revolutionary democracy also tend to underline its supposed failures (though this is not inherent in the endeavor shown by Fitzsimmons). Democracy failed because it was incorrectly theorized or conceptualized by the revolutionary leadership. Those who emphasize the theory of democracy and the French failures to theorize it correctly tend to associate the Revolution with terror and manipulation, envisaging it as a machine of discourse that chewed up its victims, a kind of giant bulldozer behind the text of democracy, if you will, with Robespierre in the driver's seat, maniacally building prototypes for the concentration camps of the twentieth century (whether for political opponents, Vendée rebels, or women in general). From my description, you will sense that I have some hesitations about this view.

Those who emphasize theory in the mode of Furet tend to argue that democracy was doomed to failure, not by illiteracy, inexperience, war, or even political factionalism—that is, by the nuts and bolts of social and political organization—but rather by the inadequacy of the early political conceptualizations. In Patrice Gueniffey's chapter, defects in the electoral process opened the way to manipulation by minorities. In Madelyn Gutwirth's chapter, the long intellectual tradition of misogyny culminated in the inevitable exclusion of women from full citizenship. Both offer brilliant analyses of the workings and failings of the conceptual apparatuses in question, but they should also give us pause. Is action—the messy action that comes in a period of revolution in particular—really that subject to constraint and determination by theoretical and conceptual schemas?

Most of this volume collects nearer the other pole—that is, near the various practices of democracy. Conscription, women's political mobilization, the press, workers' petitions and actions, educational reform, and voting—these are all examples of the ways in which democratic practices developed during the French Revolution. Although many interesting questions about the practice of democracy are raised, they are done so individually and separately. It may be, therefore, that we need more consideration now of the logic of practice—that is, a new marriage of theory and practice that would explain practice in more theoretical terms, and theory in more practical ones.

Although they often underline the limits on revolutionary universalism in rights, the chapters on practice underline the enormous political, social, and cultural energies that were mobilized by revolutionary democracy. Darline Levy shows, for example, the ways in which women, who were not expected to be part of the process, nonetheless found themselves caught up in democratic mobilization. These chapters demonstrate, as well, the continuation of this learning experience well beyond the Terror. After Thermidor, military service, for instance, became, if anything, even more central. The Lakanal Law set the government's sights on universal education for both sexes, and as Suzanne Desan has shown, debates on divorce went to the heart of relations among the individual, the family, and the state. The apprenticeship of democracy continued past 1794, right up to 1799. It is at least arguable that this learning in 1794–1799 had more impact on the real structures of French government than what came before.

Thus, I would metaphorize the Revolution not as a bulldozer or Kafkaesque machine, but as a hothouse in which everything grew quickly. The seeds were there in 1789, but some were choked off quickly, as in workers' organizations, allowing others to grow grotesquely, as in the institutions and practices of the Terror; still others were stunted, as were women's rights, while some grew steadily and took real roots, which I would argue to have been the case with elections in the long term of the decade. In this hothouse, no one was entirely in charge. I always like to think back to the opening pages of Robert Palmer's *Twelve Who Ruled* and that vision of twelve men in an atmosphere of some frenzy, mopping their brows, trying to see through the mist of hot humidity that engulfed their activities and ultimately overwhelmed them.

The political process triggered the hothouse effect, but once established, the

Revolution developed real social content. It fostered new kinds of social consciousness of racial, gender, and social groupings. As a result, questions arose from the beginning about the meaning of citizenship. Without citizenship as an issue, there would have been no women's movement or demands for suffrage by free blacks. Without the much-maligned universalism of men of 1789, there would have been no demands for inclusion of new groups: women, blacks, Jews, Protestants, and non-property-owners. In other words, it is easier to explain how women's rights were denied, given the past, or how difficult it was to abolish slavery, since no other country did it before the 1830s, than it is to explain how the sexist, racist, anti-ethnic deputies of 1789 maneuvered themselves into imagining a nation based on universally extendable, equal, civil rights.

Democracy, as Jeremy Popkin mentioned, is the ability to tolerate the gap between an event and its cultural and political framing. It is the willingness to abide with the uncertainty of meaning that is inevitably unleashed in society. Put in other terms, it is the continual struggle over the boundaries of citizenship. That uncertainty, that gap, those struggles are not the reason for the Revolution's failure, but rather the essence of democracy itself. In semiotic terms, it is possible to define the Revolution as conflicts over signification, but the conflicts were never limited to words or signs in the narrow sense. If we are to develop a fuller understanding of the logic of the revolutionary practices of democracy, we need to pay more attention to the political and social modes of conflict, not as separate instances but as parts of a whole revolving around the uncertainties of citizenship and democracy. The chapters in this book point the way to such a reexamination, and at the same time they show us that much remains to be done.

SELECTED BIBLIOGRAPHY

NATIONAL ASSEMBLY, 1789–1791

Applewhite, Harriet B. *Political Alignment in the French National Assembly, 1789–1791*. Baton Rouge: Louisiana State University Press, 1993.

Baker, Keith M. *Inventing the French Revolution. Essays on French Political Culture in the Eighteenth Century*. Cambridge: Cambridge University Press, 1990.

Fitzsimmons, Michael P. "Privilege and the Polity in France, 1786–1791." *American Historical Review* 92 (1987): 269–95.

Furet, François, and Halévi, Ran, eds. *Orateurs de la Révolution Française*. Vol. 1, Les Constituants (introduction). Paris: Gallimard, 1989.

Griffiths, Robert Howell. *Le Centre perdu: Malouet et les "monarchiens" dans la Révolution française*. Grenoble: Presses Universitaires de Grenoble, 1988.

Higonnet, Patrice. *Class, Ideology, and the Rights of Nobles during the French Revolution*. Oxford: Clarendon Press, 1981.

Lemay, Edna Hindie, et al. *Dictionnaire des Constituants, 1789–1791*. 2 vols. Paris: Universitas, 1991.

Lucas, Colin, ed. *The Political Culture of the French Revolution (The French Revolution and the Creation of Modern Political Culture, II)*. New York: Pergamon Press, 1988.

Palmer, Robert R. *The Age of the Democratic Revolution*. 2 vols. Princeton, N.J.: Princeton University Press, 1959–1964.

Tackett, Timothy. "Nobles and Third Estate in the Revolutionary Dynamic of the National Assembly, 1789–1790." *American Historical Review* 94 (April 1989): 271–301.

CARICATURE

Agulhon, Maurice, *Marianne into Battle. Republican Imagery and Symbolism in France, 1785–1880*. Cambridge, U.K.: Cambridge University Press, 1981 (trans).

French Caricature and the French Revolution, 1789–1799. Los Angeles: Grunwald Center for the Graphic Arts, Wight Art Gallery, University of California, Los Angeles, 1988.

Henderson, Ernest. *Symbol and Satire in the French Revolution.* New York: G.P. Putnam's Sons, 1912.

Hunt, Lynn. *Politics, Culture, and Class in the French Revolution.* Berkeley, Calif.: University of California Press, 1984.

Paulson, Ronald. *Representations of Revolution (1789–1820).* New Haven, Conn.: Yale University Press, 1983.

Vovelle, Michel, ed. *La Révolution française: Images et récit. 1789–1799.* 5 vols. Librairie du bicentenaire de la Révolution française. Paris: Livre Club Diderot/ Messidor, 1986.

THE THEATER

Carlson, Marvin. *The Theatre of the French Revolution.* Ithaca, N.Y.: Cornell University Press, 1966.

Chazin-Bennahum, Judith. *Dance in the Shadow of the Guillotine.* Carbondale: Southern Illinois University Press, 1988.

Collins, Herbert F. *Talma: Biography of an Actor.* London: Faber and Faber, 1963.

Isherwood, Robert M. *Farce and Fantasy: Popular Entertainment in 18th Century Paris.* New York: Oxford University Press, 1986.

Lough, John. *Paris Theatre Audiences in the 17th and 18th Centuries.* London: Oxford University Press, 1981.

Root-Bernstein, Michele. *Boulevard Theatre and Revolution in 18th Century Paris.* Ann Arbor: University of Michigan Press, 1984.

ELECTIONS

Crook, Malcolm. "*Aux urnes, citoyens!* Urban and Rural Electoral Behavior during the French Revolution." In *Reshaping France: Town, Country, and Region during the French Revolution,* edited by Alan Forrest and Peter Jones, 152–67. Manchester: Manchester University Press, 1991.

Edelstein, Melvin A. "La Place de la Révolution française dans la politisation des paysans." *Annales Historiques de la Révolution Française,* no. 280 (April–June 1990): 135–49.

Fournier, Georges. "La Participation électorale en Haute-Garonne pendant la Révolution." *Annales du Midi* 101 (1989): 47–71.

Gueniffey, Patrice. "Elections" and "Suffrage." In *A Critical Dictionary of the French Revolution,* edited by François Furet and Mona Ozouf. Cambridge, Mass.: Belknap Press of Harvard University Press, 1989.

Lancelot, Alain. *L'Abstentionnisme électoral en France.* Fondation Nationale de Sciences Politiques, Cahiers 162. Paris: A. Colin, 1968.

Woloch, Isser. *Jacobin Legacy: The Democratic Movement under the Directory.* Part 3. Princeton, N.J.: Princeton University Press, 1970.

THE PRESS

Censer, Jack. *Prelude to Power: The Parisian Radical Press, 1789–1791*. Baltimore: Johns Hopkins University Press, 1976.

Darnton, Robert, and Roche, Daniel, eds. *Revolution in Print: The Press in France, 1775–1800*. Berkeley, Calif.: University of California Press in collaboration with the New York Public Library, 1989.

Gough, Hugh. *The Newspaper Press in the French Revolution*. Chicago: Dorsey Press, 1988.

Labrosse, Claude, and Rétat, Pierre. *Naissance du Journal Révolutionnaire, 1789*. Librairie du bicentenaire de la Revolution française. Lyon: Presses Universitaires de Lyon, 1989.

Murray, William. *The Right-Wing Press in the French Revolution, 1789–92*. Woodbridge, Suffolk (U.K.): The Boydell Press for The Royal Historical Society, 1986.

Popkin, Jeremy. *Revolutionary News: The Press in France, 1789–1799*. Durham, N.C.: Duke University Press, 1990.

———. *The Right-Wing Press in France, 1792–1800*. Chapel Hill, N.C.: University of North Carolina Press, 1980.

PRIMARY EDUCATION

Baczko, Branislaw. *Une Education pour la démocratie: textes et projets de l'époque révolutionnaire*. Classiques de la politique. Paris: Garnier, 1982.

Furet, François, and Ozouf, Jacquest. *Reading and Writing: Literacy in France from Calvin to Jules Ferry*. New York: Cambridge University Press, 1982 (trans).

Gontard, Maurice. *L'Enseignement primaire en France de la Révolution à la loi Guizot, 1789–1833*. Paris: Belles Lettres, 1959.

Grew, Raymond, and Harrigan, Patrick. *School, State, and Society: The Growth of Elementary Schooling in Nineteenth-Century France, a Quantitative Analysis*. Ann Arbor, Mich.: University of Michigan Press, 1991.

Palmer, Robert. *The Improvement of Humanity: Education and the French Revolution*. Princeton, N.J.: Princeton University Press, 1985.

Vignery, Robert. *The French Revolution and the Schools: The Educational Policies of the Mountain, 1792–94*. Madison, Wisc.: State Historical Society of Wisconsin for the Dept. of History, University of Wisconsin, 1965.

MILITARY SERVICE

Bertaud, Jean-Paul. *La Révolution armée. Les soldats-citoyens et la Révolution française*. Paris: Robert Laffont, 1979.

Forrest, Alan. *Conscripts and Deserters: The Army and French Society during the Revolution and Empire*. New York: Oxford University Press, 1989.

———. *The Soldiers of the French Revolution*. Durham, N.C.: Duke University Press, 1989.

Lynn, John A. *The Bayonets of the Republic: Motivation and Tactics in the Army of Revolutionary France, 1791–1794*. Urbana: University of Illinois Press, 1984.

Scott, Samuel F. *The Response of the Royal Army to the French Revolution: The Role and Development of the Line Army, 1787–1793*. Oxford: Clarendon Press, 1978.

Woloch, Isser. *The French Veteran from the Revolution to the Restoration*. Chapel Hill: University of North Carolina Press, 1979.

WOMEN'S CITIZENSHIP

Bourdin, Isabelle. *Les Sociétés populaires à Paris pendant la Révolution française*. Université de Paris, Centre d'études de la Révolution française, Documentation (v.3). Paris: Librairie du Recueil Sirey, 1937.
Fauré, Christine. *Democracy without Women. Feminism and the Rise of Liberal Individualism in France*, translated by Claudia Grobman and John Berks. Bloomington: Indiana University Press, 1991.
Godineau, Dominique. *Citoyennes tricoteuses. Les femmes du peuple à Paris pendant la Révolution française*. Aix-en-Provence: Alinéa, 1988.
Landes, Joan M. *Women and the Public Sphere in the Age of the French Revolution*. Ithaca, N.Y.: Cornell University Press, 1988.
Levy, Darline G., and Applewhite, Harriet B. "Women and Political Revolution in Paris." In *Becoming Visible: Women in European History*, 2nd ed., edited by Renate Bridenthal, Claudia Koonz, and Susan Stuard. Boston: Houghton Mifflin, 1987.
Levy, Darline G., Applewhite, Harriet B., and Johnson, Mary Durham, eds. *Women in Revolutionary Paris, 1789–1795*. Urbana: University of Illinois Press, 1979.
Rose, Robert Barrie. *The Making of the Sans-Culottes. Democratic Ideas and Institutions in Paris, 1789–92*. Manchester: Manchester University Press, 1983.

PARISIAN WORKERS

Andrews, Richard M. "Social Structure, Political Elites and Ideology in Revolutionary Paris, 1792–1794: A Critical Evaluation of Albert Soboul's *Les Sans-Culottes parisiens en l'an II*." *Journal of Social History* 9 (1985–86): 72–112.
Kaplan, Steven L., and Koepp, Cynthia J., eds., *Work in France: Representations, Meaning, Organization and Practice*. Ithaca, N.Y.: Cornell University Press, 1986.
Leith, James A. *Space and Revolution: Projects for Monuments, Squares and Public Buildings in France, 1789–1799*. Montreal: McGill-Queen's University Press, 1991.
Soboul, Albert. *Les Sans-Culottes parisiens en l'an II. Mouvement populaire et gouvernement révolutionnaire, 2 juin 1793–9 thermidor an II*. Paris: Clavreuil, 1958.
Sonenscher, Michael. *Work and Wages: Natural Law, Politics, and the Eighteenth-Century French Trades*. Cambridge: Cambridge University Press, 1989.

DIVORCE

Dessertine, Dominique. *Divorcer à Lyon sous la Révolution et l'Empire*. Lyon: Presses Universitaires de Lyon, 1981.
Garaud, Marcel, and Szramkiewicz, Romuald. *La Révolution française et la famille*. Paris: Recueil Sirey, 1978.
Phillips, Roderick. *Family Breakdown in Late Eighteenth-Century France: Divorce in Rouen, 1792–1803*. Oxford: Oxford University Press, 1980.

Ronsin, Francis. *Le Contrat sentimental. Débats sur le mariage, l'amour, le divorce de l'Ancien Régime à la Restauration*. Paris: Aubier, 1990.

Théry, Irène, and Biet, Christian, eds., *La famille, la loi, l'état de la Révolution au Code civil*. Paris: Imprimerie nationale, 1989.

Traer, James F. *Marriage and the Family in Eighteenth-Century France*. Ithaca, N.Y.: Cornell University Press, 1980.

INDEX

ABOUT THE EDITORS AND CONTRIBUTORS

HARRIET B. APPLEWHITE is Professor of Political Science and Director of the Honors College at Southern Connecticut State University. She has co-edited with Darline G. Levy *Women and Politics in the Age of Democratic Revolution*. Another book, *Political Alignment in the French National Assembly, 1789–1791*, is due in 1993. She is currently working on a book with Darline G. Levy on citizenship and gender in revolutionary Paris.

ANTOINE DE BAECQUE is Assistant at the Université de Paris I–Sorbonne. He has published *La caricature révolutionnaire* and *Le Corps de l'histoire. Les métaphores face à l'évènement politique 1770–1800* (1993). He is presently working on the representation of the body at the end of the eighteenth century, in particular on attitudes toward corpses and organic secretions.

MARVIN A. CARLSON is Sidney Cohn Distinguished Professor of Theatre and Executive Officer, Ph.D. Program in Theatre, at the Graduate School and University Center of the City University of New York. His latest books are *Places of Performance* (1989) and *Theatre Semiotics: Signs of Life* (1990).

PHILIP DAWSON is Professor of History at the Graduate School of the City University of New York and Brooklyn College. He edited *The French Revolution* and was a contributor to the *Historical Dictionary of the French Revolution, 1789–1799* (Greenwood Press, 1985). His area of specialization is French Revolutionary history, and his latest publication is "Parisiens, acheteurs de biens nationaux dans les districts de Melun et de Versailles," in *Paris et la Révolution Française* (1989).

SUZANNE DESAN is Associate Professor of History at the University of Wisconsin–Madison. She is the author of *Reclaiming the Sacred: Lay Religion and*

Popular Politics in the French Revolution (1990). Currently she is working on the impact of the French Revolution on divorce and the family.

MELVIN EDELSTEIN is Professor of History at William Paterson College of New Jersey. He has published in the areas of the revolutionary press, especially the diffusion of the Revolution to the villagers, and revolutionary elections: *La Feuille Villageoise: Communication et Modernisation dans les Régions Rurales pendant la Révolution. Commission d'Histoire Economique et Sociale de la Révolution Française. Mémoires et Documents*, XXXIV (1977) and "La Place de la Révolution Française dans la Politisation des Paysans," *Annales Historiques de la Révolution Française* (1990). His current research topic is France's Apprenticeship in Citizenship: The Origins of Mass Electoral Politics during the French Revolution.

MICHAEL P. FITZSIMMONS is Associate Professor of History at Auburn University. His publications include *The Parisian Order of Barristers and the French Revolution* (1987) and "Privilege and the Polity in France, 1786–1791" in *The American Historical Review* (1987). Currently he is working on a study of the National Assembly and its remaking of France from 1789 to 1791.

ALAN FORREST is Professor of Modern History at the University of York, England. His books include *The French Revolution and the Poor* (1981), *Conscripts and Deserters* (1989), and *Soldiers of the French Revolution* (1990). His research interests focus on French Revolutionary History, especially the areas of social policy, military, provincial history and counter-revolution.

PATRICE GUENIFFEY is Maître de Conférences at the Ecole des Hautes Etudes en Sciences Sociales. He is the author of "Cordeliers et Girondins: La préhistoire de la République?" in *Le Siècle de l'avènement républicain* (1993). He is finishing a book on elections to be published in November 1993, *L'Invention de l'électeur. La Révolution française et les élections*.

MADELYN GUTWIRTH is Professor Emeritus, West Chester University and Research Associate at the Alice Paul Center for the Study of Women, University of Pennsylvania. Her recent books are *The Twilight of the Goddesses—Women and Representation in the French Revolutionary Era* (1992) and *Germaine de Staël—Crossing the Borders*, with Avriel Goldberger and Karyna Szmurlo (1991). She is working on women in the late eighteenth century, women and fiction, and Germaine de Staël.

LYNN A. HUNT is Annenberg Professor of History at the University of Pennsylvania. She is the author of *The Family Romance of the French Revolution* (1992) and *Politics, Culture, and Class in the French Revolution* (1984). She is preparing an edited volume on the early modern origins of pornography.

DARLINE GAY LEVY is Associate Professor of History at New York University. She is the author of *The Ideas and Careers of Simon-Nicolas-Henri*

Linguet: A Study in Eighteenth-Century French History (1980) and has co-edited with Harriet B. Applewhite *Women and Politics in the Age of the Democratic Revolution* (1990). She is presently collaborating with Professor Applewhite on a book about citizenship and gender in revolutionary Paris.

JEREMY D. POPKIN is Professor of History at the University of Kentucky. He has published several books on the history of the press, including *News and Politics in the Age of Revolution* (1989) and *Revolutionary News: The Press in France, 1789–1799* (1990). He is currently working on a study of the role of the press in revolutionary crises in France since 1800.

ALLAN POTOFSKY is an Instructor at Columbia University. He is presently writing a book entitled *The Builders of Modern France: The Organization of Labor, From Turgot to Napoleon*, a study of transformations of Parisian work sites in the revolutionary era. His current research interests include the relationship between the revolutionary state and social change and the impact of political theory and state policy between 1770 and 1830.

PIERRE RETAT is Professor at the Université de Lyon 2. He is an authority on the development of the press during the Old Regime and the Revolution. The latest of his numerous books is *Naissance du journal révolutionnaire 1789* (1989). He is presently engaged in research on gazettes from the seventeenth to the early nineteenth century, focusing on the form and function of the political journal during the Old Regime.

RENEE WALDINGER is Professor of French and Executive Officer, Ph.D. Program in French, at the Graduate School of the City University of New York. Her area of specialization is French literature of the eighteenth century and her publications have focused on various aspects of the works of Voltaire, Diderot, and Condorcet. Her first book was entitled *Voltaire and Reform in the Light of the French Revolution* (1959), and her latest book is *Approaches to the Teaching of Voltaire's CANDIDE* (1987). She is presently working on Frédéric-Melchior Grimm's *Correspondance littéraires*.

ISSER WOLOCH is Professor of History at Columbia University. His most recent book is *The New Regime: Transformations of the French Civic Order, 1789–1820s*, to be published in 1994.